FRACTURE

ALSO BY MATTHEW PARRIS

FRACTURE

Stories of How Great Lives Take Root in Trauma

MATTHEW PARRIS

PROFILE BOOKS

This paperback edition published in 2021

First published in Great Britain in 2020 by
Profile Books Ltd
29 Cloth Fair
London
ECIA 7JQ
www.profilebooks.com

1 3 5 7 9 10 8 6 4 2

Typeset in Dante by MacGuru Ltd
Printed and bound in Great Britain by
CPI Group (UK) Ltd, Croydon CRO 4YY

A CIP catalogue record for this book is available from the British Library.

ISBN 978 1 78125 724 1
eISBN 978 1 78283 293 5

To the creator of my *Great Lives* radio series,
Miles Warde

CONTENTS

ACKNOWLEDGEMENTS

Fracture has been a long time in the making. The idea began forming five years ago as I noticed a pattern in so many of the lives we were covering in *Great Lives*, my BBC Radio 4 series. From there to conversations with Andrew Franklin at Profile Books, and finally to a formal proposal, took long enough. But once I started on the manuscript the tentative and incomplete state of my own argument fast became clear to me.

Without the industry and guidance of my researcher Robbie Smith I would have found no compass in the huge and hazy field that any study in 'greatness', 'genius' and 'childhood trauma' must lead us into. Robbie has helped direct my endeavours, and himself undertaken a huge amount of the research and much of the drafting too, as we made our way through scores of biographies and the literature on the subject. Without his work, his ideas and his organisation, I doubt this book would have happened.

If Robbie has laboured mightily to good effect, then it was with only the lightest of touches that another friend nudged me in the best direction. Alison Parente heard my outline of the argument this book would pursue, and responded with a single sentence: '[m]y advice would be to go light on the theory, and heavy on the real-life stories; let the theory arise naturally from these.' She was right.

The real life stories, of course, did not write themselves. I needed help with the many mini-biographies that form the backbone of this book, and for this I'm grateful to Susan Chambers, Morgana Edwards, Ian Johnston, Keir Mather, Tom Mitchelson, Rachel Parris and Claudia Williams. I was also so grateful for Sir John Major's guidance in my chapter on Rudyard Kipling.

I've been so lucky Profile Books sent me Fiona Screen and Paul Forty: two ace and patient wordsmiths with the intellect that goes to meaning as well as sentence construction. And as to my publisher, what can I say? To acknowledge the help and forbearance of one's publisher may sometimes be a routine courtesy. Not in this case. My publisher, Andrew Franklin, has doubled up as a benevolent but merciless Oxbridge don in helping me sort out my own argument, reserving his mercy for my periodic pleas for more time. This book owes a good deal of its shape to Andrew. My editor, Cecily Gayford, has been so much more than an editor. For her presiding intelligence, her rigour, and her weeks of work knocking an unwieldy and over-long manuscript into shape, both Robbie and I are enormously grateful.

A flash of insight is one thing. A proper argument, proper evidence and finally a proper book is quite another. I should never have proceeded from the former to what – I hope – is the latter without a little platoon of kind and clever helpmates. To all of them, thanks.

Matthew Parris
Derbyshire, July 2020

CHAPTER ONE

AN ATTACK OF THE MORBIDS

The clowns tumbled and fooled across the green field in the sinking sun. Happy music drifted over as the afternoon slipped into twilight: a twilight that would never be forgotten by the seven-year-old standing next to his father, looking on.

All was merry. On that evening in 1819 the two had made the short journey up to Highgate from their home in the nearby village of Holloway on the outskirts of London. As the light faded father and son returned home. The boy went up to his room, alone. There he sat – and wept for half the night.

Something had shattered the 'scene of gaiety' (his words) at the rural show: something would henceforward cut into his memory with a bitter clarity. In the dark of night, peaks of happiness turned into troughs of misery. The memory tormented him cruelly for days afterwards and marked the start of an affliction which would dog him for the rest of his life.

Our age has found a name for it. But what we would now call acute depression was to the boy almost a creature, a sort of living thing – and though he could not explain it or understand it, he named it: The Morbids. This terrifying low after every high, this consuming misery, this happiness lost, remained forever a thorn in his side. As an adult he would keep himself constantly on the move and 'look ahead as little as possible' for fear of The Morbids smothering his thoughts. The Morbids and their heart-eating melancholy were among the chief struggles of this young boy's life. But they were far from the only ones.

His earliest memories were happy. Born in 1812 he could recall, aged three, being rolled in a rug and lifted to the window to watch fireworks exploding over London after the victory at Waterloo. But even this joy spelled trouble. The boy's father was a stockbroker and in the tumult that followed Waterloo he defaulted on the Stock Exchange. His debts were not quite big enough to be fatal so, helped by a friend, he was just about able to go back into business, though not before the loss of the family's large house in Holloway. Bowman's Lodge stood on the junction of the Holloway Road and Seven Sisters road: now it is a roaring multi-lane thoroughfare of buses, cars and exhaust fumes, but then it was considered higher ground with good, clean air, at a premium as London grew.

The house had to be let, and the boy and his family decamped from what had been a happy home. That might have been tolerable. Happy families have coped with worse. But when the family returned to live more frugally in their old house the boy's mother (perhaps exhausted by childbirth, her husband's woes, the loss of domestic help and a souring marriage) rejected her little son, the twenty-first of her twenty-two children and one for whom it seemed she had no time or love left. He was palmed off on his eldest sister. The effect on the boy was sharp. Four was an age at which he could feel in full the hurt without being able to grasp what lay behind it. Now he developed asthma.

But his eldest sister and foster mother, twenty-two years his senior, was caring and devoted – mothering, schooling and tending to this frail child. She was also a devout Christian, and this had sadder consequences. Even before The Morbids struck, the small boy had encountered a darker terror, just as inexplicable to him.

He was five or six when he suffered his first attack. Had you been watching, you would have seen him stop dead, his eyes blanked with a glassy stillness, his hands and lips fluttering and shaking and his whole body beginning to sway. We now know this as epilepsy: specifically the *petit mal* form.

But that little boy in a big, now shabbier Georgian house knew nothing of the affliction's hazy pathology: only the fear that gripped him. And shame, too, because his pious sister led him to believe the seizures were somehow demonic. For the rest of his life he would call his fits visits by The Demon.

The boy's and later the man's relationship with The Demon was (so far as possible) hidden from others but not unacknowledged by him. The visits mark his diaries in a coded refrain, quietly staining the days when they troubled him. He would inscribe each seizure in his diary with only an X, followed by a number indicating the number of seizures that month or that day. Sometimes comment would be attached, often it would not. These silent black marks were The Demon's visits. Sometimes he called it The Terrible Demon.

His illness made him reclusive and secretive. Yet because

it was the *petit mal* form of epilepsy – rather than the *grand mal* form which causes full-body seizures – he was able to hide it from all but close family. His practice, and he grew adept at this, was to make himself scarce just before an attack. He had learned the warning signs, and it became a central but almost secret part of his life to navigate the affliction.

The Demon and The Morbids were just names: names by which the boy gave a shape to his interior struggles. It was, in a way, an explosion of creativity. He was creating monsters out of his sadnesses and magic out of his monsters.

It was they that made him the man he became. This was the genius he bequeathed his age and the ages to come. From the sorrow and seclusion came words and worlds, clownings and grotesqueries bursting with imagination and laughter. From the rejection and self-doubt came kindness and vigour. From the shy child came an adult who understood children and their interior lives. From that childhood came a famous painter, a respected, imaginative and successful travel writer, a musician, the survivor of a doomed and unrequited homosexual yearning, and the finest author of English Nonsense there ever was.

Forged in the wreckage of a childhood, fractured and then re-made, came Edward Lear.

*

For over a decade I have presented a biographical programme, *Great Lives*, on BBC radio. The format is simple. We choose as our guest someone of some present distinction. My guest then chooses from the past (ancient or modern) a great life they wish to champion. They make their case in our studio alongside a witness who is expert in the life in question. Our only stipulations are that the individual must no longer be alive, our guest must believe this was a great life, and our expert witness must know a lot about them.

Our series has covered more than four hundred lives: so many that names slip from the mind. These lives have been plucked from every age and every field of human endeavour, and they've been enormously various – from soldiers to composers to explorers to poets, politicians, brave feminists, early apostles of black emancipation, revolutionary military strategists, singers and scientists.

And so many of them have something in common. This began to dawn on me early: at first as a vague impression, then as a growing observation, finally as something approaching a theory. At first I simply thought 'how odd, how apparently unlikely'. Now, looking back, the link seems to me to leap from the evidence. Time after time, life after life, my hypothesis had become harder to ignore. Genius was linked to childhood trauma.

So, this book is about wrecked childhood – or 'fracture' as we call it here – and the great men and women who crawled from the wreckage. But my theme is not the emergence of genius *despite* early troubles, but the emergence of genius *because* of those torments. It is my belief that calamitous early years in a person's development can – *can* rather than must – release those extraordinary qualities to which we give names like 'genius', 'greatness,' 'exceptional creativity' or 'originality'.

That the wreckage of a childhood could bring the gift of extraordinary powers of imagination or reasoning, or of artistic and intellectual courage, at first glance runs against ordinary common sense. But things that seem unlikely are not necessarily untrue: there are Eucalyptus trees in Australia whose seeds will not germinate unless burned by fire, cracking what encases the kernel. What we mean by 'genius' is that kernel; what we mean by 'greatness' is too various to be captured in words; yet the terms have meaning, and rarely mean less than a kind of rejection of the familiar, and a lashing out for the new and different.

Of course, no childhood is without sorrow or difficulty, and many, many people can wax tragic about their lonely youth, bullying at school, cash-strapped circumstances or an unkind or uncaring parent. They are not making this up: childhood is a raw thing and for most of us memories are often cruel and sharp. But the lives I'm describing have been marked by experience when young that's in a different league of anxiety and horror. Over the last thirteen years, folded into the pages of my own happy and undistinguished life, I have listened to many hundreds of the kind of lives I'm describing.

Something went so badly wrong for these individuals, usually in infancy, childhood or youth, that you may wonder how they survived at all. A striking proportion lost one or both parents. Some came from families whose circumstances were shattered by illness, war, drugs or financial ruin. Some were pulled between two parents from different cultures speaking different languages; others wrenched from one culture and taken to another. Trouble may come to the young of our species in an infinity of guises, but so many of these are exceptional. See and judge for yourself as we proceed.

If that is what I mean by 'fracture', what do I mean by 'genius', a term that has been done to death as few others have? All I can do is reel off a thesaurus of synonym words and phrases. An inner flame, a one-off quality, *sui generis*, a pusher of the boundaries, a capacity for the imaginative leap, for thinking laterally, 'outside the box' ... but there we go again: the clichés begin to roll. Perhaps, though, you sense what I am getting at. Deep exceptionality. Originality. Brave new thinking. These are the kinds of greatness I believe are so often linked to early fracture. But the honest answer is that I cannot entirely define what such very fuzzy expressions as 'genius' or 'great life' mean; nobody can.

So I shall hardly try. Instead, I have left it to others – my radio guests on the *Great Lives* programme. Asked to nominate a 'great' life my radio guests have hardly ever complained that they don't know how to use the word – and hardly ever have they nominated a life where listeners would protest that they don't see how anyone could call it great. We know it when we see it even if we find it hard to define.

However, I have not entirely sheathed my critical faculties in selecting examples for this book, and in cases where I'm simply unable to see why a life has been called great, you will not find it in these pages. Importantly, I've also excluded another class of women and men we'd call great: those to whom it was all handed on a plate.

As a wag once wrote: 'The Hall of Fame is high and wide, and the waiting room is full / And some go in by the door marked "push" and some by the door marked "pull".'

Lives may achieve greatness mainly because of where fate placed a person: history handed them their robes, and they wore them well. But they themselves did not make their own place in the human story: good fortune did. Many (not all) monarchs are obvious examples, but wealth and position may come in other ways – by inheritance, by chance or by appointment. The silver spoon in the new-born's mouth is sometimes the only explanation we need for their later success. So this book looks mostly at those who came in by the door marked 'push'. In some important way my examples are people who – whether their origins were humble or lofty – made their own distinction.

This does not mean the chosen individual must have started poor or in obscurity: look, for instance, at the 7th Earl of Shaftesbury (see p. 163). But at the root of their modern fame lies something extraordinary about the individual, something outstanding, that broke through: a life that seems to be more than the sum of its parts – even to defy its own ingredients.

To my evidence, then, in a moment – because correlation is not necessarily causation, and a list is of limited interest without a theory.

Here's mine.

Right at the centre of mankind's self-knowledge is the understanding that few break new ground, see new worlds, dream of new continents, reach for new revelations, without being kicked hard by fate, often to the ground. An early trauma can trigger the mould-breaking characteristics we associate with human greatness. Something in these young lives has broken. Familiar certainties have been ripped away. The security of the hearth and the moral and intellectual shelter lent by what we call a 'stable' upbringing has been shattered in the way a Kansas tornado shattered Dorothy's constricting girlhood and hurled her through the heavens to Oz.

Instinctively we know that old habits of thought and belief may need to be shattered, often violently, before the new can be born. The phoenix wings upward from the flames. To rise again we may first have to be broken down. At some deep level we know this, and all through history we say it to ourselves in legend, in religion, in fiction and in fable. That's why Jesus and Mohammed began their lives in trouble and distress. That's why Romulus and Remus were abandoned and suckled by a she-wolf. That's why the Ugly Duckling becomes a swan, and Simba returns to rule over his father's lands in *The Lion King*.

Deep down we know that easy mental habit suffocates, know we are in some sense prisoners of untroubled childhoods. We know we're stuck in a comfortable mental groove, know that the longer we stay in it the harder it becomes to break away, know that the earlier we are knocked out of it the better the prospect of permanent escape.

Nor do we ourselves necessarily wish to explore these possibilities of escape. They're for others. Most of us just want to jog along comfortably within the assumptions – moral and practical – we were born to.

Indeed, doing so is a survival mechanism. Darwinian forces favour the moulding of offspring into conformity with the ways and mental habits of the larger group. A tribe would not function well if most individuals broke ranks and marched to the beat of their own drums. Upbringing is designed to squeeze and restrict – and sometimes to stifle – pure individuality; and life will usually be easiest and happiest for those who conform. We don't want our private selves to chafe too hard or too often with the times we live in and the people we live among. We've no intention of breaking away. But we're drawn by stories about those who did. Myth and legend show this.

I am not suggesting that the breaking of a child will usually launch creative genius. A damaged child most often becomes a damaged adult. Of course, I absolutely don't advocate messing up your child's early years in hopes of triggering genius. There is no guarantee that they would find, as the individuals whose stories I will tell here have found, the disregard and the personal autonomy – the sense of self-worth – to wake in the dead of night and hear the blackbird sing and at some almost mystical level know – while knowing it to be literally untrue – that the blackbird is singing to them alone.

*

By way of evidence, I will introduce you to the stories that first convinced me of my theory. First to real people, real reports, divided into six rough-and-ready categories of calamity that emerge as typical among their childhoods. The book will then move on to fiction, legend, myth, religion, and those age-old stories which have somehow lodged themselves in our culture down the ages. For these stories – fireside tales, tales told at a mother's knee, readings from the pulpit – be they fiction or reality, speak to a belief in the unbinding of the spirit by escape from the suffocation of 'the world'. Break out! Run free! In the human imagination, largely ignored in commonly expressed theories but betrayed in the stories we remember, sits a deep understanding of the link between breakage and transcendence, between calamity and epiphany.

But before leaping in, there's something I want to make absolutely clear. What I am talking about is – at least – mental torture and spiritual despair. I'm not talking about the kind of challenges that simply toughen a person up, troublesome though these may be. Boot camps do not breed genius. This is a confusion with Friedrich Nietzsche's maxim: '[w]hatever doesn't kill you makes you strong.' The nineteenth-century German philosopher is not wrong, but he's talking about something different.

Nietzsche's idea and mine have a striking but superficial similarity, and his expresses a truth we've all seen demonstrated – including in ourselves. It has become almost a cliché, a slogan associated with the self-help industry. But we should not sneer. Nietzsche was only crystallising what is no more than a piece of common sense. Adversity can toughen us, arm us for combat; trouble is a great teacher; we know this. Any number of summer camps, Duke of Edinburgh Award route-marches, army training 'yomps' and corporate bonding weekends testify to humanity's faith that facing difficulty can be good for us. Nietzsche is talking about capacity building: the acquisition of mental and physical resilience; of learning from experience; and of life skills. His well-crafted soundbite struck a chord. Since then many voices, good and bad, have borrowed the theme. The Hitler Youth used it as a slogan. In his autobiography Richard Nixon's assistant, Gordon Liddy, popularised it (after Watergate, and prison) when he wrote 'that which does not kill us makes us stronger'.

Not the insight of fascists and tricksters alone, it has been co-opted by international singers and popstars, too. Sinatra's 'My Way' relies upon the picture of someone who 'took the blows', who 'ate it up and spat it out'. His imagined hero is a tough old thing, not an original thinker or creative genius but an alley cat that's lost an ear or two but learned to survive. But my purpose in starting with the story of little Edward Lear is to suggest a less obvious idea. Lear was never resilient and never could become so. He was wounded and exposed, and from this experience an imaginative genius flowed.

So I'm talking about strength not in Sinatra's sense, not in the sense of muscle, callouses, toughness or experience, but in the sense of genius. Genius may be a guttering candle, a fragile and flimsy quality whose strength is not to be measured in horsepower. Among 'great' men and women are many who were not tough at all. Some – indeed a pretty striking proportion of them – were a bundle of neuroses.

Coping with adversity is a kit for survival, not a catalyst for genius. We do not remember Lear for his pluck – plucky though he was – but for early misery and the singularity of his talent. Endurance, stamina, steadiness under fire, the ability to plough on … these are admirable attributes but billions of human beings display them. They should be distinguished from a very different class of qualities: the qualities that make a person stand out from those billions; that make a person one-in-a-million, paradigm-shifting, original. The things to which we give names like 'genius', 'creativity', 'inspiration'; the things that make a person great in that most cosmic of senses.

For genius to emerge, we may not need to be toughened up; we may not need to win a childhood battle. We may need to be broken. We may even need to lose. Only after much damage has genius often taken wing. That's why I argue that, in the most exceptional sense of the word 'strong', it is not what doesn't kill you that makes you strong. It may even be what does.

*

Here are the five categories of misfortune that (to me) emerge as typical among those traumatic childhoods we later see heralding the emergence of genius. Yet such pigeonholing can never be exhaustive, and much calamity defies easy definition. Most of the lives in this book will have been hit by more than one of these miseries. So, though categorisation lends shape and gives us something to hold on to, please don't accuse me of hanging each story on a single hook when in reality it could be hung on more than one. To that I plead guilty at once.

Nor is the categorisation I've hit upon of much importance to the theory being illustrated. You may feel that some of the lives described here don't fit neatly into the compartments, or into any compartment at all. But it's what the stories all point to that matters: those tremendous shocks to the system, or longer-drawn-out episodes of utter wretchedness, which whatever their cause are linked to the emergence of genius.

These are my five categories, our five horsemen of childhood apocalypse:

Affliction – physical and mental
Isolation – and dislocation
Chaos – and family dysfunction
Cruelty – and oppression and prejudice
Shock – ruin, death, suicide

Each category will be accompanied by one in-depth story of a life that illustrates it well, plus a range of further life stories told more briefly. The many examples I shall set before you represent only the tip of the iceberg of the evidence available.

One other thing. Plenty of examples of great women will follow on these pages, but there are not as many women as men. The likely reason will be immediately clear to you. For women, and until relatively recently, there's been such a ceiling to achievement outside hearth and home that the number who could break through has been limited. It's notable that among my female examples many who lived before the 19th century got their start in life by accident of birth, for instance to royal lineage, and only thereafter could shine brightly in their era.

I must add as an embarrassed footnote that virtually all the men we've invited onto *Great Lives* have until quite recently chosen to champion other men. By contrast our women guests have chosen women and men in roughly equal numbers. In response to this we've in recent years actively sought great women as our subjects, and guests who want to champion them. I make no apology for this.

Where genius has been buried you have to dig harder to find it.

CHAPTER TWO

AFFLICTION

Affliction is a misery tied to terrible childhood problems of body, or mind, or both: to physical and mental difficulty. Like Edward Lear, whose childhood story I outlined at the beginning of this book, we are all trapped in our bodies with no means of escape. Financial ruin can be surmounted, the death of a parent transcended, loneliness cured. Shock can be survived and cruelty put behind us. But – especially to a child – illness in body or mind might seem final. Inexplicable, too. To the child's 'Why?' comes no reply. The injustice is mysterious, and permanent.

A sense of fairness develops surprisingly early in infancy. The child may disapprove, but already knows that bad people as well as good exist, and can hope and dream that the bad ones will get their just desserts – and even plan to do something about it. But if you are five and (say) Edward Lear, what moral knowledge arms you to face epilepsy and severe depression? If you are the six-year-old Frida Kahlo how do you explain the polio that has left one leg withered, and the taunts of your schoolmates – let alone, later in your teens, the bus accident, the iron spike through your pelvis and the life of pain and disability that followed? If you are the young Carl Jung and your mother goes mad, where, in your own mind, do you fly?

Why, then, might this be the kind of fracture that can unlock genius? Each case will have its own unique characteristics, each will affect the developing child differently, but there strike me as three effects in particular that serious childhood affliction may visit upon the mind and imagination of the child.

First (as I've suggested) is a massive sense of injustice. A scream against life itself, against fate, against the world. Yet despair, fury, alienation, rejection ... these can mark the beginnings of genius. I defy anyone to maintain that the brilliant and contrarian Marxist thinker and brave fighter against Italian fascism, Antonio Gramsci, would ever have gone into battle with his era in Italy if he had been tall, healthy, good at sport and popular at school.

Second, loneliness. My study gives this woe a category of its own ('Isolation'), but it is so often the first and unavoidable consequence of illness. The child misses school and the companionship of their age group; or is bullied like Frida Kahlo for being different; or is unable to play, as physically normal children can play. There's so much that the well and able-bodied child can do that the afflicted child simply cannot, and, typically among our great lives, these latter escape into their own imagination and learn to create their own world away from other children, because the world where other children live is closed to them. In the imagination is made a secret place where only the afflicted child can dwell: a private, personal place. Edward Lear is a vivid example.

Third may come the feeling of being special. Though

much derided because of overuse in social science's vocabulary of 'special needs', the idea of being special can be life-saving and sanity-saving to afflicted children, and a source of self-respect. Set apart by others, they can set *themselves* apart with pride. Thus can begin the disregard for conventional wisdom and conventional approval that marks so many great lives.

There now follow five stories all illustrating that strand of affliction which is woven into the childhoods of so many great men and women. Beyond Lear I offer the lives of Ada Lovelace, Antonio Gramsci, Carl Jung and Frida Kahlo.

Ada Lovelace

What is imagination?

'What is Imagination?', mused Ada Lovelace, the mathematical prodigy and protégée of the polymath Charles Babbage. 'Imagination', she continued, 'is the Discovering Faculty ... It is that which penetrates into the unseen worlds around us ... It is that which feels & discovers what is, the real which we see not.'

Such contemplation might be more readily expected from a poet than a mathematician, but Lovelace was no ordinary academic. Born in 1815, the only legitimate child of the Romantic poet and infamous prodigal, Lord Byron, and Annabella Milbanke, a reserved but mathematically gifted woman, Ada Lovelace was a contradiction from her very beginning. Existing where mathematics and poetry, engineering and imagination, cross, Lovelace would go on to apply her poetic imagination to the disciplines of mathematics and logical reasoning, earning her the title of the first computer programmer. Although hardly recognised in her lifetime, Lovelace's groundbreaking understanding of the wider horizons of computing make her the patron saint of all who champion women's increasing role in today's STEM (Science, Technology, Engineering and Maths) subjects.

But Ada's early years were marked by fracture before emerging brilliance. Her parents' marriage was brief and unhappy. Byron and Milbanke separated just weeks after Ada's birth. Months later Byron left England, never to return to the family home. The globe-trotting poet was not indifferent to his child; he apparently kept a portrait of her with him on his travels, and his letters often asked for her news. But, forever unwell and isolated at home with her austere mother, Ada felt Byron's absence keenly. She would never meet her father. He died in Greece when she was eight years old.

Childhood for Ada was shaped by repeated illnesses and debilitating afflictions, physical and mental. She suffered from asthma and chronic digestive problems. After a severe attack of measles when she was twelve, she was semi-paralysed. For three long and painful years, worn down by all these ailments, the little girl was largely bed-ridden and half-blind.

Her troubles were psychological as well as physical. The young Ada had a fierce temper and her mood swings were wild and unpredictable. Starved of simple affection, her childhood years were passed in isolation from her peer group, and in recurring pain and physical distress.

Nevertheless (but is 'nevertheless' the right word?) she fast became a brilliant and determined student. In the hope that rigorous study would prevent Ada from developing her father's moody and wild character, her mother insisted she be tutored in mathematics and science, highly unusual for a young aristocratic girl at that time. Her resulting education was unconventional and intense. Her mathematical gifts were obvious from early on, but she was more than good at arithmetic. Intellectually ambitious and deeply curious, she seemed to develop an ever-deeper relationship with numbers, with the meaning of numbers and the meanings to be found within the world of numbers; and with language. Not just calculation, then, but concept. She was destined to break new ground.

Ada was only twelve when, already fascinated by mechanical engineering, she wrote and illustrated a book, *Flyology*, which detailed her plan for constructing a flying machine. Not least but not only by her own reckoning, there was a spark of brilliance in her intellect. In a letter entreating Charles Babbage, the renowned inventor of mechanical computing, to become her mentor, the young Lovelace wrote of 'some portion of natural genius' that existed in her passionate pursuit of science and mathematics.

Her self-confidence was well placed and Babbage did indeed mentor her. It was through him and with him that Ada moved on to the study of advanced mathematics and when, in 1843, she translated an article on Babbage's Analytical Engine – famously thought of as the first computer – not only did she translate the French into English, but she also added her own thoughts and ideas, tripling the length of the original work. It is for these notes, containing groundbreaking concepts now considered to have shaped the birth of the modern computer, that Lovelace is most celebrated.

It would be easy to suggest that her father's abandonment was the thorn in her side that spurred her on to make a name for herself in mathematics; an act of rebellion against Byron's world of romantic poetry and sensual pleasure. But this would misunderstand the complexity of her genius. Lovelace was brilliant in many ways because of, rather than in spite of, her father. Though her mother desperately tried to purge Ada of her father's unruly nature (in an attempt to encourage the young Ada to develop self-control, her mother reportedly forced her to lie still for lengthy periods), the Byron bloodline seems to have run deep; Ada was erratic, highly strung and independent. She had her father's capricious temperament as well as his romantic tendencies. As a teenager she had an affair with a tutor and ran away from home. But, perhaps most importantly, she also inherited something of Byron's creative imagination: that 'Discovering Faculty' that made her intellectually curious, willing and able to cross boundaries of discipline and study. In a moment of teenage rebellion she wrote to her mother: 'You will not concede me philosophical poetry. Invert the order! Will you give me poetical philosophy, poetical science?'

Although she is celebrated today, Ada's work – like her recognition that Babbage's Analytical Engine could be applied beyond mathematics, to musical notes, for example – drew little attention while she was still alive. Her attempts to develop mathematical schemes to win at gambling left her perilously close to financial ruin, and her many afflictions as well as her violent mood swings dogged her all through her short life, each attack leaving her with apparently 'mad eyes' and swollen facial features. In 1837 she contracted cholera. Laudanum and opium, prescribed to her as painkillers, brought about changes in her personality; her mood swings intensified and she began to hallucinate. She died of uterine cancer in 1852 aged just thirty-six.

It was Lovelace's positioning at an intersection between mathematics and poetry, and the friction generated at the rubbing point of engineering and imagination, which we should credit for her bold and prescient mind: that all-important 'discovering faculty' to penetrate 'the unseen worlds around us'. A child of the Industrial Revolution, Ada saw beauty and poetry in science, and she saw science in poetry, in society, in everything. Her most outstanding imaginative journey was grounded in more than academic reasoning. It was rooted in a willingness to take conceptual leaps. She saw more than mathematical possibility in Babbage's machines, more than poetry in the possibilities of the human imagination. She was fusion, contradiction, a reconciliation of opposites; the yield of an equation no ordinary, contented childhood could have framed.

Antonio Gramsci

Can man dominate his own destiny, can he 'make himself', can he create his own life?

Antonio Gramsci was an unlikely hero. Born in 1891 in impoverished Sardinia and the fourth of seven children, the great Marxist thinker was a frail child. A malformation of the spine stunted his height to less than five feet and left him severely hunchbacked. When his father was arrested for alleged fraud in 1897 the family became destitute and Gramsci was forced temporarily to abandon his studies and take work at the local Land Registry, carrying files equal to his own weight for nine lire a month. Nevertheless he was a brilliant student. He kept up privately and alone with his studies and, with the help of his mother and government scholarships, eventually made it to the University of Turin. There he lived on a pittance, almost starving and too embarrassed by the state of his clothes to go out with friends; his health worsened and he suffered from nervous exhaustion.

Though Gramsci did not complete his degree he would go on to become a well-regarded writer and cultural critic, seminal Marxist thinker, outspoken opponent of fascism and leader of the Italian Communist Party. As a student, Gramsci had discovered Marx, signed up for the Socialist Party and organised protests. By the time he was thirty, his politics were considered so radical that he was arrested and incarcerated by the fascists. Scribbling in a prison notebook later, he asked: can man dominate his own destiny? The question was apposite: how had this man taken wing to become a political revolutionary that Mussolini feared enough to imprison?

Dante Germino, a professor and biographer of Gramsci, has suggested that the answer lies in the thinker's past. 'To understand Gramsci's designs for a new politics,' Germino says, 'one must go in search of Gramsci himself.' And where might Gramsci be found if not at the margins of society? He had begun life as an outsider: geographically as he was born in isolated and peripheral Sardinia, but also physically as a severely disabled boy in a rural village, at a time when to be so was seen more with disfavour than with sympathy. He was terribly bullied by his classmates and was appalled by his own disability and poverty. 'For a very long time,' he said, 'I have believed it was absolutely, fatally impossible that I should ever be loved.'

This difficult start to life is reflected in his later thinking. Gramsci's driving political concern was always that the *enmargenati*, the marginalised, should be brought to the centre of politics. He questioned the accepted wisdom whenever possible, be it the growing fascism of interwar Europe, the increasing totalitarianism of Soviet communism, or even the political opinions of members of his own party. Gramsci's upbringing exposed him to social realities that his fellow students in Turin could have only read about. The young Gramsci saw first-hand the harsh poverty of peasants' lives and their struggles against the brutal disregard of central government.

These struggles also strengthened his character. In spite of, perhaps because of, his difficulties, Gramsci grew into a determined and uncompromising man. He wrote that his childhood troubles had created within him an 'instinct of rebellion' and a determination to feed his intellectual and political hunger by any means, and at any cost. He considered himself to be man of action: the ten years that he spent in prison, often in such poor health that he needed to be propped up by fellow inmates during the recreational period, must have been agonising. He was a political organiser and militant by temperament and he was interested in intellectual thought only in so far as it was put into practice.

At his trial, Gramsci's prosecutor famously argued that he was so dangerous that 'for twenty years we must stop this brain from functioning'. Yet in spite of his worsening physical condition and the intense loneliness of prison, Gramsci could not be deflected from his ambition to agitate for social and political revolution. During his imprisonment he wrote tirelessly: personal letters and over three thousand pages of political notebooks in which he mapped out most clearly his political ideology and revolutionary designs. These notebooks, sprawling and fragmentary, were smuggled out of prison and later assembled and published in compilation. They are now his best-known and most influential works.

Upon his release, Gramsci intended to return to Sardinia to convalesce before resuming his work. This was not to be. He'd been born crippled and isolated and he would die in the same way, less than a week after the expiry of his prison sentence. Before imprisonment he had married a young violinist, Julia Schucht; and he never got to see his second son.

Today the legacy of Gramsci's politics is more intellectual than material, and the fragmentary nature of his writing has left it open to interpretation, indeed appropriation, by both the Left and Right; but all his thinking and writing is shot through with the rebellious spirit born in his childhood. In a letter to his mother from prison he wrote that 'I've always refused to compromise my ideas and am ready to die for them.'

And in a way he did. He broke not only with what he

would have called the economic oppression and exploitation of the poor and the working class but also with the Russian-dominated version of communism that saw 'struggle' as a conflict between forces, to be resolved by the victory of the greater force. The real battle, thought Gramsci, was not between opposing forces arrayed, as it were, on the political or economic battlefield, but a battle for men's minds and often within men's hearts.

Key to this new interpretation of the Marxist struggle was the idea on which Gramsci's fame and influence still rests: the concept of 'cultural hegemony'. The failure (he would argue) of communism to make the progress expected elsewhere after the Russian revolution of 1917, was because bourgeois society had won the cultural battle of ideas. What (he would say) we loosely call common sense in bourgeois liberal society is in fact steeped in cultural assumptions about earning, deserving, respecting, deferring. We think of these ideas as obvious, objective truth; but they have been embedded by a 'hegemonistic' cultural tradition (a tradition of authority, rank, deference, social stratification) that favours the status quo. Religion, folklore, fairy-tales, novels, myth, legend and proverbial wisdom – our whole background culture – have been weaponised to reinforce the existing social and economic order.

Though by no means an entirely new perspective on politics and history, Gramsci's idea was powerfully developed and cogently expressed. It has (and for Marxists still maintains) the enormous advantage of appearing to explain why communism has met such resistance over the last century, and why the masses have not flocked to join the revolution. Disappointment with the response of the masses is a major and baffled strand in the Left's world view. 'Cultural hegemony' seems to offer an explanation: people can't think straight because their way of thinking, even of speaking, and so many of their unconscious assumptions, have been manipulated by the boss culture. While this author is anything but a revolutionary Marxist I see at once the power and appeal of Gramsci's idea. So much in politics is bound up with understanding failure. Gramsci found an explanation. It is no exaggeration to call this genius. And it was in alienation, despair, pain and even self-loathing that Gramsci's genius was born.

Carl Jung

Why was he so interested in himself?

The childhood of the second father of psychoanalysis, after Freud, was disfigured by isolation, loneliness, and – more than anything – the severe mental illness of his mother. Remembered for revolutionising analytical psychology, Carl Jung and his profoundly original theories changed the field entirely, introducing concepts such as the collective unconscious, and the extrovert and introvert personalities. His work was almost insanely ambitious in its attempted reach. Into it he wove a wider and deeper enquiry into personhood than has perhaps ever been attempted: myth, religion, mysticism, philosophy, art, literature, folk-memory, dreams and even dance. A charismatic but self-centred man, much of his thinking was grounded in introspection, and continues to influence contemporary art, literature and religious studies. He was famed for his relationship, and later disagreements, with Freud. Writing in the *Guardian*, Adam Phillips, the eminent child psychotherapist, said: 'If the question we are likely to ask of Freud now is "why was he so interested in sexuality?", the question we are likely to ask of Jung is "why was he so interested in himself?"'

Carl Jung was born in 1875, in Kesswil, Switzerland. He was the first child of his parents to survive, and experienced a solitary youth. In her biography *Jung*, Deirdre Bair writes that he spent hours observing the behaviour of the adults he was surrounded by yet somehow set back from, developing an impressive 'self-reliance' and 'intense concentration on the inner life'. Even when his sister was born in 1884, Jung remained detached – he'd been kept away from her by his mother as she was a frail baby, and the sibling bond never recovered.

His father Paul was a Protestant clergyman, who had occasional crises of faith which worried his son. Carl's mother, Emilie, however, was more than an eccentric woman: she was fitfully lunatic, believing she was visited by ghosts, and suffered other serious mental health problems. She would spend evenings alone in her bedroom with (she believed) the ghosts. Today her visions might be described as psychotic. So – almost – might the young Carl's: he was later to report that he once imagined he saw his mother coming towards him with her head disembodied and floating in front of her.

When Jung was three, his mother was committed for a spell to a psychiatric hospital. He found her absence devastating, worrying that it was his fault. He suffered from anxious and confusing dreams of dark figures and inexplicable images, and was scared by the similarity to his mother's night terrors. He also experienced what he later described as 'unconscious suicidal [urges]' – or 'a fatal resistance to life in this world'.

At school, Carl, who had scant experience of the company of other children, did not fit in. Early in 1887 when he was twelve he was pushed to the ground by a fellow pupil, hitting his head so hard that he almost lost consciousness. Later, he remembered having only one thought: '[n]ow you won't have to go to school anymore.' He began to suffer from fainting spells whenever he returned to school or tried to do his homework. He stayed at home for six months, luxuriating in his solitude. His parents sought the advice of various doctors to no avail.

A point of fracture occurred as he overheard a conversation between his father and a friend. Mentioning his financial difficulties, his father confessed his fears for his troubled son's future if he proved unable to support himself. Carl was thunderstruck – his pride likely damaged – and from that moment was a changed child. He started work immediately, fighting for hours through fainting spells to teach himself Latin, until he felt he had overcome the attacks. He dedicated himself to academic excellence, now a driven youth studying for long periods before school; and later identified the fainting spells as a neurosis (in other words, as psychosomatic). At the time, overcome with shame, he felt he had caused the whole situation; he was determined to make something of himself, and never to be pitied again.

Following his father into the clergy seemed an unsuitable choice, and it was decided Carl would become a

doctor. So he could afford to study, his father had to peti-
tion Basel University for a 'sizeable stipend', betraying the
family's poverty and shaming his son. Jung's mother again
deteriorated, and now his father too began to sink.

Paul died in 1896, prompting yet another psychological upheaval for Carl. Though his mother did her best the
family was destitute. Carl was told to give up his training to provide an income. He was furious, and refused,
instead taking a loan from an uncle. Committing himself
to his work with renewed vigour, he stormed through
his studies and medical training in five years. Pulled now
towards spiritualism, religion and introspection – and suddenly disgusted by physiology – he began in 1908 to devote
himself to psychiatry.

His ferocious work ethic, his drive to prove himself
and his need to support his family might have spurred any
capable young man to conventional professional success.
But with Carl Jung there was an extra fire: his wild, strange
and revolutionary ideas about human beings' relationship
with themselves, with their psychological inheritance from
the human race, and collectively with their fellow humans.
Genetics was hardly established as a science in Jung's day
but there are powerful intuitive resonances between its
findings and Jung's near obsession with inheritance and
the individual mind as part of humanity's collective mind.
Set against the collective is his work on what he called
'individuation' – a person's recognition of themselves as
an individual entity. It is hard to imagine that this didn't
stem from a moment or moments of bewilderment and
despair in Jung's solitary childhood, almost certainly
associated with the derangement of one of the only two

people he loved and knew and who loved and knew him, without which he would never have posed to himself the fundamental question of who we are, who anyone is, and where this knowledge comes from.

Central within the whole argument this book presents is the point in childhood at which we (metaphorically) look in the mirror and recognise, know, and embrace, the person we see. Jung stood before that mirror earlier than most, and it never left his sight.

Frida Kahlo

Things are worse than we know, and, second, they're all right.

Frida Kahlo is a radical political and artistic icon for millions. Since her death she has taken her place among Mexico's greatest artists. Her unflinching self-portraits, once seen, never leave the mind's eye. Works such as *Henry Ford Hospital* and *A Few Small Nips* are famous for their unflinching portrayal of pain. They confront the viewer – often in an uncomfortable manner – with the artist's intimate world. Her husband, the muralist Diego Rivera, whose repeated infidelities were at the root of much of Kahlo's later suffering, described her as 'the only artist in the history of art who tore open her chest and heart to reveal the biological truth of her feelings'. And Kahlo's unique work – and the inspiration for it – stem from harrowing experiences in her youth.

Kahlo was born in Mexico City in 1907 to Guillermo Kahlo, a German photographer, and Matilde Calderón y Gonzalez, who was of Spanish and indigenous descent.

The family's home life was shaped, Kahlo said, by a cold and loveless marriage. Her parents were often ill, her father struggled financially, and though her mother could be 'kind, active and intelligent' she was also 'calculating, cruel and fanatically religious'.[1]

When she was three years old, her country was torn apart by revolution and civil war. But what truly marked Kahlo was the pain and violence of her personal life. At six, she contracted polio. She recalled 'a terrible pain in her right leg' and spent nine months in bed.[2] Muscle atrophy left her right leg shorter than her left. The resulting pelvic imbalance would cause a curvature in her spine, which led to a lifetime of chronic pain. Partly due to her disability, the sickly Frida grew closer to her father, who suffered from epilepsy and identified his own pain with his daughter's. As others bullied her and nicknamed her 'peg leg', Guillermo loved his child with ever-greater affection. As a result, said one art critic, 'for the rest of her life, Kahlo would associate pain with love'.[3]

Intermittently home-schooled because of her illness, she was then sent to a German school in Mexico City. Kahlo excelled academically but was deemed unable to take part in sports. Her gym and anatomy teacher declared her 'too frail' to participate in lessons. She pulled the thirteen-year-old Kahlo out and began what was later described as a 'physical relationship' with her. Compromising letters were discovered by Frida's mother, and the girl was immediately withdrawn from school.[4]

Despite this, she went on to become one of only 35 girls to enter Mexico City's prestigious National Preparatory School, where she excelled. But her first dream, of becoming a doctor, was wrecked in a bus crash when she was seventeen. A number of passengers were killed; Frida's right foot was crushed; a handrail 'pierced me as the sword pierces the bull',[5] passing right through her pelvis. She developed peritonitis and cystitis and was bed-bound for three months. Vertebrae had also been displaced and she spent three further months in a rigid corset.

The accident had a lasting impact on Kahlo's life and work. She underwent over thirty operations in the years that followed, but none relieved her unremitting pain. In 1953, after gangrene, her right leg was amputated. She also suffered a series of miscarriages, harrowing experiences that would inspire works such as *Henry Ford Hospital*.

But the bus crash and its consequences marked a new point in Kahlo's life. She abandoned ambitions to be a doctor and began to pursue painting seriously. Previously Kahlo had hidden her pain, wearing billowing dresses to cover her 'peg leg'. Now she wore it openly, depicting it in her work. She tried 'to begin again, painting things just as [she] saw them, with [her] own eyes and nothing more'.[6] Her left-wing political activism (alongside Diego Rivera) became a lifelong pursuit.

She invented her own style, fused her own artistic influences, lived life according to her own command, and followed her beliefs where they led her. You can see – or sense – in her work a Mexican nativist, the inspiration of indigenous culture; a world of the spirit; a naivety which borders on the cruel, and a terrible and striking realism. They call her a magical realist. Something in her work breathes honesty and defiance. The breaking of her body is the making of her spirit.

Over the coming thirty years, the self-taught Frida would create 143 paintings. Fifty-five were self-portraits and it was in this genre that she excelled. Her fans included Pablo Picasso, André Breton and Diego Rivera himself. Only a few, Vincent Van Gogh among them, have succeeded in portraying themselves with the same level of intimacy as Kahlo. In every portrait the same monobrowed face stares impassively at the viewer. *The Broken Column* (1944) portrays a naked Kahlo, with her torso split open to reveal a metal shaft in place of her spine. The body is barely held together by a corset, and countless nails pierce the exposed flesh.

But what is perhaps exceptional is that the unflinching depiction of pain is pitiless: entirely devoid of sentimentality or self-absorption. There is no call for sympathy. Instead, the impassive Kahlo stares out and dares the viewer to feel sorry for her, with a look as piercing as the handrail that had gored her. Pain confronts the viewer as a tragic but necessary part of life: to be lived with. In the words of art critic Peter Schjeldahl, Kahlo's gaze assures us, first, that 'things are worse than [we] know, and, second, that they're all right.'

CHAPTER THREE

ISOLATION

'Alone in the world'. The sentence sounds self-pitying, and the way most of us use it, it usually is. But contrast the whimpers to which we are all of us prone at moments when we feel insufficiently loved or supported, with the reality of our lives. How often have most people so much as approached – let alone fully experienced – having nobody at all to turn to, nobody who cares? Even the more solitary among us tend to have a fine if invisible web of friendship and mutual obligation to sustain us as we sustain others, however alone we sometimes feel.

Maybe we're not getting as much companionship or tender, loving care as we would like – but what would it be, particularly for a small child, to be genuinely abandoned, lost in a big, wide world we hardly knew and didn't understand, unable to reason out our situation, unloved by anyone at all? A striking number of great lives I've covered in my radio series have, at some point and usually in childhood, come very close to that state of isolation.

I include in this chapter experiences of 'dislocation' – which is not the same thing as loneliness, but works upon a child in the same way. To be wrenched early from one culture, one way of life and perhaps one language, and thrust into another, alienates. 'Alienates' not necessarily in the sense of generating hostility to the new circumstances, but in causing the child to step a little back from both: to distance themselves from total absorption in any culture.

Whether through abandonment, bereavement or dislocation, all the lives in this chapter are distinguished by having turned their back on something big, and as a result, seeing the world anew. Easy deference to the status quo need no longer bind a man or woman who has known utter rejection. They're equipped to stand forever apart. Such experiences need not be a negative thing, and in lives that later prove great their effects so often prove creative. It's a matter of being able to step away and to think things through from first principles, as Napoleon did. The adult is lent the moral confidence to swim against a tide, to follow their own hearts and heads, as they were forced to do when young.

That is true of the great black American rapper and musician who was a thinker and a poet too, Tupac Shakur. It is also true of the comedian who was so much more than a clown, Charlie Chaplin.

And certainly it's true of the small girl who in her later thoughts was to anticipate exactly what this book is trying to say – and whose remarkable story follows in more depth.

The waif who had to say no

On this dismal night, she needs to say no to something, to say no passionately to everything around her ...

A lone abbey stands on a rocky outcrop, looking over the thickly forested gorges of France's Massif Central. The monastery, founded by Stephen of Obazine in the twelfth century, lasted five hundred years before it was seized by the government in the French Revolution, briefly turned into a brothel, and then abandoned. Religious worship, though, proved harder to dislodge from this isolated place, and the nuns of the Sacred Heart of Mary found their way back. In the 1870s they added an orphanage.

And here – 'Aubazine' as it was now called – was where a destitute twelve-year-old girl and her two sisters arrived in 1895. The little girl would one day command global attention, not as a piteous orphan of ill-starred parents, but as the woman who changed the way the world dressed. She would modernise, re-imagine the idea of beauty in women's dress, create entirely new styles, revolutionise fashion, and design a logo synonymous with elegance and class. She would design the simple pink dress that Jacqueline Kennedy was wearing on the day her husband was assassinated in Dallas, Texas. By the time she invented the perfume for which she is perhaps most famous, she had spent much of her adult life trying to forget and erase her past.

But that girl on the orphanage doorstep was not called Coco Chanel, not then: that would happen later. As she stood on the steps of Aubazine she was Gabrielle: Gabrielle Chasnel.

Her mother had just died, on a cold February morning, in a freezing room in a lonely, shabby house in a nondescript French market town. The girls' father, an unsuccessful travelling salesman, had been away on the road, as usual. He was a man who had perfected the art of not being there. He hadn't been there for Gabrielle's birth, and nor was he there for his wife Jeanne's death.

Returning to his now motherless children, three girls and two boys, their father gathered them up and scattered them about the countryside like the tat he hawked for a living. The two brothers, aged six and ten, were given to peasant farms to be 'brought up'; as manual labour not far removed from child slavery. The three girls would at least be educated, though when they arrived at Aubazine in that mid-winter, bleak would have seemed the only word for their circumstances.

And now Gabrielle was in the middle of nowhere, in a small and remote village, on the doorstep of the nuns who were to replace her parents. But despite her circumstances she did not sink into self-pity: not now, not later, never. Fired up by her experience of a cruel and haphazard world, a shift seems to have taken place deep within her. It is impossible to say at what point the personality, revolutionary creativity and ambition which were to mark her life germinated, but we may speculate that it may well have been here on the threshold of Aubazine that something snapped. Something within her rejected the destiny life seemed to have chosen for her.

Gabrielle herself certainly thought so. She was later to report (speaking about herself in the third person as she so often did) that when she and her sisters turned up the nuns had finished their meal and seemed irritated that the three girls had not eaten.

This disturbs their routine and their household management, but eventually they overcome their harsh, provincial austerity and say reluctantly: 'We shall cook you two boiled eggs'. Little Coco can sense their reluctance and is offended; she is dying of hunger, but at the sight of the eggs she shakes her head, she refuses them, she declines, she states in a loud voice that she does not like eggs, she loathes them; in actual fact, she loves them, but after this first meeting, on this dismal night, she needs to say no to something, to say no passionately to everything around her …

It was a lie about the eggs, she continues. Her first big lie, the first of many.

In fact, her account of this episode is also a lie. Or, rather, truths are re-constituted, identities concealed. Gabrielle fought hard against the truth that she was sent to an orphanage. In her account she was sent into the care of aunts, not nuns, and it was at her aunts' doorstep that she had arrived. In later life she would refer to her time at the monastery in elliptical fashion, never once letting the word orphanage pass her lips.

Chanel's version of events and the likely truth often diverge, meet and diverge again; but always in more or less the same direction. As your narrator I have struggled with the choice between letting contradictory accounts wash over us in a flood of claim, counter-claim and supposition – or trying to catalogue for you the differences between the verifiable, the unverifiable and the frankly fictitious versions of her early life. I've done something to sift truth from fabrication, but in an important way it doesn't matter. In all essentials it's the same story: of being rejected, and – just as importantly – of rejecting.

This much we cannot doubt: her childhood is shrouded in the contradiction and mystery common to stories that are painful to tell, but we know that Gabrielle Chanel was born on 19 August 1883 to Albert Chanel, and Jeanne Devolle. Very evidently, Albert had a personal magnetism that could charm birds from trees. Many young women in the towns Albert passed through were susceptible to his patter, and there are stories about other pregnancies. It was inevitable in an age of scant contraception and censorious morality, that such a scallywag would get himself and his girl into trouble. In 1881 Albert found himself in Courpière, a commune in central France. There he rented a room with Jeanne and Marin, the young woman's brother. When Jeanne found herself pregnant in early 1882, Albert absconded.

The Devolle siblings had been orphaned at a young age but were by no means destitute. After his sister became pregnant and Albert had escaped, Marin set out to find him, and finally tracked him down in a town called Aubenas. Jeanne, then nine months pregnant, was left to journey to Aubenas alone. She made it. Perhaps she was determined not to be dishonoured by bearing a child out of wedlock. Perhaps she couldn't shake off her feelings. Perhaps Albert's true nature was not yet fully manifest. Whatever the truth, and whether through courage, love, lust or despair, she was unready to give up.

She found Albert in a tavern where he had taken a room. It was in that room that the couple's first child, Julie, was born within days. Gabrielle was the next child, born in Saumur a year later. Though listed as a married couple on Julie's birth certificate, Albert and Jeanne were not married: perhaps the first of many reasons Gabrielle felt ashamed of her childhood. As an adult she would tell different stories about her birth. We can know only that the truth must in some way have pained her deeply.

In one version of her birth, told to journalist Paul Morand, Gabrielle was very nearly born in the house of some rich, kindly townsfolk of Saumur who had taken in her mother, assuming her to be ill, and were outraged to discover that Jeanne was in fact pregnant. Having determined that Jeanne Devolle was the wrong kind of ill, they threw her back out on the street, leaving her to give birth in a hospital. The nun who cared for Jeanne was called Gabrielle Bonheur. The baby was named after her because, Coco said, that was the done thing. Coco always hated the name Gabrielle and any opportunity to palm it off onto unkind fate was willingly taken. Whether her mother's cruel treatment by the household that threw her out helped spark her inner rage at privileged hypocrisy or whether the rage caused her to invent the story matters more to historians than to students of human psychology. It's notable that neither this nor other versions of her nativity seek to dignify or even normalise her start in life. All versions, however, sensationalise it. In a different story told to a fabric wholesaler friend, Coco dispensed with the sneering citizens, the hospital, and Sister Gabrielle Bonheur. She moved her mother instead from the hospital ward to the carriage of a train that was travelling to Saumur. Gabrielle was born, Coco claimed, in that very carriage.

It seems one story was false, another only partly true. Gabrielle Chanel was almost certainly delivered in a Saumur hospice (the hospital of the earlier story) by two care workers. The next day this pair went to the town hall to notify the authorities; they were illiterate, so the deputy mayor, François Poitou, wrote down the young girl's name – and did so with an extra 's', as 'Chasnel'.

Between her birth and her mother's death the outlines of Gabrielle Chanel's life are clear even if the detail is not. In the first eleven years she lived in awful squalor interwoven with happier moments with her father's extended family. She spent much of her early childhood in another nondescript French town, Issoire, where her father left her, her mother, and her siblings, as he traced the rail network, selling his wares at towns up and down the lines. The Chanels, her biographer Axel Madsen says, lived in neighbourhoods that 'belonged to the dying crafts – ropemakers, nailsmiths, potters and hemp weavers and chandlers'. It was here, in this fading world soon to be eclipsed by advancing industrialisation, among the backstreets of Issoire, that two more children, Alphonse and Antoinette, were born within four years. Then, two years later, with the family back on the road, a son Lucien, was born near Limoges.

Any woman's health would have suffered, and Jeanne was already sickly and racked by coughing. She tried to give up following Albert and settle, but within two years, devoted to him, she and her five children were on the road again. One day in 1895 Jeanne's breath was particularly short, her temperature particularly high, and she fainted in the room she was in. She would never leave it. She was found dead there one February morning. She had been the one fixed point in her children's peripatetic life; their shock and anxiety must have been made worse by their father's callous response. From his very first entanglement with

Jeanne he had evidently wished to avoid being tied down by her. Now he was free to dissociate himself from his children too.

At this bitter moment in Gabrielle's life, her later (and alter) ego Coco dissimulates. Her father, she told friends at the time and journalists later, had gone to America to seek his fortune. Her father, in fact, had not left the country. He was last seen by his son Lucien performing a ridiculous salesman's ruse in Brittany in 1909 and living with a woman who was far younger than him, but an equally prodigious drinker. Albert's trick was to parade loudly through the streets of villages with a hired horse and claim he was the retainer of a local nobleman, the marquis of Barrucan, who was suddenly cash-strapped and needed to sell his high-quality crockery at conveniently affordable prices. Gullible villagers duly bought up Albert's stock of distinctly ignoble plates and pans. His family never saw him again, after that. It's fitting that Albert Chanel, after living the kind of carefree, irresponsible life he had, should march out of history in a whirligig procession of exotic lies in the company of his latest drunken squeeze.

Here, then, are some of the many facets of Coco Chanel. It's the story of how Gabrielle became Coco. Nowhere is the refitting of history more apparent than in her references to herself. Her use of the third person in her story about refusing the eggs distances her from her own past; in fact the very name she uses, Coco, does the same: no aunt would then have called her Coco, they would have called her Gabrielle – the name Coco came later, perhaps as a result of the 1920s equivalent of a karaoke party she attended with some cavalry officers, at which she sang a song, to whoops of applause, about a lost little dog named Coco. In her own imagination she was surely that little lost dog.

It seems impossible to escape from the conclusion that her time at Aubazine shaped her sense of identity and of purpose profoundly. Less dwelt upon in her recollection is the fact that she did not spend all her time at Aubazine. There were happier interludes spending holiday time staying with her real aunt, the childless Louise Costier, and her husband. The couple also intervened to rescue Gabrielle's two young brothers from the farmhand serfdom and set them on the road to becoming market retailers. Though later their sister sent them money, Coco pushed them out of her life and her life story. Madsen suggests that later in life, as a romance with the Duke of Westminster deepened, she became afraid of her own back-story, and so bought her brothers' silence: and it is true they (both) died in the 1940s, having not seen her for years, and thereafter she refused to have anything to do with their children or their grandchildren. My own guess, however, is that the inconvenience of her siblings' existence was as much psychological as practical. In her story, she wanted to be alone.

Holidays away from Aubazine nourished Gabrielle in ways the orphanage could not. She started to devour the women's romance novels of 'Gyp' and Pierre Decourcelle, banned at Aubazine, where she hid them in a loft – until she was rumbled by the nuns, who noticed entire passages in one of her creative writing essays that seemed too polished and too purple for a little girl. She was ordered to throw out her books, but not before she had been inspired by one literally purple passage in a Decourcelle novel where the lead female character wears a purple dress. As a teenager Gabrielle later persuaded a local seamstress to make her something similar. Coco described the dress: 'It had a high neck with flying ribbons and matching slip, purple, and underneath a ruffle. I was perhaps fifteen or sixteen, although I looked twelve. I chose a clinging linen, not that I had anything to mould or underline.'

One Sunday morning before church Gabrielle duly presented herself at the top of the stairs – but her grand reveal misfired: they were running late; she was hurried downstairs without a glance; her relatives, suddenly confronted with what appeared to them an outrageous costume, ordered her to take if off and dress properly. Worse followed – the poor seamstress was asked never to work for the family again, and turned angrily against Gabrielle.

Gabrielle spent five years at the monastery, leaving when she was eighteen. It was a place that had formed her, not least by the way it had repelled her. But things were looking up. Her grandparents' circumstances had improved over their lives, and they were now able to send her to a finishing school in Moulins. A year later the chief friend of her childhood, Adrienne, joined her. The girls were becoming young ladies now. Slowly the outside world was opening up. After school they got jobs together in an outfitters shop in town, and took lodgings there. Now the sewing she had learnt at the orphanage became useful, though later she wrote the shop, Desboutins, out of her life. Even more useful was Gabrielle's talent for socialising with the officers of the cavalry regiment, the Tenth Horse, stationed in the town. There she would begin the first serious relationship of her life, which opened many doors. There was a long way to go – and a name still to change – but Gabrielle was well set when she finally departed a period of her life she would never revisit.

Or would she? The austerity of the monastery was a very long way from the stardust that settled upon her later life. It is hard to believe that the young girl who, dressed in only the simplest clothes, washed linen for years among the nuns could be the same woman as the fashion designer who changed the way women dressed, dallied with English lords, and was saved from prosecution after the overthrow of the Vichy regime thanks to her personal friendship with Winston Churchill. Yet to emphasise the difference is to ignore the link between those two lives.

I'll turn in a moment to the profound sense of rebellion, the tiny raised fist of the little girl who wouldn't admit to liking eggs, the consciousness of being alone in the universe, and the capacity to shrug off conventional wisdom, that both inspired and branded her work in fashion. But it's worth mentioning first that echoes of the austerity and asceticism that surrounded her at Aubazine may be detected in the look she came to define as her own.

Coco Chanel's modernisation of fashion was characterised by her pared-down style. Looking back to the Edwardian tastes of the Europe she burst upon, we can call her a revolutionary. It was Chanel who invented the now ubiquitous 'little black dress' that in 1926 *American Vogue* predicted, accurately as it turned out, would be a 'frock that all the world would wear'. At Aubazine not only was Coco confronted daily by the simplicity of the nun's dress, but also the usefulness of being able to make do. As Madsen notes, this was particularly useful after the Great War:

> By upbringing, if not inclination, Gabrielle was trained to 'make do'. The orphanage and Aunt Louise had taught her to improvise with bits and pieces, to find ideas in what was handy, to work with what was available. She understood that the war demanded a fashion of rummage, of salvage, a fashion that was simple and functional, and could be made up with opportunities and remnants.

Another of her biographers, Edmonde Charles-Roux, similarly believes her love of purity and simplicity can be traced back implicitly to the years spent at Aubazine:

> And whenever she began yearning for austerity, for the ultimate in cleanliness, for faces scrubbed with yellow soap; or waxed nostalgic for all things white, simple and clear, for linen piled in high cupboards, whitewashed walls, an enormous padded table above which starched wimples and ruff wings fluttered like weightless petals, one had to understand that she was speaking in a secret code, and that every word she uttered meant only one word. Aubazine.

The experience of growing up affected not just her sense of style and elegance; it profoundly affected her drive. She hated her childhood. The fabrications of her own life that she wove only make that even more obvious. And she didn't just want to mythologise it – she half wanted to jettison it, half clutched it to her bosom. 'Depend upon it,' said Samuel Johnson, 'that if a man talks of his misfortunes there is something in them that is not disagreeable to him.' The poverty, the loneliness, the hardness of the life all lit a fire underneath her:

It is loneliness that has forged my character, which is bad-tempered, and bronzed my soul, which is proud, and my body, which is sturdy.

My life is the story – and often the tragedy – of the solitary woman, her woes, her importance, the unequal and fascinating battle she has waged with herself, with men, and with the attractions, the weaknesses and the dangers that spring up everywhere.

That is my childhood, the childhood of an orphan, retold by a girl who knew no home, no love, no father and mother. It was terrible, but I don't regret a thing. I have been ungrateful to the wicked aunts: I owe them everything, a rebellious child makes for a well-prepared and very strong human being. (Aged eleven, I had much more strength than I do now.)

It is kisses, hugs, teachers and vitamins that kill children and prepare them for being weak or unhappy. It is wicked aunts who make conquerors of them ... And who develop inferiority complexes in them. In my case, this gave me the opposite: superiority complexes. Beneath maliciousness, there is strength; beneath pride, there is the taste for success and the love of importance. Children who have teachers learn. I was self-taught; I learnt badly, haphazardly. And yet, when life put me in touch with those who were the most delightful or brilliant people of my age, a Stravinsky, or a Picasso, I neither felt stupid, nor embarrassed. Why?

Because [my italics] I had worked out on my own that which cannot be taught. I will return to this frequently. For the time being, I want to end on this important aphorism, which is the secret of my success, and perhaps that of civilisation; confronted with ruthless techniques of doing things: it's [her italics] *with what cannot be taught that one succeeds.*

After Coco Chanel, fashion was different. In 1915, when she had only been in business for a few years, *Harper's Bazaar*, the fashion magazine, said '[t]he woman who hasn't at least one Chanel is hopelessly out of fashion ... This season the name Chanel is on the lips of every buyer'. Her career was just getting started. Before her, much of women's fashion had been restrictive and stuffy. She liberated women from frilliness and dressed them instead in clothes that actually paid attention to their figures. Her biographers, of whom there are many, may have an interest in promoting her, but the uniformity of their judgement throws her achievement into clear relief. André Malraux, the eminent French historian, wrote: '[f]rom this century, in France, three names will remain: de Gaulle, Picasso, and Chanel'. Axel Madsen's remarks are similarly a little overblown, perhaps, but have the ring of fairness: 'Some twenty years after her death, the timeless appeal of Gabrielle Bonheur Chanel reigns supreme. The Chanel look is everywhere, canonized and copied with more fervor than ever before. Fashionable without being forward, the Chanel suit achieved new currency and appropriateness, a look that was rich, refined and, above all, dressed.'

There were surely many other factors in her rise and her success – not least, as is always necessary, a prodigious amount of luck and timing. But in the facts of her childhood it is possible to see how what broke Gabrielle made Coco.

Coco Chanel's childhood was without question a fractured one. Shot through with loneliness, betrayal, isolation and despair, her early life didn't just damage, didn't just grind, didn't just 'toughen up' Gabrielle. It energised and drove her. It illuminated her imagination. Being solitary and unloved became for her a creative impulse. In each type and episode of suffering – the death of her mother, abandonment by her father, the hated life at the orphanage – seeds were sown that grew her future genius. This can be understood not least in her own words, drawing the thread between deprivation and genius. I repeat: 'Children who have teachers learn. I was self-taught; I learnt badly, haphazardly. And yet, when life put me in touch with those who were the most delightful or brilliant people of my age, a Stravinsky, or a Picasso, I neither felt stupid, nor embarrassed. Why?'

From our own schooldays all of us can remember this: the view out through the windows of the prison that was our childhood classroom. At that orphanage in Aubazine there are patterns of interlocking letters on the stained glass. The famous Chanel logo, the interlocking pair of Cs, now an instantly recognisable symbol copied around the world, were her own design.

Charlie Chaplin

The school was a place of humiliation and suffering ... when he returned to visit in 1931, he was overwhelmed by the 'same sensation of oppression and confinement [he] had then'.

Arguably the most famous silent film star of all time – and the inventor of a whole genre of comedy – Charlie Chaplin began his journey to these heights in rags, from a workhouse, and the gates of the mental asylum where his mother was incarcerated.

Chaplin is universally acknowledged as one of the finest and most original comic performers in history. He rose to fame in the era of silent film, and became a global icon with his character 'the Tramp'. His life was a remarkable story of poverty, chaos and despair in childhood, and command, creativity and moral courage in the soaring career which followed. It spanned more than seventy-five years, and encompassed acting, filmmaking, directing, composing, and acts of brave political resolve.

Charles Chaplin Jr was born on 16 April 1889, probably just off the Walworth Road in south London, although his birth was never registered. His mother was Hannah Chaplin, a music-hall singer with a history of mental illness. His father, Charles Chaplin Sr, was also a successful music-hall artist, though his son questioned his own paternity. Charles Sr left the family the year after Charlie was born, and it's possible his mother turned to prostitution to support herself. Soon she started a relationship with singer Leo Dryden, and the family moved neighbourhoods, but as Charlie reached his fourth birthday Dryden left, taking the couple's six-month-old son with him and leaving Charlie, his older brother Sydney and their mother behind.

It was around this time that Chaplin's 'Dickensian period' started. Hannah's mother had just been committed to a mental asylum, leaving Hannah to cope alone. Hannah's own health collapsed, beginning a continuous cycle of upheaval for the children. When their mother was in hospital or institutionalised, the boys were sent to the workhouse or residential schools like the Central London District School for paupers, which Chaplin remembered as 'a forlorn existence'. They were so poor that Sydney was forced to wear his mother's heeled boots and jackets. Missing a father figure, Charlie in particular idolised his mother, and his attachment to her at that time was very strong. In a 1915 essay for *Photoplay* magazine he wrote that she 'was the most splendid woman [he] ever knew'. The pair bonded over their love of the music hall, and she used to refer to him as 'the King'. In the spring of 1896, Hannah succumbed to illness again (she was to develop an apparent psychosis, possibly brought on by syphilis and malnutrition) and the boys went back to the workhouse. They were then sent to Hanwell School, an institute for destitute children just outside London, after Charlie's father refused to take them in.

Amid what was never less than a distressed and disjointed upbringing, this episode of Charlie's life can be considered the greatest fracture. He later referred to it as the moment when his childhood ended; or as his period of 'incarceration'. Aged seven, he was immediately separated from his older brother, and subjected to harsh punishments. Unwell and alone, he experienced the school as a place of humiliation and suffering. His eighteen months there had such an impact on him that when he returned to visit the school in 1931, he found himself, at the very sight of his old surroundings, overwhelmed by the 'same sensation of oppression and confinement [he] had then'. For a seven-year-old, misery was only made worse by the failure of his mother to visit. He experienced a profound sense of betrayal. When she did visit the following year, he was embarrassed by her behaviour. As an adult he would never entirely shake off a difficulty in trusting women.

The little boy survived this experience by trying to make himself invulnerable, and thinking of himself 'as the greatest actor in the world'. This invulnerability became a crucial part of his most famous onscreen persona, the Tramp, a figure who keeps going because he has to, and is rarely the object of pity. In the early films especially, the Tramp is angry, craving food and security. Sheer survival is a key theme throughout Chaplin's work.

Within six months of leaving the school, the family were back at the workhouse again. When his mother was committed again, Charlie perceived it as another betrayal. The boys went to live with Charles Chaplin Sr, but by then he had become a severe alcoholic and died a few years later of cirrhosis of the liver. For the remainder of Hannah's life she would be in and out of institutions. Charlie rarely visited or wrote to her when she was away, and as an adult seemed to fear that he, too, would lose his mind. At fourteen, he had to take her (after a period of remission) back to the mental asylum and, awaiting the return of his older brother, spent time sleeping rough on park benches and looking for food.

His last recorded day in school was in November 1898 – he left aged nine. He had already sought occasional work in music-hall theatre, and in time his talents were spotted, though it was in America (where he finally made his career) that he was to break through and achieve worldwide fame. He had been introduced to the stage by his parents, and it was a natural environment for him to be in, but, as the people who met him later recalled, there was something different about Charlie – 'something intense and unbroken within him'.

The depth of his ambition and the power of his will had set him apart early, but he had something more than that: comic genius. His Tramp was never just a clown. The tragic absurdity of his comic creations (including his brave portrayal of Adolf Hitler in his satire, *The Great Dictator*, first screened in New York in 1940 when the United States was still a neutral country) invited something other than pity, and more than laughter. It's in some ways regrettable that people of this writer's generation were introduced to him through slapstick films hired out for small children's birthday parties. Chaplin might have smiled to note the irony. Indeed, it was in the depths of his own childhood misery that some kind of internal cosmic smile, tinged with melancholy, was born in Charlie Chaplin.

Napoleon Bonaparte

I was a quarreller, a fighter; I feared nobody, beating one, scratching another, making myself redoubtable to all.

'Never interrupt your enemy when he is making a mistake.' Napoleon's famous remark to his officers at the

Battle of Austerlitz showed not only his calmness under pressure, but his strategic genius. The allied forces occupied a high point – the Pratzen Heights – and Napoleon knew he had to lure them from it. He withdrew men from his right flank, making it appear weak and unprotected. When the allied forces rushed down to engage, he ignored his excited marshals and waited. Only once the allied forces had fully entered his trap did he counter-attack, deploying his left flank with decisive speed to seize the heights and turn the tide of the battle. His cavalry pursued the fleeing Russians and put an end to the fighting. Napoleon had lost 9,000 of his 60,000 men over the course of the fighting. The allied forces had lost 36,000 of their 89,000. Through military manoeuvre, deception and sheer nerve, Napoleon had destroyed a far larger force. The young Tsar Alexander rued his bad luck: 'We are babies in the hands of a giant.'

But Napoleon's first encounter with the nation he was to lead was steeped in anger, loneliness and isolation. Aged nine, he and his older brother Joseph were sent from Corsica to mainland France. Napoleon spoke no French, and was sent to a school in the centre of the country to learn the language. Born in 1769 just after the French annexation of Corsica from Genoa, Napoleon followed his proud father as a Corsican nationalist and supporter of Pasquale Paoli, the famed Corsican leader. He'd been brought up speaking Corsican and Italian and his father had encouraged him to consider the French as foreign usurpers. Not surprising, then, that Napoleon was made wretched. 'He was pensive and moody, he looked unhappy and never took part in any games, almost always going around alone,' wrote an early biographer, Arthur

Chuquet. His naturally abrasive character further pitched him into angry resistance to the place where fate had sent him.

Throughout his childhood in Corsica, the second Bonaparte son behaved as if he were the first. He recalled: 'I was a quarreller, a fighter; I feared nobody, beating one, scratching another, making myself redoubtable to all. It was my brother Joseph who most often had to suffer. He was slapped, bitten, scolded ...' The boy's perhaps innate fearlessness and pugnacity were coupled with a consuming hatred of losing. Chuquet describes a game between Napoleon, Joseph and his classmates in which the boys re-enacted Hannibal's battles with Rome. Napoleon, desperate to be on the winning side, was outraged when he was handed the flag of the Carthaginians. He begged Joseph to swap places with him and let him join the Roman side. Affable Joseph obliged.

But, uprooted and deposited in a French school, Napoleon's light seemed to dim. He fared even worse when, a year later, at the age of ten, he was sent to Brienne Royal Military School. Napoleon was one of the first Corsican children to enter Brienne and he cried all the way there, devastated to leave his brother and longing to return to his parents in Corsica. The rules of the school said otherwise: students were not to leave Brienne from the moment they entered the school to the day they graduated, six years later. The brutality of these six years went a long way to forming young Napoleon's character.

The school followed the theories of Abbé Fleury, a seventeenth-century pedagogue, who called for strict, serious education in 'useful' subjects, and few private pleasures.

The students were taught classical studies, history, geography, mathematics, foreign languages and all that was useful to the '*art militaire*'. They were also deprived of luxuries, prevented from playing, going for walks, or eating with their friends (says Chuquet). Thanks to this upbringing – the teachers argued – the trials of later life would seem a breeze.

But Napoleon was badly bullied. He sulked and grew to hate his classmates. Even his teachers taunted him, identifying Corsica as a foreign land and Napoleon, by extension, as a foreigner. His classmates jeered at him for being, whatever his pretensions, a subject of the French king. Naturally, the 'mockery of his peers only affirmed and deepened his Corsican patriotism', says Chuquet. He was an outsider. He now understood that only by individuation, and not by association with his mainland classmates, could he be a winner.

He did this first through military prowess. Chuquet describes the snowy 1783 winter during which Napoleon, inspired by engineering classes, built a small fort in the courtyard and organised a snowball fight. The Corsican ordered his classmates on both sides around, inspiring them to defend the fort with all their might, and hold it. When the day was done, however much they disliked him, all had to admire his bravery and sheer imagination. Napoleon's rise to giant status was the result of a gruelling military education and an abnormally fierce will to succeed but, more than anything, an immensity of imagination and an almost limitless audacity. Whatever box contained conventional military thinking, Napoleon could think outside it. Along whatever lines the law and governance of France had conventionally been conceived, Napoleon broke through them.

Were I to choose a phrase that best indicates what set him apart from contemporaries, it would be the Latin term, *a priori*: taking things back to first principles; discarding the encrustation of custom and practice and, in an imaginative leap, starting from scratch. It was just such a leap, just such a sweeping away of the certainties of his age and culture, that marked the boy Napoleon's tormented younger years.

As the twentieth-century French poet André Suarès wrote, 'he was France's idol. The passion he inspired in so many Frenchmen … is one of the noblest poems ever to have emanated from the valiant heart of man'. Is it strange, as some have thought, that such a fierce Corsican should have come to embody all things French? I would argue the opposite. Only by standing outside France – as perhaps in his heart he always had from the moment he landed on the mainland to face the miseries of a new language in a strange school – could a man know France, re-imagine France, and then re-make France, as Napoleon did.

After his military campaigns abroad he was to transform the legal and administrative framework of his country and its empire, its education system and its economy; and to set in place a meritocratic system that lasts to this day. He remained an outsider all his life – an upstart who overturned habits of mind still tangled in a monarchical history. If the word 'genius' has any application to statesmanship and command, Napoleon is the outstanding modern example. And his genius was born in his isolation, dislocated to a strange land and speaking a strange tongue.

Orson Welles

Some said he never really was a child; others that he remained one all his life.

As a boy Orson Welles was visited by a psychologist who wanted to include him in a study of 'fate-marked children' so unusual that they seemed destined to lead extraordinary lives. The prodigy treated his observer with disdain. To the psychologist's various stimuli and measurements he replied with cryptic wisecracks, citing Oscar Wilde and Shakespeare. The psychologist gave up; the 'subject' seemed more interested in testing the questioner than answering the questions.

None can doubt that this child began his life with bags of intelligence and talent. But what gave him the almost outrageous apparent carelessness of the world, of fate, of the opinion of others, that propelled him to the top in so many fields?

He was always a performer. He acquired an almost bloated confidence that would enable him to excel in almost every genre of modern entertainment: theatre, radio, television and, of course, cinema. Frank Brady, his biographer, believes 'the story of his life is the story of dramatic performance in twentieth-century America'. This may be so, and the works he left behind – from *Citizen Kane* to his radio play *The War of the Worlds* – bear witness to his talent.

Being a performer, however, Welles was also a notoriously unreliable interviewee. The American film critic Jonathan Rosenbaum reports that some labelled him 'a compulsive liar'. Biographical details are to be taken with a pinch of salt. What we do know is that his childhood was a wreck.

Neither Welles's cultural hinterland nor his prodigious personal confidence came from nowhere. His pianist mother, Beatrice, is said to have read Shakespeare and other literary greats to her son from infancy. By the age of two, the boy was speaking in fully formed sentences. The family doctor and friend, Maurice Bernstein, was astonished by the toddler's intellect. The boy accompanied his mother everywhere, soon familiar with local artistic and intellectual circles. He longed to converse as an equal, shunned the very idea of childhood and swore to grow up as quickly as possible. If Brady's reports are to be believed, he sipped wine at five, applied make-up to age his face and, by ten, tried to roughen his voice with smoking.

Unsurprisingly, Welles showed no interest in children of his own age and was both bullied and bored at school. His mother, father and Dr Bernstein became his real teachers.

Until, at the age of seven, a cycle of loss began. Beatrice contracted hepatitis. She fell fast into a critical condition and Orson last visited her bedroom on his eighth birthday. Her death marked the boy deeply; he was left, he said, with a sense of 'anguished loss'.

Then the chaos started. In a period of his childhood that Welles later described, with understatement, as 'somewhat hectic', he went to live in a Chicago apartment shared by Bernstein and his father, Richard Welles, who had been a successful inventor in his younger days. Then with his (now) heavy-drinking father he toured Jamaica and the Far East, the boy (according to one account) taking care of the father as much as the father the son; and then to an Illinois hotel room with his father, who had by then become a hopeless alcoholic.

The hotel burned down, and the pair took to the road again. At eleven Orson was sent to a private school, where the headmaster, Richard 'Skipper' Hill (a lifelong mentor) took him under his wing and gave Orson free rein over dramatic productions, of which he mounted many every year.

Back in another hotel room, his father descended ever further into alcoholism. Finally, hoping to stop his drinking with the threat, Orson refused to visit him. Richard then drank himself to death in his Chicago hotel, aged fifty-eight. Orson, then fifteen, was inconsolable and blamed himself for his father's self-destruction.

We can only imagine the effect on a child who'd seen the early death of his mother, watched his father destroy his own life, and was now wracked by guilt for not stopping it. He had lived (said others) for adult approval, and now the principal adults in his life were gone. Some (like Hill, his headmaster) said he never really was a child; others that he remained one all his life – a precocious, energetic, *wunderkind*.

But Welles's exuberant confidence was a facade. It served – like the make-up he had applied as a boy – to cloak his insecurities. He had lived in constant fear of disappointing the adults in his life. Biographer Barbara Leaming commented: 'to understand Orson Welles, his formative early years as a cosseted prodigy should be kept in mind. The brilliant expectations of others ... and the expectations he had for himself, are what he has struggled to live up to all his life.'

Live up to them, though, he did. The story of how Orson landed his first professional role as an actor shows how effective his blustering confidence could be. At eighteen the young Welles had travelled to Ireland hoping to become not an actor but a painter. He had moved round the country and was on the point of finishing a spell in Dublin when he visited the famous Dublin Gate Theatre. Impressed by the lead actor, Michael MacLiammoir, Orson was seized with the conviction that he must star alongside him. He left a note to the director: 'Orson Welles, star of the New York Theatre Guild, would consider appearing in one of your productions and hopes you will see him for an appointment.'

In the resulting audition Welles delivered a performance of such energy and weight that he was cast as an elderly gentleman in the next production. MacLiammoir hadn't been taken in for a moment by the bluster, but recognised the boy's talent. The crowd did too. The opening night was a roaring success.

He went on to success in fields and in ways too various to list; and, besides, it is not in the end the length of the list but the depth of the originality that marked him out as (in the words of two British Film Institute polls) the 'Greatest film director of all time'. His innovative use, for instance, of a non-linear narrative form – scenes do not necessarily appear in chronological order – is now a familiar, almost standard technique; but the literary and theatrical tradition had always been to start a story at the beginning and follow it to the end. Welles took control both as a director and as an actor, brushed convention aside, and did it his way. To watch a Welles-directed performance – whether or not Welles himself is also the performer – is to feel the presence of an author, not just an actor or director. The author is in charge; his voice can be heard beneath and behind all the others.

There exist two types of self-confidence: the showy self-confidence, close to boastfulness, that so often betrays a secret fear; and the real self-confidence of a guiding mind that knows how do to it. Orson Welles displays both. A rocket our age has never seen the like of, had risen.

But what was the launchpad? Not really that cheeky note to an old pro from a precocious eighteen-year-old: the youth was fully formed by then, his talents already evident. Nor either, I believe, the careful coaching from his mother or the clever grown-ups and shiny society that formed the backdrop to his boyhood. Countless other boys and girls have such advantages. If you seek not his genius but the launchpad to his genius, seek out his sick and sallow mother's deathbed when he was eight; the realisa-tion as his father sank that the son must now take control or nobody would; the sordid circumstance of the hotel room in which his father drank himself to death when Orson was fifteen; and the guilty belief that he had killed his father that was to haunt him for the rest of his wildly successful, hard-driving and extravagantly varied life.

It was the boyhood realisation that the grown-ups were not in charge, nobody was in charge, and that if you knew what to do you had to take control of it for yourself, that unlocked Welles's genius.

Tupac Shakur

Through the imagination of this troubled man, the
imagination of a whole generation had been captured.

On 7 September 1996, the hip hop artist and actor Tupac Shakur was shot several times while riding in a car in Las Vegas with the record producer Suge Knight. Six days later, he died in hospital. Among the most successful rappers in history, Tupac has sold more than 67 million records and is considered one of his generation's most gifted and influential lyricists. To some he was a controversial figure who drew criticism for the content of some of his lyrics and his association with violence. To others he was a revolutionary thinker who expressed the fears and hopes of young, disadvantaged people and worked hard to confront inequality. Neither friend nor foe questions his genius.

Such is his cult status that there are many convinced he is still alive. He has been projected in hologram at music festivals. By his genius as a rapper, by the dizzy complexity of his art and his activism, and by his early death, Tupac Shakur has joined the ranks of the deathless.

But it all started in confusion.

Tupac was born in June 1971 in Harlem, and named after Túpac Amaru II, an eighteenth-century Incan revolutionary who fought Spanish rule in Peru. His mother, Afeni Shakur, an active member of the Black Panther Party, was released from prison one month before his birth after being acquitted for her role in the Panther 21 trial, a plot to bomb public spaces in New York City. His stepfather was involved in the Black Liberation Army, and spent years on the FBI's Ten Most Wanted Fugitives list. His godfather,

Geronimo Pratt, was a high-ranking Black Panther convicted of murder (later overturned) before Tupac's birth, and his informal 'godmother' was Assata Shakur, one of the FBI's 'Most Wanted Terrorists'.

Tupac's exposure to radical black thought was crucial to the development of his own political ideas, and he was involved in political activism from the age of seven. However, his home life was enormously disrupted: the family moved between the Bronx and Manhattan about eighteen times before he was ten years old, and experienced periods of homelessness. The child was forever being required to reinvent himself, make new friends and try to fit in, and he felt isolated. His mother was often unemployed, and later developed an addiction to crack cocaine, sending Tupac out to buy her drugs. This was during President Richard Nixon's war on drugs, heavily concentrated on poor black communities. Young black men in particular were doubly hit, both victims of the crack cocaine epidemic and the militarised, racially charged policing of the period. They were imprisoned in unprecedented numbers, and the homicide rate for young black men skyrocketed. As a teenager Tupac would carry a video camera around with him to make sure any encounter with the police would be on record. These themes found their way into Tupac's lyrics, attacking the crack trade, mass incarceration and police brutality.

The family moved to Baltimore in 1986, and at the age of fifteen Tupac began writing and performing tracks whose lyrics looked at social problems. He became involved with the Young Communist League, and began organising grassroots activity while in high school. As he grew older his ideas developed and he became more politically independent from his parents. He attended Baltimore School for Arts, where he met Jada Pinkett (now married to the actor Will Smith) and began studying poetry, ballet and Shakespeare. He began performing more, and made close friends.

But when his mother found they were to be evicted in 1988, she sent Tupac and his younger sister to live with a friend, Assante, in Marin City, California – known then as the Jungle. This forced move, with the misery it caused, is one of many possible fractures: he was heartbroken, and the move changed the course of his life. Assante was a verbally abusive alcoholic, and Tupac didn't fit in; a bohemian more interested in creative arts than basketball, he was a target for street gangs. He said of the time that writing poetry made him think he was 'weird'. He hated himself, he said. He even tried to keep his poetry a secret. His mother's crack addiction returned, he dropped out of school and had nowhere to live: he had few options and the circumstances of his life appeared to be closing in on him.

But he started rapping to anyone who would listen. He was gaining a reputation for his talent. His fortunes lifted further when he met music promoter and poetry teacher Leila Steinberg, who took him into her care and filled an almost maternal role, as well as becoming his first agent. With her help, he was set on a course to stardom.

Tupac was talented, certainly: but something set him apart from the common run of clever, streetwise artists. It's true that his rap fundamentals – bravado, lyricism and charisma – put him in the firmament of nineties gangsta rap, but it was his range, greater than any of his peers, that made him the era's shining star. Choosing people who illustrate *Fracture*'s thesis, I have had a particular difficulty with black American heroes whose childhood, in common with millions of their race and nationality, was marked by racial oppression and its consequences: poverty, poor education, dislocation and dysfunctional family life, and who succeeded despite this, as humans commonly do. Shakur, however, succeeded because of it. There is something transformative in his work. He could do emotion, lyrical terrain that would have killed a lesser rapper's credibility stone dead. Instead, on songs like 'Dear Mama', he raps with a deftness about the trickiest of subjects – love.

He describes how he and his mama fell out when he was seventeen and he was kicked out onto the streets – and he believed he'd never see her again. Yet still he loved and missed her. He despaired. Afraid to go home and excluded from school, he was, he raps, a fool, running wild with older boys.

The dislocation of his childhood crops up again and again in his songs. And on 'Papa'z Song', Tupac inveighs against his absent father and his mother's string of brief relationships: every weekend it was a different father, he raps. Yes, there is self-pity here, but also tenderness, ruefulness and self-knowledge. The bravado falters and one senses that the teenage poetry was not a phase of childish self-absorption. It was what he was – despite, but also, and in an important sense, because of the mess that was his youth.

Tupac's art had a depth that lifted him to the pinnacle of his world. That depth was shaded by his childhood, how he understood it, how he made use of it in his art.

On top of that, somewhere amid the drugs, the violence,

the constant dislocation, the bullying and the loneliness, he had also conceived a real belief that he could – and should – change the world. Could such singularity have germinated in a calm and secure childhood? Shakur was a complex character and not without his own demons: in 1995 he was sentenced to prison for sexual assault. Many of his lyrics are full of misogyny. But through the imagination of this troubled man, the imaginations of a whole generation had been captured.

Freddie Mercury

At eight, the little Farrokh was summarily sent to a new continent, a new culture, with new languages. Everything he had known fell apart.

The image of Freddie Mercury at Knebworth in 1986, proudly moustachioed, wearing a yellow leather jacket, collar turned up, microphone stick in hand and strutting around conducting 120,000 people (some claim many more) in singing his songs sums up the very notion of 'having the audience in the palm of your hand'. Freddie Mercury's sheer exuberance, swagger and – yes – mercurial vivacity demanded the world take notice. And they did: nearly thirty years after his death, a film of his life and his band, Queen, has scooped Oscars; and the musical based on the songs went on tour after twelve years in London's West End.

Queen sold millions of albums worldwide and broke the mould for pop videos. Mercury's virtuoso turn at Live Aid in 1985 is widely regarded as one of the greatest musical performances ever. Queen – which was always a melody-led band with a foot in glam rock, another foot in plain old rock and roll, one ear open to opera and a nose for the possibilities of prog rock – had an unlikely breakthrough in 'Bohemian Rhapsody'. This wasn't the first song to break the three-minute pop-hit rule but it was arguably the most extravagant. Yet there is no time wasted: attack piano, human tragedy, lyrics with more feeling than meaning, a baroque backstory and a tight guitar solo, it manages to cram a mini-opera into the time it took some bands to change key. One DJ, playing the track for the very first time, reached the end of the record, lifted the needle, and played it again from the beginning. And then did it again. After all, how do you follow that?

The music – all pomp and bravado – matched the preposterously overblown, irresistible confidence of frontman, Freddie. Yet the man behind this audacious stage persona that came so extraordinarily to life in public performance was intensely shy, almost secretive, in private. Mercury himself alluded to this: 'On stage I'm a big macho, sexual object and I'm very arrogant, so most people dismiss me because of that. But I'm not like that really. They don't know what I'm really like underneath.'

It was both these sides of Mercury's character that began to surface when as a little boy a sudden change in his surroundings forced him to face the world alone.

This is a story of dislocation. It is not a story of destitution, abuse or abject misery, and the young Freddie was neither poor nor neglected. He was a confident, normal child. But his world was turned upside down when his family sent him away from their African home.

Freddie Mercury was born Farrokh Bulsara on 5 September 1946 in the former British protectorate of Zanzibar, just off the east coast of what was then Tanganyika, another British territory. His mother and father, both born in India, were practising Parsees, the monotheistic Zoroastrian faith whose followers are sometimes called 'sun-worshippers' or 'Manichees'. Zoroastrianism goes back to sixth-century Persia.

Young Farrokh's father worked as a cashier for the British colonial authorities so the family had a relatively privileged life, with servants and a nanny. Asian immigrants to Britain's African colonies, often in clerical or retail jobs, occupied a middle position between the 'colonials' and the 'natives' but they were not quite part of white society. Farrokh's early years were spent splashing in the Indian Ocean, playing on the beach or walking along the streets of Stone Town, where (under the noses of Zanzibar's British-backed rulers and until shockingly late in the nineteenth century) the world's last slave market had thrived.

Mercury's biographer, Lesley-Ann Jones, quotes his former lovers, Barbara Valentin and Jim Hutton, reporting Mercury's lament that his parents were very reserved and physically undemonstrative. Hutton said Freddie would occasionally wonder out loud whether 'a disproportionate obsession with physical love in adulthood … a craving which all too often manifested itself in meaningless sex' was the result of being starved of affection as a child. Possibly; but a lot of people of Freddie's generation might make similar complaints about their parents. As for the meaningless sex, this was the 1970s, and in the 1970s, if you were famous, meaningless sex is just what you did.

Seemingly with the best intentions for Farrokh's future, the decision was made for him to be sent to school 3,000 miles away at a well-respected Church of England school, St Peter's, in Panchgani, India.

Quite what the eight-year-old Farrokh made of being separated from his baby sister, his friends, his parents, his culture, in fact, all that he had ever known, can only be guessed at; but Jones writes about how (Freddie remembered) he would cry himself to sleep at night surrounded by other frightened young boys, and how those close to him said he harboured a deep resentment towards his parents. The lack of one-on-one affection at this formative stage in his life would have been felt keenly.

There may be more in this than the homesickness that has afflicted millions of little boys sent to English public schools over the centuries, most of whom did not become great men. At eight, the little Farrokh was summarily sent to a new continent, a new culture, with new languages. Everything he had known fell apart.

When for my *Great Lives* programme I discussed this with Lesley-Ann Jones, she spoke of 'a void that was created in Freddie by this massive separation. Anxiety was the thing that drove him. I believe that [wanting to become] a rock star [was] because he needed something massive to fill that void.'

Farrokh rarely returned home. During holidays he would stay with an aunt who lived nearby. In later years he displayed a rather stoic attitude to his banishment: 'Of course there were feelings of being sent away from my parents and sister whom I missed very much – feelings of loneliness, feelings of being rejected – but you had to do what you were told. So the sensible thing was to make the most of it.'

For the rest of his life, a shadow falls across this period of his childhood. The adult Freddie hardly ever spoke about his time in India. It was as if he swept this traumatic experience under his own mental carpet. Bonzo Fernandez, a school friend from when he returned to Zanzibar at the age of sixteen, remembers, 'I knew he had been away at school in India, but he never spoke about his years there.'

In their book about Mercury, *Somebody to Love*, Matt Richards and Mark Langthorne cite *The Making of Them: The British Attitude to Children and the Boarding School System*, whose author, Nick Duffell, argues that sending a child away at that age is tantamount to child abuse. Duffell claims that children this age do not have the maturity to deal with the sense of loss they feel. They develop a 'strategic survival' personality. To the outside world they are competent and confident but privately they're deeply insecure. I would not go so far, but Farrokh's loss was sharper and more complete than that of an English child sent to an English public school, within a few hours' drive of his parents.

It's not hard to imagine the sense of dislocation the young Farrokh must have felt but he took from it at least the lesson that: 'One thing boarding school teaches you, is how to fend for yourself, and I did that from the start. It taught me to be independent and not to rely on anybody else. All the things they say about boarding schools are more or less true, about the bullying and everything else.'

It certainly wasn't an easy experience and he was

dubbed Bucky by the other kids on account of his protruding front teeth, but Farrokh's sudden exile was forcing him to sink or swim.

At first he retreated into his shell. But then a more confident Farrokh was born. It was at this time he changed his name. He started calling himself Freddie, perhaps rejecting the old life that had rejected him. He made himself proficient at boxing and became the school table tennis champion. He began to master the piano and took on a range of roles in school plays, frequently playing female parts. Janice Smith, the daughter of his art teacher, recalled him referring to other children, both boys and girls, as 'darling' or 'dear'.

One school friend, Zahid Ali Abrar, noted how the usually quiet Freddie would morph into an almost entirely different character once he took to the stage to perform. 'When he went on to the keyboard he would be in a bliss playing and, I would put it crudely, like getting multiple orgasms.'

The realisation that he was homosexual would have been challenging enough but his isolation must have compounded his sense of dislocation. He was reaching an age when he could begin to understand the cultural taboos around sexuality: and both Zoroastrianism and Christianity were unambiguous about its sinful nature.

Manichees believe that the universe is in perpetual contention between the forces of light and those of darkness. Neither wins. It's just a matter of whose side you are on. Farrokh's religion and upbringing taught him that to be gay cast you into darkness.

And at the same time, alone in a boarding school, he

was having to self-define. Being true to himself in an alien environment must have been a challenge: nobody would have expected the sports star to be gay. And the school ping-pong champion calling other boys 'darling' is a sort of ambiguity young gay teenagers have often sought: people who know the signs can read them, and those who don't will see what they want to see.

This was an ambiguity he was to play with, consciously or not, for the rest of his life. Mercury invited speculation. He became a puzzle for others to work out. No doubt anyone who questioned why that boy called the others 'dear' would be told by those who thought they knew him better: 'Oh that's just Freddie.' He was perfecting the art of hiding in plain sight. When Freddie Mercury died, some were genuinely unaware that the man who fronted a band called Queen was homosexual.

The sense of rejection and feelings of isolation seem to have stayed with him all his life. 'Sometimes I wake up in a cold sweat, in fear because I'm so alone.' You wonder if he stared at the ceiling on those long nights, next to a stranger, feeling eight years old again.

Despite the adulation and fame, loneliness was a recurring theme. He watched himself from the outside. 'Most people wonder how someone like Freddie Mercury can be lonely?' he remarked. 'He has money, he has cars and chauffeurs, he has the lot. You can seem to have everything, and yet have nothing. Maybe one day I'll catch up with myself and that'll be my downfall. In fact, sometimes that kind of loneliness is the hardest to bear because within all that, all the people around you, you're still lonely.'

The song 'Living On My Own' is a big clubby dance

number guaranteed to fill the floor. The lyric is about Freddie, isolated, time on his hands, and yet too distracted to fill out the tune with proper lyrics. Every element of the production – the drum beat and the bass line – are there to distract you from the message of the words themselves. It's Freddie Mercury, the man in a song, insisting you have a good time; while the person behind it all is less than happy about his situation. This is hiding in plain sight, again.

Mercury must have had an innate resilience to get him through this period of teenage banishment. He failed his school exams, and for a smart child at a good school, this was a surprise to his family and teachers. But perhaps he wanted to fail. The young Freddie was turning the tables on a world that told him what he should and shouldn't do, should and shouldn't be. Rejected, this was his way of rejecting.

He returned home. He spent two years at school in Zanzibar before the violent political revolution that came after independence from British rule in 1964. For Freddie it was another huge cultural and geographical shift – but one he embraced. The move this time was from the coral beaches of Zanzibar to the working-class suburb of Feltham, near Heathrow.

But he loved it. Peter Freestone, his personal assistant, explained that all at once, he felt at home. 'If Freddie had the choice, he would have been born, at the age of about twenty-one in Feltham.' And in a way he was. Exotic, colourful, eccentric, and with that survival core instilled by boarding school, Freddie could make a huge impression in a drab environment. Suburbia is an unlikely training ground for star quality, but in a culture that thrives on gossip and values uniformity, where else is it easier to stand out?

He went on to flourish musically and become one of the world's most famous performers; but it is impossible to study what we can learn about the private man without suspecting that he was still trying, and failing, to reconcile himself to that early rejection. Freddie hid away the boy he was and his creation, Freddie Mercury, mercurial showman, became his greatest invention, his trademark, and his dominating idea. It was born, though, in dislocation.

CHAPTER FOUR

CHAOS

There are dysfunctional families and childhoods that can only be filed under the word 'chaotic'. Other more specific woes may be present – bereavement, abandonment, destitution, illness, cruelty – but such ills are all tangled up with a complete lack of structure to the child's (and often the family's) life. The chaos that the children whose stories I will tell in this chapter had to navigate seems to defy the vast achievements we now know they were headed for. Where did they find their bearings? How, ducking all the blows, was self-confidence ever born in their troubled breasts? What was it in Eva Perón that helped an actress of modest talents and passable good looks claw her way out of the Argentinian slums and then – and it's this that distinguishes her – use her fame to help the poor?

Well, by now you cannot have missed the emerging theme: that there's reason to suppose these eruptions of genius were not despite but because of wrecked childhoods. Something was released in every case. John Lennon's rich imagination, his yearning for a better world, and his search for meaning in life; the inimitable pathos yet defiant spirit in Piaf's voice – regretting (as runs her most famous song) nothing; the damaged Louise Bourgeois' fiercely personal sculpture ... these are not 'despite' but 'because'. It is all but impossible to imagine the singularity of each genius chronicled here as emerging from conventional, ordered home lives.

Or conventional educations. A surprising proportion of both the lives in this book and the hundreds of *Great Lives* covered in the radio series have a story to tell – of little schooling, of learning at home, or being self-taught. School can be the site of inspiration and a great expansion of horizons – but it can also stifle originality, suffocate the free spirit, head the child off from new paths of thought and expression. The boy with whose story we start was reduced to reading the same book over and over again, for want of any new ones, and writing on any crude surface he could find, for want of writing paper, yet became one of America's wisest and more erudite presidents.

The panther's scream

O Memory! thou midway world
'Twixt earth and paradise,
Where things decayed and loved ones lost
In dreamy shadows rise.[7]

'I am going away from you and I shall not return.' The boy was nine when his mother uttered her last words to him. He knew already the pain of loss. He had watched his great-aunt and great-uncle succumb to the same illness that now afflicted his mother. The sickness had spread fear through their community. Its origins were unknown, its course rapid, its result fatal. One doctor of the period described attending to a man thus stricken:

> I was called to him about eleven o'clock at night – he was attacked at dark, and according to the description of the bystanders complained at first of giddiness and weakness, became stupid and indisposed to move. In the course of an hour he said he was burning up at the stomach, and shortly afterwards vomiting commenced. This continued till near the time of my arrival, when he was so completely exhausted that he could not speak. I could scarcely feel his pulse – the extremities were cold, and his breathing scarcely audible. In about an hour from the time that I reached the house he died.[8]

Within days the boy's mother was dead. For the boy the loss sunk deep. The scars can be traced years later in poetry he wrote on his return, as an adult, to the place of her death:

> I range the fields with pensive tread,
> And pace the hollow rooms,
> And feel (companion of the dead)
> I'm living in the tombs.

This place was, in his memory, rough, wild country. It was thick with memories of a childhood on the edge. In another poem he recalled:

> When first my father settled here,

'Twas then the frontier line:
The panther's scream, filled night with fear
And bears preyed on the swine.

What a place, then, for the boy to be left in by his father, just a few months after the death of his mother. Yet for the family to survive in the harsh environment they inhabited, his father needed a new wife to share the burden – and set out to get her. That meant leaving behind the nine-year-old boy, his twelve-year-old sister, and their cousin, himself just eighteen, to fend for themselves. When the father returned with his new bride in tow, she found them living like animals, 'wild – ragged and dirty'.[9]

Her arrival, though, marked the beginning of an improvement in their circumstances. In time they got by, but scratching out an existence on untilled soil deprived the boy of things others his age enjoyed, like education. What good was knowing geometry if, with winter howling, you couldn't split a log?

Subsistence farming – or something like it – has been the lot of so many. For this boy it was certainly tough, as it is for billions; but his external circumstances were grinding rather than desperate. There was something within, though, that brought him close to despair; this was a young man who knew loss and pain. Yet, in later life, he translated the pain into an abiding insight into human nature; he became wise, not morose; he pushed back hard against his lack of education and threw himself obsessively into whatever books he could find, repeating, writing, and memorising huge chunks of text. His hunger for the thoughts and words of others helped make him one of the greatest orators of his generation, perhaps one of the greatest the world has seen. This alloy of sagacity, fluency and oratory, stiffened by the iron self-confidence that formed in a person who had forged his own way, turned him from boy to the leading figure of the American epoch that he himself was to help define.

By now you realise who is standing, his face in shadow, before you. If I were to show him in front of his place of birth, a one-room log cabin on an American prairie, you would doubtless then know that the little boy who struggled against so much loss, and against such severe poverty, was the man with a strong claim to be the greatest president yet of the United States, Abraham Lincoln.

*

When America fractured on 12 April 1861, it looked as if the noble dreams of its founders would go up in the gun smoke. It was Abraham Lincoln who was commander-in-chief, and president, at that moment. The Civil War was, in personal terms, just the latest challenge in a life full of setback, violent obstruction and melancholy; but a challenge, yet again, that the sixteenth president could rise to. He had (his biographers note) an extraordinary capacity for growth.

It was during the Civil War that, like Pericles in Athens over two thousand years before, Lincoln delivered a funeral oration which was soon accepted as being the greatest speech of the age. The Gettysburg Address, delivered on 19 November 1863, was only ten sentences long, but it has come to embody democratic ideals as no other text before or since.

Lincoln's rousing conclusion is worth quoting in full:

It is rather for us to be here dedicated to the great task remaining before us – that from these honored dead we take increased devotion to that cause for which they gave the last full measure of devotion – that we here highly resolve that these dead shall not have died in vain – that this nation, under God, shall have a new birth of freedom – and that government of the people, by the people, for the people, shall not perish from the earth.

His talent, not just for oratory but for lyricism, had, as we shall see, deep roots. It also fuelled much of his success. Politics in mid-nineteenth-century America made much of speeches. Large, boisterous public rallies called for speakers who could persuade, command and amuse. Abraham Lincoln proved more than capable of this. When he spoke before a crowd of 1,500 in New York at a rally in 1860 during his campaign for the Republican nomination, a local paper declared it 'one of the happiest and most convincing political arguments ever made in this City'.

It was as an Illinois lawyer that Lincoln first made his name as an unequalled speaker. But his judgement, even temper, and deep psychological insight were just as important as his oratorical skills. Lincoln had these in spades and displayed them to the fullest by defining and deepening the dream of America's founders at a time when it had seemed to falter. He was valiant but he was deft. He proved himself a master in navigating complex, strongly felt issues, especially concerning slavery.

The record is not unblemished. Lincoln's own words on the racial divide make for uncomfortable reading today. At a debate with the Democrat Stephen A. Douglas in 1858 he said this: 'There is a physical difference between the two, which in my judgement will probably forever forbid their living together upon the footing of perfect equality, and inasmuch as it becomes a necessity that there must be a difference, I, as well as Judge Douglas, am in favour of the race to which I belong having the superior position.' Set these words against the background of the woes and oppression black Americans faced following the Civil War and one may conclude that Lincoln could see his way through that convulsion, but not far past it.

Some limited defence is possible. Though a soaring orator, Lincoln always weighed his words carefully. The inclusion of 'probably' slightly trips the rhetorical flow so we should note its insertion. And what he said next was this: '... but ... there is no reason in the world why the negro is not entitled to all the natural rights enumerated in the Declaration of Independence, the right to life, liberty and the pursuit of happiness'. There is evidence that before he died he was considering granting the vote to black men who had fought in the Union Army. But his murder, by the Confederate fanatic John Wilkes Booth, put an end to that. A possible evolution in his thinking was frozen forever, and so Abraham Lincoln's record on race will have to stand where it stood at his death.

None should doubt his greatness, however. Even to win the presidency as he did, coming from where he did, is an achievement that would have qualified him for the pantheon. But his actions, his character, his remarkable kind-heartedness, his decency, and his saving of his country make this a life almost without equal.

The question, though, is how he ever got through his childhood.

Abraham Lincoln was born on 12 February 1809. His parents, Thomas Lincoln and Nancy Hanks, were poor, but not paupers. Abraham was their second child, after a daughter, Sarah. They had the 300 acres of Sinking Spring Farm, a thin and unproductive patch of land, swathes of it unable to be worked. Thomas Lincoln hunted on much of the land. The sole dwelling was the building in which Abraham was born: a rude, one-room log cabin that, thanks to its roughness, and the fame of the child who grew up there, has tumbled into the folklore of America.

But what (in replica) is now an object of intense interest and a destination of political pilgrimage was in its day thought unremarkable. Abraham certainly held no affection for it. Nor did the person who bought the land from his father; one of the first things he did was dismantle the mean dwelling.

Yet in many ways to be born in a one-room log cabin was not so much a sign of wretched deprivation as it was the mark of pioneering stock. None of them had it easy. Abraham's father Thomas had himself experienced at first hand the brutality of frontier life when his own father was killed in front of him by a raiding party of Shawnee Indians. The consequences of Abraham Senior's murder were dire for Thomas. Kentucky primogeniture gave everything to the eldest and Thomas's brother Mordecai inherited not just Abraham Sr's land but his money too. Mordecai was able to educate himself well, but seemed not to have granted the same to his brothers. Landless and illiterate, Thomas had to fend for himself: as he said ruefully, Mordecai had run off 'with all the talent in the family'. As an adult Thomas would often use Mordecai's mark to sign documents. As Abraham Jr grew up, Thomas's lack of education – despite the painful explanation for it – caused increasing tension between son and father.

Antipathy towards his father may have been among the reasons why, for the rest of his life, Abraham appeared to have what amounted to a mental block when it came to talking about his early years. Asked later in life for an autobiography, he told the *Chicago Tribune* that wished to print it that 'it is a great piece of folly to attempt to make anything out of my early life. It can all be condensed into a single sentence, and that sentence you will find in Gray's *Elegy*, "The short and simple annals of the poor".' As any politician then as well as today could tell you, a 'back story' of struggle is a positive advantage to statesmen, once they have become statesmen, but Abraham couldn't seem to bring himself to celebrate this.

When he was four years old, the family left Sinking Spring for another patch of land in Kentucky. At Knob Creek Thomas had thirty acres of land, but he could cultivate only a part of it, for it was as 'knotty – knobby – as a piece of land could be, with deep hollows and ravines, cedar trees covering the … Knobs as thick as trees could grow.'[10] The pattern at Sinking Spring was repeating itself. Thomas Lincoln found himself unable to make much of his land and was reduced to farming little parcels of it, eking out the family's subsistence by hunting.

Though Knob Creek was beautiful, and the land better

than that of Sinking Spring, the life of a pioneer was restless. Thomas Lincoln upped sticks once more in 1816.
Sarah and Abraham had attended a small school within
the relatively populated valley, but in the manner typical
of frontier children they spent only months there, and
Abraham probably hadn't yet learnt to write by the time
they left. Their father, though, was concerned more with
making a living than with education – or so his son believed.
But there was also trouble in Kentucky. The state had been
subject to a serious inflow of population as American citizens began to wake to the possibilities out west. It was also
a slave state, which presented two challenges to the Lincolns. The first was ethical. As Separate Baptists, Thomas
Lincoln and Nancy Hanks were anti-slavery (the result of a
rigorous moral code that also prohibited profanity, gossip,
intoxication and much else). The second was economic.
As self-employed farmers they could not compete with
the grim 'efficiency' of slave labour. A final complication
was that Thomas was being sued by people from outside
the state: a daunting and draining legal battle loomed. The
Lincolns sold up and left Knob Creek and Kentucky, to try
again elsewhere.

Thomas built and then loaded up a raft with all his family's worldly possessions before floating down the Ohio
into the heavily forested semi-wilderness of Indiana. The
site Thomas had found was known as Pigeon Creek: so
isolated that as the family journeyed overland the father
had to hack part of the trail himself. Contemporary
reports of the state describe it as teeming with the wildlife
so evocative of 'untapped' America: flocks of geese and
ducks flying overhead, wild turkeys charging about the

forest floor, and bears lurking behind trees. Lincoln later described it sparely: as settling 'in an unbroken forest'.

At Pigeon Creek the Lincolns first lived in a 'half face camp'. This crude structure of trees, sticks and canvas with three sides enclosed and one open represented a backward step even from a log cabin. But there was a community here, and neighbours quickly helped the Lincolns build a new log cabin. The construction, though, in icy weather was difficult and the gaps between the logs could not be filled. During that first winter the wind whistled through the gaps. Farming would have to wait. This was a life little more developed than that of a hunter-gatherer.

But 1817 brought brighter prospects. New neighbours arrived early in the year. Elizabeth and Thomas Sparrow, Nancy's aunt and uncle, had been forced from Kentucky by an ejectment suit (suggesting Lincoln Sr was perhaps wise to jump when he did) and joined Thomas and Nancy out in Pigeon Creek. They brought with them Dennis Hanks, then eighteen and the (illegitimate) nephew of Elizabeth. Their arrival helped the Lincolns settle in and make a home where they'd previously made a stand.

By the following autumn, however, an outbreak of milk sickness was ravaging the community. The illness was later to be traced to the consumption of milk from animals that had eaten the wild snakeroot plant which grew freely on forest floors in Indiana. Milk sickness sent Elizabeth and Thomas Sparrow to their graves. Then it killed Nancy Hanks.

Thomas Lincoln returned to Kentucky, where he married a widow he knew called Sarah Bush Johnston. Thomas brought Sarah back to Indiana, along with her three children, Elizabeth, John, and Matilda. As we saw at the beginning of this chapter, Sarah Bush Lincoln found a pitiful scene, her new husband's children neglected and unwashed. She fast helped put the family back on its feet. What she brought with her was not just her own children, and fine goods, such as cutlery, which the Lincoln children had lacked, but energy and love. The Lincoln household had more than doubled in size, swelling from three children fending for themselves to two adults and six children. Abraham's stepmother was one of the brightest lights of his childhood. She loved him as her own, and later, when discussing her son and stepson, said 'Both were good boys, but I must say – both now being dead that Abe was the best boy I ever saw or ever expect to see.'.

Between Nancy's death and Sarah Bush Johnston's arrival, Abraham's sister Sarah had acted as mother. When Sarah Lincoln married in 1826, Abraham would have been sad to see his sister depart the family home. They had lived their whole lives together, sharing times of happiness, calamity and sorrow. And two years later, in January 1828, Sarah Lincoln died in childbirth. One of her husband's relatives speaks of Abraham's grief: 'I will never forget that scene. He sat down in the door of the smoke house and buried his face in his hands. The tears slowly trickled from between his bony fingers and his gaunt frame shook with sobs. We turned away.'[11]

Lincoln was seventeen. He'd seen three of his immediate family die, as well as his aunt and uncle. One of Abraham Lincoln's chief gifts was his remarkable way with words and his penetrating insight into the human psyche. His personal experience and direct knowledge of great sadness helped the young boy see into himself, and from that, into others.

But, for the meantime, the family's circumstances remained hard. Added to the grind of scraping a living on the land was a growing sense of unfairness for Abraham. The law stipulated that until he was twenty-one he legally owed his labour to his father. This constriction became ever more unbearable as Lincoln grew into adolescence and his father slipped into senescence. Thomas Lincoln's life had been one of almost unbroken toil. He had been forced to fend for himself after the murder of his father. He built five homes, each by his own hand, for his family to live in. He suffered the death of his first wife and then supported the family of his second wife – an extra three children – as well as Dennis Hanks, the nephew of the deceased Sparrows.

These labours took their toll in the end. Thomas started losing his sight and began making greater demands of his son. As the 1820s drew to a close, Abraham's work was 'farming, grubbing, hoeing, making fences'.[12] But he began now to earn money through his own efforts. Once, using a boat he'd built himself, he rowed two men out to another vessel on the river. As they crossed over, they casually tossed a couple of coins back into the boat. 'I could scarcely believe my eyes as I picked the money,' Lincoln later wrote, 'I could scarcely credit that I, a poor boy, had earned a dollar in less than a day … The world seemed wider and fairer before me.' And it would have seemed narrower again, as soon as he had to give that money to his father.

The poverty he'd lived with all his life was now brushing up against a world where money was there to be made; where money represented a way out. Before, the word 'money' had been synonymous with 'worry', but in moments like those in his little rowing boat it spoke of 'hope': a world far beyond the confines of Pigeon Creek, beyond the limitations and struggles of his father. Yet just as his world seemed to be opening up, his father was asking more and more of him.

*

The adult Abraham Lincoln was prone for the rest of his life to serious bouts of depression and long moods of melancholy. Barack Obama, writing about Lincoln's relationship to slavery and his mixed views on race, described eloquently his wrinkled skin and haunted eyes. As a grown man he had much to trouble him, but it's an intuitively persuasive idea that these dark moods put their roots down into a childhood shaped by an indelible sense of both injustice and loss.

The deaths of the Sparrows, Elizabeth and Thomas, and a younger brother who died in infancy, must have troubled Lincoln. But seeing even close relatives perish from the mysterious milk sickness could not prepare him for the death of his mother. Nancy Hanks remains a historical figure who stands more in darkness than light. Lincoln himself rarely spoke of her – in the short autobiography he wrote for the *Chicago Tribune*, he devoted only a single sentence to her death – and when he did so it was in elliptical terms. Dennis Hanks, Lincoln's cousin, offered this description:

Mrs Lincoln, Abraham's mother, was five feet eight inches high, spare made, affectionate – the most affectionate I ever saw – never knew her to be out of temper, and thought strong of it. She seemed to be immovably calm; she was keen, shrewd, smart, and I do say highly intellectual by nature. Her memory was strong, her perception was quick, her judgement was acute almost. She was spiritually and ideally inclined, not dull, not material, not heavy in thought, feeling, or action. Her hair was dark hair, eyes bluish green – keen and loving.

Much of what Hanks said here has to be treated with caution. Nancy has been described as tall, short, ugly, pretty, skinny, fat. But about her judgement and sharp intelligence, other sources agree with Dennis. In retrospect, Abraham made his mother the source or conduit of his greatness. He believed all his best characteristics were inherited from an unknown grandfather on his mother's side, a 'broad-minded, unknown Virginian'. Lincoln's dislike of his father, and shame at his intellectual failings, keeps poking through his account. His mother gave him a way to claim he was superior, his gifts owing nothing to Thomas. As far as his biographers have been able to discover, Lincoln's hopes were fantasies, and no patrician grandfather lurked in his past to give him the Virginian lustre that adorned Presidents Washington and Jefferson.

Thomas Lincoln was, in fact, a greater influence on his son than Abraham would have liked. In Abraham's eyes his father was little more than an unschooled backwoodsman. When a relative wrote asking for some detail of family history, Lincoln replied, 'Owing to my father being left an orphan at the age of six years, in poverty, and in a new country, he became a wholly uneducated man; which I suppose is the reason why I know so little of our family history. I believe I can say nothing more that would at all interest you.'

We know that Lincoln was fond of emphasising the uselessness of his father, and talked up, perhaps dreamed up, his mysterious Virginian ancestor. When he left home aged twenty-two he broke with his father, to all intents and purposes permanently. Later in his life he grudgingly gave him money; wrote sarcastic letters, so different to his usual style; even failed to see Thomas before he died; and didn't mark his grave despite promising to do so.

It is possible to conclude that Abraham Lincoln was simply ashamed of his father and wished therefore to be dissociated from him. I find that explanation unsatisfactory. Lincoln was a big-hearted and dutiful man, and no snob. He had the common touch, and his fair-minded openness to people of all walks of life was part of what modern journalists would call his brand. He understood this – even cultivated it. He was not known and would not have wanted to be known for airs and graces. Cruelty towards his own uneducated father went right against the brand, and, I would guess, his natural bent. It was in both his interests and his nature to play the part of dutiful son who does not think himself too good for his humble dad. So why couldn't he spare a little kindness to Thomas, and Thomas's memory? Why couldn't he even pretend?

My hunch is that there was something traumatic buried in the relationship between son and father. Not necessarily an event (though there might have been events we don't know of) but an emotional convulsion, a deep chaos, cause unknown, that left young Abraham in almost physical revolt against his father for the rest of his life, unable to embrace him on any level, unable even to simulate filial affection. It is not uncommon for a repulsion between two people to leave one of them all but unable to look at, let alone speak genially to, the other. Something had gone horribly wrong, probably quite early, between Thomas and Abraham, blocking Abraham's reason and smashing all possibility of bonding. Even as president, Lincoln found himself helpless: unable to go through the motions.

Here I must interrupt the chronology to report a battle still rumbling among historians, biographers and the literature that has grown up around Abraham Lincoln. It has been argued that Lincoln was gay, bisexual, or sexually confused.

The debate has been marred by everyone tending to take sides, social conservatives among his admirers anxious to resist the suggestion, modern controversialists anxious to 'plant the rainbow flag' (as Louis Bayard, author of *Courting Mr Lincoln* puts it) on the great man's reputation. There's plenty of evidence, but none of it conclusive. Most compelling is his lifelong love of the man who was undoubtedly his best friend, Joshua Speed, the 'handsome shopkeeper' (says Bayard) with whom, needing lodgings, he shared a small bed for more than three years. It was Speed who (reports Bayard, who has studied the huge, lifetime correspondence between the two) '... once declared that "no two men were ever more intimate";

who confessed that, if he himself hadn't gotten married, Lincoln wouldn't have; who promised Lincoln that he would write back the morning after his wedding night to report how it had gone; and who, for reasons unclear, never had children'. Even conservative biographers had to acknowledge Speed's primacy in Lincoln's heart, and Carl Sandburg, tiptoeing as far out on the limb as a hagiographer could in the 1920s, suggested that the Lincoln–Speed relationship had 'a streak of lavender and spots soft as May violets'.

Abraham always ended his letters to Joshua 'yours forever', a sign-off that he apparently never employed in correspondence with anyone else.

In *The Intimate World of Abraham Lincoln*, C. A. Tripp, a Kinsey Institute sex researcher, collected evidence that appears to me intuitively persuasive. Tripp lists (writes Bayard) Lincoln's male bedmates, 'from Billy Greene in New Salem (he and Lincoln, according to one neighbor, "had an awful hankerin', one for t'other") to, late in life, David Derickson, the bodyguard who supposedly shared Lincoln's bed while the first lady was away'. Tripp quotes the twenty-year-old Lincoln's jokey poem about two boys who, having tried 'the girlies', opt to marry each other instead – '[a]s far as we know' (says Bayard) '[this was] the first suggestion of same-sex marriage in U.S. history'. The poem was dropped from later editions of an early biography by Lincoln's friend (and also, some have claimed, lover) William Herndon.

Interestingly, Herndon was also the originator of various stories about Lincoln's philandering with the opposite sex, none of which can be verified. They sound unlikely. Contemporaries noted that as a youth and young man, he seemed to have little time for girls.

But he did marry (rather late and after an on-off engagement to her) Mary Todd Lincoln and there's no suggestion that this was an incomplete or loveless marriage, though Bayard says that as a young lawyer, Lincoln (with work to do all over the country) does not appear to have made much effort to return often to his wife. The sudden, apparently impulsive and inadequately explained breaking off of Lincoln's first engagement to Mary is also odd. With perhaps revealing cattiness, William Herndon's biography claims that Lincoln never meant his courtesies to Todd to be taken as a proposal and was persuaded by Speed to visit her to say so – but lost his nerve.

In the end, who knows? Men shared beds with other men frequently in those days, entirely for convenience, and affectionate letters between two people of the same sex were often extravagantly but innocently expressed. The suggestion that Lincoln might have been bisexual does help answer questions about his behaviour, but every one of them can be answered in other ways. My own tentative conclusion is that we'll never know if anything overtly sexual ever passed between Lincoln and Speed, but that the hint of homo-eroticism is very strong.

Why, then, do I say that the 'gay Lincoln' theory might help explain his uncharacteristic and almost cruel dislike of his uncultivated father? Because if the contemporary report is true that the youth was always uninterested in girls, and if Thomas was the kind of rough, garrulous audience-pleaser that Lincoln's biographers describe, then it's highly likely the younger Lincoln will have endured a good deal of banter from his father, which would have left him in no doubt how Thomas felt about his true – if unacknowledged – self.

For a sexually confused youth, this will have cut deep. Uncountable numbers of gay men from my generation and earlier have winced and gritted their teeth or grinned awkwardly while a parent lets fly with jokes about gays, or with diatribes against homosexuality, unwittingly wounding their child deeply. Thomas's jokes might not have taken quite the same form, in a time when being gay was an unthinkable sin rather than a punchline, but the substance would not have been dissimilar.

I remember my own almost ecstatic relief when my businessman father, who laughed at all the pretty-boy jokes that fathers of his generation did laugh at, reacted to a newspaper report that the chairman of the Post Office, who had been sacked for not being up to the job, was complaining publicly that his dismissal was intolerable: it was hardly as if (said the ex-chairman) he had been discovered to be a homosexual. My father retorted that that was the stupidest remark he'd heard in a long time, and itself justified the man's sacking. It was with a surge of admiration that I heard Dad say this.

Whether Abraham's father might have suspected latent homosexuality in his son, or simply enjoyed a rough joke, one can be fairly sure that his son would have winced – and perhaps eventually turned against him decisively.

I speculate wildly, of course. But not wholly wildly. Because if anything like this had indeed taken place, you can be almost sure that it would not have been reported.

*

Until very recently (and, even now, only to some degree) biography has but rarely known or been able to prove that somebody placed by history on a pedestal was gay; and even where this is suspected, biography has often been disinclined to mention the fact, or, if mentioned, inclined then to dispute it or brush it embarrassedly aside. It will seldom be hard to do so: the individual will usually have hidden his or her sexuality and often be on record as denying it. On the internet you will find lists of possibly gay heroes in history, and the names on the lists mostly share this: the very idea would have been vehemently denied, particularly by friends, and never committed to paper.

What this reflects – and it puts me in mind of Lincoln – is that at least until the present generation, being gay has made people, perforce, outsiders. Throughout history, a gay man or lesbian would have had to struggle all their life with the central fact that the rest of the world judged what they felt – what they were – to be a dangerous and socially destructive sin. It would seem the whole world was against them.

That is a fracture. It can cut a person off – drive a wedge between them and their families, friends and workmates. Being private and usually undisclosed, the separation has not worked both ways. A gay person feels separated from others, but those others may be unaware of this. It's a secret separation. Your inner life, like a teenager's bedroom, becomes your very private world. You have secretly self-isolated, yet are still engaged with the world.

And because you know you are not a wicked person,

nor warped, nor ill-intentioned, nor mentally disturbed, you draw from this experience a series of conclusions, all related. That most people understand less than they think. That the world talks an awful lot of rubbish. That an intense moral certainty, endorsed by leading authorities in religion and morality (and sometimes medical science) and deeply imbued in almost all your heterosexual contemporaries, can be completely wrong. That criminal justice can be grotesquely unjust. And that popular theory propagated by doctors, academics and experts and given the name of science can be nonsense nevertheless.

From my own experience and from close acquaintance with the experience of many others, I've become certain that homosexuality can set a person apart in his or her own imagination; can root in a mind and heart a profound doubt about the world, about justice, about the wisdom of the era or the ages, and about what others may choose to think. It can place people at one step removed from the moral certainties of their contemporaries and set them – just a little, but to them importantly – apart. A gay man or lesbian woman, in an age of persecution, will always feel to some extent an observer: less so a participant.

And this sceptical self-isolation will not be restricted to matters of sexual attraction. 'If', you tell yourself, 'the experts and the moral authorities are so wrong about this, what else may they be wrong about?' In Nevil Shute's 1948 novel, *No Highway*, colleagues of the hero (who has concluded that an aircraft is about to break up due to metal fatigue) doubt his science because he is also a believer in the paranormal. Through the ages, secretly gay men have felt empowered to doubt the judgement of their age because their age has reached a spectacularly wrong judgement about something they intimately know and understand.

So I'm not making any case for innate genius in gay people, but pointing out that, in the past at least, same-sex sexual attraction has often made people secret loners; and that this in turn, a variety of fracture, can sometimes liberate.

Such fractures with one's era can be a freedom, illuminate, release. I speculate – but no more than speculate – that bisexuality or sexual confusion may well have haunted but will also have liberated Abraham Lincoln, setting him apart from other sons in his own mind. Of one thing I have no doubt: Lincoln, clubbable as he could be, was always a secret loner.

*

But that clubbability was a gift (beside, perhaps, the hurt) that father gave son. Thomas Lincoln was a raconteur, and Abraham became one too. Dennis Hanks, though, claimed it was a skill in which Thomas was superior, for the father 'could beat his son telling a story – cracking a joke'.

Growing up at Knob Creek farm, Lincoln sat by the fire listening attentively to talk between his father and passing travellers. He absorbed the stories they traded, and how they told them. In his early life, though, Abraham's tongue brought him more trouble than success, especially from his father. Young Lincoln was cocksure and learnt how to needle his father. He made a point of being the first to speak when a new face appeared on the farm, getting a word in before Thomas. For this impudence Thomas used to strike his son. Abraham didn't react, stayed silent, but (wrote Dennis Hanks) 'dropt a kind of silent unwelcome tear, as evidence of his sensations'.

Like his father, Lincoln received little formal schooling: the sum total over his life amounted to less than a year. In later life he was dismissive of his formal education, saying: 'There were some schools, so called; but no qualification was ever required of a teacher, beyond "readin, writin, and cipherin," to the Rule of Three. If a straggler supposed to understand Latin, happened to sojourn in the neighborhood, he was looked upon as a wizard.'

His first succour, familiar to many in similar situations, was reading. I remember in one of my *Great Lives* programmes the council-estate-to-Privy-Council former Labour politician, Alan Johnson, describing the same sense of an escape hatch. Lincoln devoured books, what few there were. A common pose in which young Lincoln could be discovered was with his feet raised above his head, reclining in a chair, nose-deep in some tome.

These books were the gift Sarah Bush Lincoln, his stepmother, brought with her from Kentucky. Works like *The Pilgrim's Progress* and *Aesop's Fables* made that fateful journey, much to Abraham's good fortune. Along with the loving affection she showed her stepson, these were Sarah's greatest contributions to his progress.

For a mischievous child who liked to wind up his father, these books were a boon. That there were only a handful of them was no matter. Once Abraham got to the final page he could just shift the weight of the book into the other hand, flick back the pages, and start again from the beginning. He polished off the *Fables* so many times he was reputedly able to copy the entire work out from memory.

He didn't just read and talk, he wrote, too. Sarah Bush Lincoln recalled that 'frequently, he had no paper to write his pieces down on. Then he would put them with chalk on a board or plank'. He used to write out quotes and ciphers on a shovel before scraping it clean with a knife when it got too full. If he'd been writing words, he'd often memorise them before erasing them. His stepmother said that '[W]hen he came across a passage that struck him, he would write it down on boards if he had no paper and keep it there till he did get paper – then he would re-write it – look at it [and] repeat it.' Jesse William Weik, who, with William Herndon, wrote one of the earliest biographies of Lincoln, records him as writing on all the boards and 'flat sides of hewn logs' in the cabin, 'when every bare wooden surface had been filled with his letters and ciphers he would erase them and begin anew'.

The energy he devoted to his own education was as remarkable as it was sustained. But it would not have been possible without the support of his parents. This support came from his three parental figures each in their own, unorthodox way; for they were unable to provide him with a steady school, let alone the chance at university.

Nancy Hanks, Abraham's mother, seems to have encouraged his early study. But unfortunately her contribution must remain vague for so little is spoken of her in relation to Abraham's learning, or indeed early life. Sarah Bush Lincoln was a potent influence, supportive emotionally and more prosaically with her (relatively) impressive book collection.

And finally there is Thomas Lincoln.

Believe his son and Thomas Lincoln wanted nothing more than to beat his boy for his big lip, workshy nature and love of books. He was contemptuous of his son's intelligence and disdained his lack of physical application. Believe also some of Lincoln's earlier biographers, like Albert J. Beveridge, and the same view of Thomas Lincoln as a latter-day Philistine appears. Read instead the testimony of his second wife, Sarah, and a different man emerges from beneath the scorn. Thomas did what he could to help his boy get the education that he was denied, she said: 'As a usual thing, Mr Lincoln never made Abe quit reading to do anything if he could avoid it. He would do it himself first.' Some of Lincoln's more recent biographers have pointed out that these are the later recollections of a wife on her long-dead husband. Time can brush away sharp edges. Even though his father perhaps did what he could to help his boy, what matters is that Lincoln had come so unbendingly to dislike his father and his father's world. Young Lincoln constructed himself against his father as a way to leverage an escape. For while Lincoln's obsession with reading and writing is a mark of the playfulness of a very able mind, it had a darker side, which was aimed at his father. His embrace of learning wasn't just a way out of a stultifying hicksville where Latin-literate wizards were supposed to wander. It was a way not to be Thomas Lincoln.

What Abraham found in Kentucky and Indiana were scraps, nods in the general direction of education, but they were offerings Lincoln gobbled up as if he were already, at a young age, preparing for a life among the stars. At each turning point, the death of his mother, the death of his sister, the breakdown in the relationship with his father, the meagre opportunities for escape, he could have turned and wept, broken by the harsh world of the frontier. But at each moment he coiled tighter, assessing the world, expanding his mind and redefining his limits. As the vices tightened, the adamantine core was ready to break through, and out.

At the age of twenty-one, as he'd done aged nine, Lincoln boarded a flat-bottomed boat and escaped across a river. Perhaps on that very first trip into Indiana he had seen in the craft the means for freedom. He didn't hesitate and took his chance as soon as he could, sailing away from his father, and what remained of his family, into New Salem, and into the new life that eventually, many years and twists and turns later, led him to the famous house on Pennsylvania Avenue, and made him his country's sixteenth president – and its saviour.

Eva Duarte de Perón

I cannot betray the people because it would mean a betrayal of myself.

Think Diana, Princess of Wales; add to this a sustained, serious, lifelong and working commitment to the problems of the poor; and subtract every advantage that might come with a privileged start in life; and you have Eva Duarte de Perón. If any First Lady ever crawled from the wreckage of a chaotic childhood, it was Argentina's beloved 'Evita' (little Eva).

Until the late-twentieth-century musical of the same name hit the world, Evita was hardly famous outside Argentina. But she has been the most important female figure in that country's popular history since. As the glamorous third wife of the populist demagogue Juan Perón after the Second World War, she made herself the human face of a political movement's commitment to the poor, the *descamisados* – the 'shirtless ones'. Eva and her husband remain controversial figures in Argentina: leaders today still tend to define their politics by reference to the Peronist ideal, for or against. But her own convictions were never in doubt: she had lived through poverty and was determined to improve the lives of the poor, by whom she came to be adored, almost worshipped. As a recent president of Argentina, Cristina Kirchner, was to remark, 'Evita' established herself in the collective national imagination 'for her passion and combativeness'.

She was certainly brave. On her famous 1947 tour of Europe, in which she charmed the continent's elite, Eva made a first stop at Madrid's Barajas airport. She was greeted by 300,000 people, including General Franco and his wife, Carmen Polo, with whom she would spend the week. Eva asked to visit the working-class districts of Madrid. Carmen Polo consented reluctantly, recoiling from the 'red' areas, whose republican inhabitants had opposed her husband's Falangist movement a decade before. Eva snapped: 'Your husband is in charge not thanks to the will of the people, but by the imposition of a victory. Perón won elections and governs because the majority of the people wish it to be so.' Her unconcealed indignation was a million miles from stiff-necked Castilian

political convention. But Eva was an unconventional political figure. Her background was not very different from
those living in Madrid's 'barrios obreros'.

She was born in 1919 in the city of Los Toldos. Her
mother, Juana Ibarguren, was an impoverished working-
class woman, and Eva the product of her affair with a
wealthy, married landowner, Juan Duarte. Their relationship led to five children, and Eva was the youngest.
When Eva was one year old her father abandoned her
mother and returned to his wife and legitimate children
in a neighbouring town. Eva was left to live in hope of the
occasional visits of her still-adored father – until she was
six. Then he was killed in a car accident in 1926. The loss
left Juana and her children destitute, but determined they
pay their respects. She turned up at the funeral with her
five children in tow, where Eva, the youngest, was the last
to kiss her dead father's cheek. Juan's relatives looked on in
horror and scorn. It was at this point (says her biographer
Alicia Dujovne Ortiz) that Eva vowed that 'one day, she
would be first'.

Eva, like Alexander Hamilton (see p. 108) lived with
the burden of illegitimacy throughout her life, and the
words stung. At school, classmates scrawled 'you are not
a Duarte, you are an Ibarguren' across the blackboard.
When she married Juan Perón she hid her birth certificate, dated 1919, and produced another, dated 1922. This
allowed her to claim that Juan Duarte's wife – who died
in 1922 – had been her mother, which in turn enabled her
to marry a military officer. Poverty could be overcome.
Illegitimacy never could.

Poverty, though, was harsh and grew harsher for the

little girl. In 1929 when the Great Depression hit Argentina, Juana and her children had drifted to the railway hub town of Junín – a melting pot for the country's indigenous and immigrant populations. Eva, still only ten, was (in the words of Dujovne Ortiz) a 'tender but authoritarian' young girl. She had developed an interest in theatre and was a natural performer with a rebellious streak.

This emerged when as a teenager she and a young female friend made the acquaintance of two young male aristocrats who invited them on a day trip to Mar del Plata, a posh seaside resort nearby. Eva, defying her mother's rules, leapt at the chance: she wanted to see how the other half lived. But the young men's car pulled over en route at an isolated station and the two youths tried to rape their teenage passengers. When Eva and her companion managed to throw them off, the girls were thrown, stripped, onto the side of the road. The men drove away.

After this episode Eva had had enough. She aspired to, and felt she deserved, something better. The sociologist Juan José Sebreli believes that Eva was the product of 'dual membership', a descendant of rich landowners and the homeless poor, with the imaginative dislocation that this can produce.

She was determined to complete the switch. At fifteen she abandoned her family and headed to Buenos Aires, intent on becoming an actress. There she found moderate fame, working on radio soap opera and earning bit parts in plays. It wasn't until she met Juan Domingo Perón, a burly, popular socialist politician, twenty years her senior, that her life began to change. In time she would run the ministries of Labour and Health, found and lead the charitable

Eva Perón Foundation, champion women's suffrage in Argentina, and create and lead the nation's first large-scale female political party, the Female Peronist Party. At Perón's side she would become one of the first women in her country's history to claim a leading voice in democratic politics, and devote the remainder of her short life to improving the lives of Argentina's poor. She died of cancer at thirty-three, to scenes of tremendous and heartfelt national mourning.

It has been neither difficult nor uncommon in history for an attractive woman to find celebrity and political status after forming a relationship with a leading male politician. It is so much less common for such a person to remember where she came from and use her status tirelessly, and with such huge effect, to help those she left behind. Evita's detractors may sneer that she hooked an older man, became an inveterate self-publicist, and loved the glamour, the money and the social life that came with her celebrity marriage. All this is true. But it overlooks the iron will and the unwavering determination to use her new life to avenge – for herself and others – the nightmares and indignities of her old one. 'I cannot betray the people,' she said to a women's movement assembly in 1949, 'because it would mean the betrayal of myself.'

Think of her, an infant kissing her faithless father's corpse as his 'legitimate' relatives curled their lips; as a schoolgirl finding her illegitimacy scrawled by classmates across the blackboard; and as a teenager thrown half-naked into the ditch by high-born louts. Something was broken by these horrors, but what was broken was resignation to her fate; and in that breakage, something was unlocked.

Alexander Hamilton

The ultimate upstart.

> How does a bastard, orphan, son of a whore and a/
> Scotsman, dropped in the middle of a forgotten/ Spot
> in the Caribbean by providence, impoverished, in
> squalor/ Grow up to be a hero and a scholar?

Thus did Lin-Manuel Miranda, writing the opening hip-hop number for the 2015 smash-hit musical *Hamilton*, frame the question that has puzzled biography since that show's hero's death in 1804.

Alexander Hamilton, a founding father of modern America, was gifted with relentless ambition, high intelligence and a run of extraordinary achievements. Powered by these talents his steep rise to the top of the American military and then politics was little short of dizzying. And it started from illegitimacy and poverty on an obscure Caribbean island.

Hamilton's father was an absent sailor. His mother, married to another man, was a Nevis woman. Born around 1755, he was orphaned at twelve and destitute by fourteen. By his mid-twenties he was in America, leading a regiment in the attack at Yorktown which effectively sealed the British defeat in the War of Independence. And his career was only starting.

Hamilton's victory at Yorktown in 1781 was a payoff for persistence. Since joining the army in 1775, he had longed for glory. Nine months after signing up he'd already been commissioned a captain. Serving alongside Washington's artillery in an attack on Trenton, New York, Hamilton helped persuade the encircled British regiment to surrender. The commander-in-chief recognised Hamilton's talent and offered him a promotion to lieutenant colonel and a role as an aide-de-camp within his inner circle. Despite the prestige of the position, Hamilton repeatedly asked to see battle first-hand; and when he was refused one too many times, walked out over a minor squabble. A year later, George Washington tempted Hamilton back, giving him a regiment to lead at Yorktown. Alongside the French General Lafayette, Hamilton routed the British forces. Glory was his. But he would not remain satisfied for long. American independence secured, he longed for political power and a stake in America's future. He would go on to shape the structure of federal government and found the national bank, leaving a system that survives to this day.

For a Broadway musical, Miranda's script portrays Hamilton's youth and life with remarkable accuracy. Historians agree that Hamilton's early life was not just fractured but nearly destroyed by tragedy. Birth records are hard to come by, but he was likely born in 1755 on the British island of Nevis to James Hamilton, a Scottish sailor, and Rachel Faucette Lavien. Rachel's estranged first husband, who had once had her thrown in prison for infidelity, obtained a divorce decree forbidding her remarriage. So, when Rachel met James Hamilton and fell pregnant, they were never able to marry. Alexander, her first son with James, was born 'illegitimately'.

Ten years later, James Hamilton abandoned the family. Rachel was struck down by disease and died with Alexander in her bed. Devastated by the loss of their mother, he and his brother were taken in by a relative, Peter Lytton, who subsequently committed suicide and left them destitute.

Ron Chernow – one of Hamilton's biographers – says Hamilton emerged from his struggle unbowed, 'with a thirst for glory, a prodigious work ethic, and a talent for attracting patrons'. He found a job as a clerk at a mercantile house on the island, and – such was his capability – was soon managing the business when the boss was away. A talent for numbers and trade which would serve him well as Secretary of the Treasury was matched by a luminous ability as a writer. He was spotted after he penned a newspaper account of a hurricane that ravaged the island. Well-off inhabitants of the island raised a subscription fund and by 1772 were able to pay his passage and send the youth (still a teenager) to the mainland: his first big break.

It is fitting that a hair-raising account of a hurricane should sweep Hamilton to success. He had only known destruction and uncertainty. His ambition and genius – be it with the pen or the sword – were accompanied by an utter and uncompromising fearlessness. He started with nothing, and carried on behaving as if he had nothing to lose even when, later, he did. His daring showed early in a series of blazing pre-war pamphlets he penned, then in his military audacity, then in his ambitious, root-and-branch structuring of the early government as Secretary of the Treasury, and finally in the formation of the federal government and the national bank.

So often on the move, on the attack, and always restless, part of his genius was never to deal with challenges by tinkering. From that moment when as a boy he realised he was alone and must not rely on providence, he just took everything head-on. He was the ultimate upstart.

George Washington became a mentor. But, as historian Andrew Trees remarks, Hamilton was 'always prone to go too far without the restraining hand of another'. The rash streak that was the making of him was also, finally, his undoing. He made enemies, not least Thomas Jefferson. Yet putting national interest over personal gain, Hamilton backed Jefferson for the presidency, against the treacherous Aaron Burr. 'Mine is an odd destiny,' he lamented. 'Perhaps no man in the United States has sacrificed or done more for the present Constitution than myself ... Yet I have the murmurs of its friends no less than the curses of its foes for my reward ... Every day proves to me more and more that this American world was not made for me.'

Burr took his revenge soon enough, duelling Hamilton on 11 July 1804. Hamilton purposely missed with his bullet. Burr was not so magnanimous, took aim, fired, and killed Hamilton.

Reading this remarkable life, one concludes that his boyhood fracture, with its dawning understanding that he was alone in the world with nothing to lose and nobody to help him, may have blunted Hamilton's instincts for precaution, but never his idealism. Perhaps it sharpened it. Few great men in history have combined such recklessness with so fastidious a sense of justice.

John Lennon

Won't you please, please help me?

As Paul McCartney and Ringo Starr drift into 'ageing rocker' territory, one Beatle has attracted the aura of untouchable myth. John Lennon, assassinated at forty, is now a cult personality, evoked as the epitome of a tortured, brilliant and politically radical musician. His music is among the most innovative the Beatles produced, inspiring a generation of artists; and his political activism against the Vietnam War made him a role model for peaceful protest across the world. You may say that Lennon, with his Indian ashrams with the Maharishi Mahesh Yogi, his transcendental meditation, and his and Yoko Ono's week-long 'bed-ins' for peace (and the world's media), invented himself. But we all invent ourselves to some degree, and an invisible rope runs from the child to the adult version.

At the child's end of that rope stands a little boy of five, weeping, as his father and mother argue about who should take him. His father wants the son to leave with him for New Zealand; his mother wants him to stay with her. As his mother walks away, the child runs tearfully after her, and thus is the choice made.

Elements and details of this story are disputed. But whether or not it happened in the filmic way that some claim, what is in less doubt is that little John Lennon's father, Alf Lennon, a sailor who had deserted during the Second World War and stopped paying for his son's maintenance but returned to try to work things out, did want to take him. His mother, Julia, did not want to let him go, and

Julia's family had never approved of Alf. The five-year-old was caught between two people.

Between more than two people, in fact. Lennon's childhood is marked – torn, ripped – by family disputes about whether his mother was fit to rear him; and, if not, who should. After the separation from his father, John was brought home to live with Julia and her new partner in their one-bedroom flat. But Julia's childless sister Mimi was determined to look after John, as she had done for much of his infancy (turning up often enough, it was said, crying on her doorstep). Mimi contacted a Housing Inspector who ruled that the flat was unfit for purpose, and took John from his mother. The boy – as he later told his half-sister – 'didn't have a bloody clue' what was happening.

He would spend his youth under the watchful gaze of his dictatorial aunt. Mimi – and therefore the child's upbringing – was middle class: middle class in Mimi's jealously guarded respectability, the gentility of the lower middle class of that era. So, though sometimes chaotic, there was flint in his upbringing, flint against which he increasingly rebelled.

But the boy was indulged by Mimi's husband, his uncle George, to whom he became exceptionally close. When Lennon was fourteen, George died of a liver haemorrhage. John's first reaction was to laugh in hysterical disbelief but he grieved privately, becoming ever more withdrawn from others.

He found solace in music when his free-spirited mother gifted him his first guitar. As the opening line of 'Mother' reveals, however, John was never able to grow close to his mother: 'Mother, you had me but I never had you.'

His longing to establish a relationship with his mother was almost Oedipal, according to his biographer Philip Norman. It would never be fulfilled. In 1958, when John was seventeen, Julia Lennon left Mimi's house after a visit, crossed the road and was run over by an off-duty policeman.

The desperate 'Won't you please, please help me?' of 1965's 'Help!' betrays Lennon's lifelong fear of abandonment. He described that track as 'the only honest song I wrote'. Songs like 'Help!' and 'Nowhere Man' portray a vulnerability that rivals the emotional pain of Kahlo's self-portraits. Lennon no doubt identified with the likes of Kahlo and Nureyev – misunderstood geniuses at the top of their field. He did not consider himself a writer of silly love songs, but an artist. Describing his work, he said 'All art is pain expressing itself. I think all life is, everything we do, but particularly artists – that's why they're always vilified. They're always persecuted because they show pain; they can't help it. They express it in art and the way they live, and people don't like to see that reality that they're suffering.'

Lennon's childhood was the opposite of stable. He told his sister 'I lost my mother twice. Once as a child and then again at seventeen. It made me very, very bitter inside. I had just begun to establish a relationship with her when she was killed. We'd caught up on so much in just a few short years. We could communicate. We got on.'

The pain caused by John's difficult relationship with his mother, the wrench from his father, the death of George Smith, the restrictive, critical atmosphere of Mimi's home, and the tension between those two chalk-and-cheese cultural estates, the working class and the lower middle class, ripped into Lennon in boyhood – not just emotionally but in his moral and philosophical interior life, his politics and his love–hate relationship with his countrymen, countrywomen and their attitudes. There was an internal mutiny that never truly abated. He shunned Mimi's forced BBC English accent in favour of Scouse. He abandoned school studies, then art school, and turned to music, forming his first group, The Quarrymen, when he was fifteen. At their second gig, Lennon met Paul McCartney.

Edith Piaf

Edith Piaf's profound virtue is her ability to drag those that admire her towards the pain that they feel and of which they feel unable to speak, nor even know how to articulate.

Edith Giovanna Gassion was born on the street (some say) on 19 December 1915, in Ménilmontant, Paris, to an alcoholic mother, Annetta Maillard, and street-performer father, Louis Gassion. She was abandoned at birth by her mother. Her father, who was serving on the Western Front, sent her to live with his mother – a Madame at a brothel in Normandy, where she came to consider the sex workers her sisters. Suffering from an eye condition, she is said to have gone partially blind for some time as a small girl.

Edith Piaf's funeral procession on 14 October 1963 marked the first time that Paris had come to a complete halt since the end of the Second World War. In France the celebrations of the fiftieth anniversary of her death rivalled those of Kennedy in the United States and Churchill in Britain. And as Paris awoke from the horror of the 11 January 2015 terrorist attacks, it was Piaf's recorded voice that blasted from loudspeakers across the city, in proud defiance of the killings. Her music is the epitome of Frenchness; songs such as 'Milord', 'La vie en rose' and, of course, 'Je ne regrette rien' are filled with pain, charm, wit, drama and romance; but she is so much more than a singer of charmingly French songs. Not just her lyrics, but her very throat, her guttural delivery, speaks of what lay beneath in her own life, touching the lives of her audience too. It will never be truer than of Piaf, that it's the singer not song.

Her attraction – as all have agreed – is the power and authenticity with which she delivered her songs. Authenticity and truthfulness are not quite the same. Truth and legend are all but impossible to disentangle from the chaos of her life. Her long-term secretary, Danielle Bonel, asked '[h]ow can anyone know who the real Piaf was? She played so many roles!'. But her authenticity was that she inhabited those roles so well. When Piaf sang of heartbreak, torture and lost love, the crowd knew that every inch of her five-foot frame meant it. Dominique Aubier, a French novelist who was by no means a fan of the *chanson populaire*, wrote that Piaf had a voice that sang beyond the words it pronounced. After watching her perform in the sixties, she remarked that 'Edith Piaf's profound virtue is her ability to drag those that admire her towards the pain that they feel and of which they feel unable to speak, nor even know how to articulate.' This virtue could only come from Piaf's own experience of pain, abandonment and loss. Her genius was to translate this into song.

As with the legends of Coco Chanel and Orson Welles, many stories from Piaf's childhood are probably far-fetched. Some report that she was born under a street light on the corner of Rue de Belleville, and that her mother was assisted by two policemen. Or that her sight was saved, as a girl, when her grandmother and 'daughters' closed the brothel for a day, and prayed at a monument to St Thérèse de Lisieux. It is known – at least – that she was kept in a miserable condition. Constantly dirty and unkempt, her poor sight may have been caused by keratitis, an inflammation of the cornea. Cared for by the women of the brothel, she was uneducated, and during the war years poorly fed. Her father returned in 1922 and, rather than attend school, she joined his street act, singing as a busker across France.

Her chaotic childhood was followed by a number of tumultuous early relationships. At eighteen she met a young delivery boy named Louis Dupont and fell in love. They found a flat together in Montmartre and had a child: Marcelle. Like her own mother, Edith was an irresponsible parent. She ignored Louis's demands that she find a 'proper job', taking to the streets instead to sing, baby tucked under one arm. Furious, Louis took Marcelle from Edith and determined to raise her alone. In his care, Marcelle contracted meningitis and died at the age of two.

Piaf was distraught, alone and penniless. It is rumoured she resorted to prostitution to pay for Marcelle's funeral. Then she returned to the streets, singing with renewed force. In 1935, she was talent-spotted on a Pigalle street corner by a cabaret owner, Louis Leplée. He made her his resident star act, outfitted her in her trademark plain black dress, and named her 'La Môme Piaf' – 'the little sparrow'. 'Môme' just means 'little one', but it was 'piaf' (slang for 'sparrow') that stuck. 'Piaf' she became. Her first performance took Leplée's celebrity audience by storm. By January 1936, La Môme had signed a record deal.

So began a musical career that would all but define French music. Piaf became emblematic of the *chanson française*: a genre distinguished by its fusion of popular song and poetry, and a symbol of the Resistance, though the Nazi occupying troops loved her too, and she always trod a delicate tightrope. In their different ways, the songs of Yves Montand, Georges Brassens, Charles Aznavour and Piaf all reflected their personalities and their search for emotional truth. Piaf, whose lyrics resonated with the tragedies of her personal life, was the truest of the lot. 'Authenticity' has become, in our era, an over-hyped word: but it is the only word for the genius of Piaf. Broken, she spilled her truth into the hearts of millions.

CHAPTER FIVE

CRUELTY

Cruelty needn't be physical and often isn't. Nobody whipped the 7th Earl of Shaftesbury – among the greatest and most admired social reformers that Britain has known – and nor did he lack the means of material support as an aristocratic boy at the very beginning of the nineteenth century. But you can be lonely as hell in a cold and loveless great house with an absent father and a callous and careless mother who seems to you like 'a devil' (Shaftesbury's words); followed by a preparatory school that's a filthy prison from which there is no escape. 'Most earnestly do I pray', the Earl later wrote, 'that no family hereafter endure from its parents what we have endured.'

'Cruelty' is an imprecise word. Sometimes it implies a cruel intention on the part of a persecutor. Sometimes no intention is implied, but only the cruelty of time and circumstance. And humans can be cruel without meaning to: Rudolf Nureyev's father probably wanted the best for his boy, and may well have had no inkling that family constraints and expectations were so very cruel for a gay son in provincial Russia who wanted to be a ballet dancer. Attitudes to homosexuality generally, and not just in Russia, bore exceptionally cruelly on the boy.

In short, the pain depends on the person. For the Brontë sisters what might, for other girls sent away to school, have been ordinary homesickness was pure torment. The lash that whipped a young Frederick Douglass ignited within him the courage and originality to imagine that black men and women might one day be free. The bullying and scorn that Nureyev faced awoke within him an aggression and assertiveness that carried his genius skyward. Sometimes, people fight back; and, fighting back they are all but reborn.

This chapter brings together some of those great lives where genius has seemed to emerge from under the crack of a whip. Pain can spawn anger, and anger can spawn courage, aggression, self-assertion. Oppression can arouse a longing to escape: escape not always outward and away, but sometimes inward, into the secret, private world of the imagination.

We start, then, with a very small boy's treatment at the hands of a sadistic foster family in Southsea, near Portsmouth. His treatment would have been appalling by any yardstick, but in a sensitive, imaginative boy, wrenched from five blithe early years in the Indian sunshine, the pain was explosive.

Yet in that explosion was born a boy forced to live in his own imagination and make things up. He was to splash his colours onto a universal canvas to universal acclaim, years later, as one of England's most famous writers and poets.

Greatness and genius, then: not always despite, but because – as you will see.

Shamed in the streets of Southsea

An immense gift for using words, an amazing curiosity and power of observation with his mind and with all his senses, the mask of the entertainer, and beyond that a queer gift of second sight.

'I had never heard of Hell, so I was introduced to it in all its terrors.' The man who wrote that was in his seventies, but the boy speaking was only six: an age when the world feels capricious, parents can be bulwarks, constant, loving, and dependable. But it was the boy's mother and father who woke him and his sister at dawn, bade him goodbye as he rubbed the sleep from his eyes, and left him in a stranger's house, waking to that nightmarish new start to his life.

Where his parents left him was, he wrote, 'a dark land, and a darker room full of cold'. He wasn't to see his mother for five years, his father for seven. They had deposited their children with another family before returning to their life in India. The foster parents had seemed decent enough, and the man was, if without kindness, at least no sadist. His wife and son were, though. This pair told the boy and his sister that their parents had left them because they were tired of them. They snapped at the children for lying, and seemed to delight in canings. The mother took something of a shine to the boy's sister, but her brother was not so lucky.

She picked on him. And where she led, her son, twelve years older than him, followed. The smaller boy was forced to sleep in the same room as his youthful tormentor. 'When his mother had finished with me for the day he took me on and roasted the other side,' he wrote in *Something of Myself.*

But it was the accusation of lying that cut to the bone. He could hardly defend himself; he was only six. Once he was paraded around town bearing a placard spelling 'Liar'. The nadir came when the words on the page before him started to blur, and the visible world began to dim. As his eyesight deteriorated, so did he. On a visit to an aunt's house, he was seen wildly slashing at trees, and sprinting towards walls to touch them and make sure that 'they were there'.[13] At last, his mother was summoned from afar to rescue her children.

What he'd known before this nightmarish land was one of 'daybreak, light and colour and golden and purple fruits at the level of my shoulder'. As an infant, and until the age of five and three quarters, he'd lived the life of a miniature king. Indulged by parents and servants, he was a chubby little terror. His birth land was beautiful, even exotic. He and his nurse went on evening walks 'by the sea in the shadow of palm-groves ... when the wind blew the great nuts would tumble, and we fled'. Frogs croaked in the night as he was rocked to sleep. These were years of light.

After the years of darkness, his mother arrived and freed him and his sister from the torture-house. His sight was restored by spectacles. But another separation loomed. His mother had found him a boarding school and sent him west, to the coast. His home was now a spartan institute, his family other boarders. He hated it, but, editing the school newspaper and winning prizes, a new boy began to emerge.

But there's no sweeping aside the darkness that came before. It had changed the boy. It broke him. It remade him. He had learnt to fantasise; learned to lie – something that, later, he called the foundation of all literary effort. And his writing came to define an era for his countrymen. His novels and poetry won fame across the world. One of his poems is considered, even today, the nation's favourite. For the child who experienced all this became the author of 'If'. Those who sneer at the poem because of its sheer popularity should consider how many millions it has touched, and be ashamed. Such was Rudyard Kipling's genius.

> An immense gift for using words, an amazing curiosity and power of observation with his mind and with all his senses, the mask of the entertainer, and beyond that a queer gift of second sight, of transmitting messages from elsewhere, a gift so disconcerting when we are made aware of it that thenceforth we are never sure when it is not present: all this makes Kipling a writer impossible wholly to understand and quite impossible to belittle.

The great twentieth-century poet T. S. Eliot, who wrote this, was as dry, as dense, as restrained a writer as Rudyard Kipling was an accessible, exuberant, even lush contemporary. You might expect Eliot to have taken a dim view of Kipling's mob-appeal; but no. Yet in the years since his death in 1936, Kipling's popularity has stayed strong but his reputation in literary circles has fallen. His support for the Empire in particular has made him unfashionable with some. George Orwell's famous charge that Kipling was a 'jingo imperialist' who was 'morally insensitive and aesthetically disgusting' was stinging. Poems about empire like 'The White Man's Burden' make for difficult reading politically, though the poetic imagination is strong:

> Take up the White Man's burden –
> Send forth the best ye breed –
> Go bind your sons to exile
> To serve your captives' need;
> To wait in heavy harness
> On fluttered folk and wild –
> Your new-caught, sullen peoples,
> Half devil and half child.

In his own time, however, Kipling enjoyed a fame as a writer that was almost unrivalled. As the nineteenth century turned he was on a roll. *Stalky & Co.* was published in 1899, *Kim* in 1901, and the *Just So Stories* in 1902. He was the first English recipient of the Nobel Prize for Literature in 1907. It was his choice of words from the Bible that adorned many of the graves of the fallen in the First World War: 'Their Name Liveth For Evermore'. His poetry, short stories and novels were wildly popular. When he and his daughter, Josephine, became ill in 1899 in New York with pneumonia it was headline news and the subject of a leader in *The Times*. Josephine died; her father lived.

This was not his only parental loss. Kipling's son John had shared his father's myopia. As the First World War dawned his attempts to join both army and navy were rebuffed on medical grounds. Rudyard went to great lengths to ensure his son could fight. An old friend got John admitted to the Irish Guards. Rudyard in late 1915 was in the thick of the war. He was commissioned as a propagandist, writing articles and cheering on the ordinary troops. Look at 'Tommy' of the eponymous poem: Kipling's jingoistic voice was always nuanced by deep personal scepticism about the competence and humanity of the country's military and political chiefs.

> You talk o' better food for us, an' schools, an' fires,
>   an' all:
> We'll wait for extry rations if you treat us rational.
> Don't mess about the cook-room slops, but prove it
>   to our face
> The Widow's Uniform is not the soldier-man's
>   disgrace.
> For it's Tommy this, an' Tommy that, an' 'Chuck him
>   out, the brute!'
> But it's 'Saviour of 'is country' when the guns begin
>   to shoot;
> An' it's Tommy this, an' Tommy that, an' anything
>   you please;
> An' Tommy ain't a bloomin' fool – you bet that
>   Tommy sees!

In the Battle of Loos that September, John was reported missing. He was never found. It is likeliest he was shot in the head and fell behind enemy lines. Rudyard and his wife were utterly distraught. In a later poem he wrote

> If any question why we died,
> Tell them, because our fathers lied.[14]

Today Rudyard Kipling is best known for 'If' and *The Jungle*

Book. The role that Walt Disney played in bringing him to a mass audience may be claimed by critics as evidence of his vulgarity, or by admirers as testament to his vivid and soaring imagination; but he is so much more than those two works. Yet still they show his qualities well: an ear for rhythm, an access to the human heart, a freshness, and a masterly grasp of imagery. This was a literary giant, his abilities no less evident now than they were when he put pen to paper. Though his views may be deeply out of fashion (and sometimes inexcusable on their own merits), he keeps his place among the masters of English literature.

But his glittering adult life obscured the dark secret of his childhood, which made and remade Rudyard Kipling. How? Where did this enigma come from?

*

In early May 1865 a young, unknown English couple stepped off their boat into the heave of imperial Bombay. The seven islands of the city were enjoying an industrial-era boom. The Civil War had cut off America's cotton from Britain where textile mills clamoured for the white gold. The British government had turned to India, and Bombay profited as the funnel through which cotton and cash passed. But the city's time was nearly up. In the month when the young couple arrived, so too did news of the North's victory in the Civil War. American cotton was back and India's boom was over. The slump set in from practically the moment they landed. Such dashed hopes, and a sense of things not quite working out as planned, would typify their early years in India.

Alice and John Lockwood Kipling had married only weeks before reaching Bombay. Alice Macdonald, as she was when they met, came from a large, garrulous family. Of all her many siblings, some of whom became notable figures in Victorian Britain, she was the most 'Celtic': hot-blooded and sharp-witted. In later years, when the Kiplings were more established in the firmament of the Raj, Lord Dufferin, the Viceroy said, 'Dullness and Mrs Kipling cannot exist in the same room'.[15]

John Kipling had met his future wife at a lakeside picnic he attended with her brother, his friend Harry. Lake Rudyard near Burslem in the Potteries was the scene. There he saw 'a beauteous creature, pensively eating salad'. Two years later the couple were married, and less than two months after that, they arrived in India so that John could take up a position at the Sir Jamsetjee Jeejeebhoy School of Art and Manufacture. John, now calling himself simply Lockwood Kipling, was to be an architectural sculptor.

Rudyard was born, just before the turn of the year, on 30 December 1865. He was placed in the care of an 'ayah': a nurse who looked after the children of Europeans, as well an Indian bearer called Meeta. The Kiplings may not have been wealthy or even of lofty status, but it was a mark of the Raj that they could afford such servants. Meeta and the ayah, whose name has remained unrecorded, became Rudyard's companions. It was with his ayah that he walked the seashore and ran from the giant palm-nuts that fell from the trees. His early memories of India are powerfully visual, as if from a paintbrush rather than a pen: 'There were far-going Arab dhows on the pearly waters, and gaily dressed Parsees wading out to worship the sunset.'

In his sparse autobiography, *Something of Myself*, written just before he died, Kipling describes a magical place. 'I have always felt the menacing darkness of tropical eventides, as I have loved the voices of the night-winds through palm or banana leaves, and the song of the tree-frogs.' These were the strong feelings of his youth, rushes of fear and delight mixing together.

When Alice Kipling became pregnant again, she elected to have her second child back home in England. Mother and son arrived in late March 1868 and stayed with Alice's parents in Bewdley near Kidderminster. Alice had been seeking some peace and quiet in which to give birth. Unfortunately for Rudyard this meant getting him out of the way. He was by all accounts something of a terror at this point. According to biographer Andrew Lycett he is said to have marched through the streets of Bewdley shouting 'Ruddy is coming! Ruddy is coming!', and when some poor soul got in his way, 'An angry Ruddy is coming!' His grandparents, Alice's mother and father, had been tasked with looking after him while their daughter stayed in London to give birth.

Little Rudyard hated it. So did his grandparents. And soon after the three Kiplings left, Alice's father George Macdonald died, his family certain the boisterous and difficult Rudyard was to blame. Louisa Baldwin, one of Alice's sisters and the mother of Stanley Baldwin, wrote in a letter to another sister 'Sorry as we were to lose her personally, her children turned the house into such a bear garden, and Ruddy's screaming tempers made Papa so ill we were thankful to see them on their way.' Whether or not he did help hasten his grandfather's death, their readiness to blame him suggests an exceptionally temperamental toddler.

In India Rudyard came back to his ayah and Meeta, with his new sister Alice (soon nicknamed Trix) in tow. The 'strong light and darkness' returned. So too did the riotous fusion of Indian and English cultures that two young Kiplings could enjoy. The ayah and Meeta would rock Rudyard and Trix to sleep while telling stories in their native tongue. And when by day the little group traipsed about Bombay they spoke in Hindustani. Rudyard and Trix picked up the language with a child's ease.

Rudyard says: 'We were sent into the dining room after we had been dressed with the caution "Speak English now to Mamma and Papa". So one spoke "English", haltingly translated out of the vernacular idiom that one thought and dreamed in.' A vivid story of Rudyard's embrace of his world comes from his mother, who, when they were at Bombay's hill station of Nassik, saw her four-year-old son walking off, holding a local's hand, shouting back 'Goodbye, this is my brother'.

*

In 1871, when Rudyard was five and Trix two, the Kiplings again boarded a steamer for England. Alice and Lockwood Kipling had decided to take their children home for the first time since Trix's birth. Lockwood had finished his three-year contract at the Sir J. J. School and before the next one started was given a six-month sabbatical. They set out in April, travelling through the recently opened Suez Canal. Trix and Rudyard had no grasp of the significance of this trip. Whether their parents did, as the small family boarded the ship, is less clear.

Reaching England the Kiplings spent a month by the seaside in Sussex, where it rained non-stop. Rudyard built sandcastles all the same and his father delighted in seeing him play. Before they returned to India the Kiplings were to make a brief stop in Southsea. This was at Lorne Lodge, the home of the Holloways: Captain Pryse, his wife Sarah, and their twelve-year-old son Harry. All seemed normal as the Kiplings put their children to bed.

From this moment, there are three narratives for what happened next. The first, 'Baa Baa Black Sheep', is an autobiographical tale Rudyard wrote at the age of only twenty-three. Its main characters are Punch and Judy, ill-disguised *noms de guerre* for Rudyard and Trix. The second narrative, 'Through Judy's Eyes', is by Trix. Probably she wrote this unpublished version of what her brother had written when she was in her late sixties.[16] And a note on the manuscript reveals that it was indeed autobiographical. Trix slips from 'Punch' to 'Ruddy', confirming what was obvious. The third narrative is Rudyard's *Something of Myself*, written in his last years.

As autobiography, the first two texts must be treated with care since they are fictional, while the third is reticent to the point of obfuscation. So what facts are certain?

We do know that six years later Alice Kipling was dashing back to England, to spirit her children away from Lorne Lodge. Rudyard had had a nervous breakdown. He and Trix had been abused. Their notional carers were the culprits and the two children, Rudyard in particular, needed rescuing. Alice arrived from India and took them away.

Or rather took Rudyard away. As we shall see, Trix would spend another two years in Southsea, and Rudyard's parents weren't to know the extent of what happened for another eleven. The reason for this murkiness is that the abuse cast a long shadow, which the children found hard to escape, or perhaps to acknowledge before escape. So in trying to understand the unfolding of events we have to use three texts together, especially since it was in their notionally fictional writings that Rudyard and Trix were probably at their most frank, though in 'Baa Baa Black Sheep' Rudyard did (Trix notes) add some 'extra tones of black'.

The moment of goodbye in Southsea shows this. His later *Something of Myself* states simply, '… a parting in the dawn with Father and Mother, who said that I must learn quickly to read and write so that they might send me letters and books'. But 'Baa Baa Black Sheep' is more expansive:

> … they roused Punch and Judy in the chill dawn of a February morning to say Good-bye; and of all people in the wide earth to Papa and Mamma – both crying this time. Punch was very sleepy and Judy was cross.

After their parents ask Punch and Judy not to forget them, the children fall back to sleep. When they wake in the morning, they discover their parents have gone to Bombay. They're told this by Harry, whose real name Rudyard did not bother to hide. It was true: Lockwood and Alice woke their children early in the morning, bade them farewell and departed for India.

The following years at Southsea were one slow trauma; but this had been a sharp initial blow. The immediate question on both pairs of lips was 'Why?' Why had their hitherto loving parents dumped them in this depressing place on the edge of Britain with these strange people? Why had they left for India without them? In 'Baa Baa Black Sheep', Punch cannot at first accept the truth. He rushes with Judy to the beach, hoping to find the ship on which his Mamma and Papa are waiting for them. They march through Southsea like two little soldiers. Punch threatens to smack Judy if she stops for even a moment. When they reach the shore they see no boat and no parents; just mud, sea, sand and crabs.

Rudyard and Trix grappled with this mysterious, awful question as well as they could. They were only five and three. Again, 'Baa Baa Black Sheep' provides an eloquent and pitiful description of their experiences:

> When a matured man discovers that he has been deserted by Providence, deprived of his God, and cast without help, comfort or sympathy upon a world which is new and strange to him, his despair, which may find expression in evil-living, the writing of his experiences, or the more satisfactory diversion of suicide, is generally supposed to be impressive. A child, under exactly similar circumstances as far as its knowledge goes, cannot very well curse God and die. It howls till its nose is red, its eyes are sore, and its head aches. Punch and Judy, through no fault of their own, had lost all their world. They sat in the hall and cried.

In a radio interview with the BBC in 1947, Trix was more direct than her brother:

The real tragedy … sprang from our inability to understand why our parents had deserted us. We had had no preparation or explanation; it was like a double death, or rather like an avalanche that had swept away everything happy and familiar … We felt we had been deserted 'almost as much as on a doorstep' … They had gone back to our own lovely home, and had not taken us with them. There was no getting out of that, as we often said.

On this wound, Mrs Sarah Holloway, their notional carer, poured vinegar. She told Trix and Rudyard their parents had left them 'because we were so tiresome and she had us in out of pity'. This was the mark of the woman, never unkind if she could be vicious. Rudyard did not believe this explanation. In that moment he showed the qualities that spelled trouble with the fostering couple. He could do little else – that was the boy he was. But it was also those qualities, obstinate pride allied to cleverness, that shaped how he survived Lorne Lodge's cruelties.

Who were these people with whom they lodged? Captain Pryse, whom the Kiplings called Uncle Harry, was an ex-navy man who'd fought in the Battle of Navarino in 1827 and been wounded. He had since worked variously for the merchant navy and the coastguard before retiring. Now he was living off his monthly pension. Sarah Holloway, his wife, was known to Rudyard and Trix as 'Aunty Rosa'. Sarah was a strict disciplinarian in the worst nineteenth-century sense. She was also a staunch Christian. It was a bad mix for her guests. Lies were her particular *bête noire*. A world divided into a strict schema of truth and falsehoods is a violent one. When people are seen through this narrow prism they are either truth-tellers or liars. Rudyard, for Mrs Holloway, was firmly in the latter group.

The Holloway's son, Harry, was twelve when the Kiplings arrived. They hated him. No description of him in their writings was complete without some reference to his greasy black hair, 'plastered with pomatum'. His mother was cruel in an astringent, religious way, but Harry was gleeful. He delighted in tormenting Rudyard especially. He was the subject, too, of some of the darkest passages of 'Baa Baa Black Sheep'.

The house itself was an unhappy building. Though Lorne Lodge was newly built, it was a dank place where toys grew blue with mould in the basement. Kipling as an adult referred to it as the House of Desolation.

Pryse Holloway showed a certain, pinched regard for Rudyard. Sarah did not. It was Sarah's obsession with lies and truth that was so cruel. In *Something of Myself* Rudyard explains:

> If you cross-examine a child of seven or eight on his day's doings (specially when he wants to go to sleep) he will contradict himself very satisfactorily. If each contradiction be set down as a lie and retailed at breakfast, life is not easy. I have known a certain amount of bullying, but this was calculated torture – religious as well as scientific. Yet it made me give attention to the lies I soon found it necessary to tell: and this, I presume, is the foundation of literary effort.

At the same time Sarah desperately tried to divide brother

and sister. Mrs Holloway took a liking to Trix, possibly seeing her as the daughter she lacked. She decided that Trix was always right and Rudyard always wrong and tried to use this to drive a wedge between them. Brother and sister slept in separate rooms. Trix stayed in the same bed as Sarah, while Rudyard slept in the same bedroom as Harry.

This was torment for Rudyard. In 'Baa Baa Black Sheep' he wrote 'Harry was at once spy, practical joker, inquisitor and Aunty Rosa's deputy executioner'. While Rudyard was forced into Harry's orbit, Trix was swept up by Sarah and her religion. Barely more than a toddler, she was soon influenced by her surrogate mother's religiosity.

One thing the two children did do together, though, was learn to read. Surprisingly, it was Rudyard who struggled here, despite being older and possessing the sharper brain. Sarah punished them if they made mistakes. Rudyard explained his learning pause as hesitation before a leap. In *Something of Myself* he wrote, '[o]n a day that I remember it came to me that "reading" was not "the Cat lay on the Mat," but a means to everything that would make me happy.' Kipling had found a way out. Like many of our other fractured lives, reading was an escape from his world and he started consuming books greedily. He read all he could in Lorne Lodge. His parents sent him more and more books, and Rudyard found he could not stop.

One particular book stands out to the modern reader. Kipling tells of how he came across 'a tale about a lion-hunter in South Africa who fell among lions who were all Freemasons, and with them entered into a confederacy against some wicked baboons'. He continues: 'I think that, too, lay dormant until the Jungle Books began to be born.'

Predictably, though, in Lorne Lodge any pleasure was precarious. Sarah saw his enjoyment of reading and turned it against him. She punished him by taking away his books and forcing him to play, strange as that may seem. Kipling loved his books too much and set up an ingenious system by which he could bang a table leg on the floor, simulating the noise of 'playing' while actually reading. Eventually, though, he was discovered, accused once more of being a liar and punished again.

Sometimes the punishments worked in favour of the boy's literary talents, though he would not have thought so at the time. Once he was questioned by 'the Devil Boy' as to why he was smiling as they left church and could not answer. Harry determined this innocent smile to be a smirk concealing some dastardly plot and pronounced Kipling's unsatisfactory response a lie. So Rudyard was sent upstairs to learn his prayers off by heart.

The light in this gloom may have made the gloom deeper. Respite came with the trips that began in Christmas 1873, when Rudyard and Trix had been at Lorne Lodge for two years. Their mother Alice had a family that was as warm as it was chaotic. Her sister Georgie had married the painter Edward Burne-Jones and set up house in Fulham, West London, in a place called The Grange. That was where Trix and Rudyard went at Christmas 1873. It had a very strong effect on Rudyard, who wrote about it in *Something of Myself*:

For a month each year I possessed a paradise which I verily believe saved me. Each December I stayed with my Aunt Georgie, my mother's sister, wife of

Sir Edward Burne-Jones, at The Grange, North End Road. At first I must have been escorted there, but later I went alone, and arriving at the house would reach up to the open-work iron bell-pull on the wonderful gate that let me into all felicity.

We know the children did not give away their secrets until later, but surely this was their moment? The answer may sometimes lie in the clinging silence that clothes many victims of abuse and cruelty. It may be terrifying to say something, easier just to stay silent. But we'll never really know the reasons for Rudyard and Trix's silence before their family.

A partial retreat for Rudyard, amid the torments of Sarah and Harry, was provided by Pryse Holloway, the stern man of the house who at least was not vindictive to Kipling. He would take the young boy on the seafront walk when he went to fetch his pension. It was on such a walk that Pryse offered a kinder reason for the departure of Rudyard's parents, telling him 'Papa had left us to be taken care of because India was too hot for small people.' Even this, though, the children knew not to be true. In India they had escaped scorching summer temperatures at Bombay's nearby hill station.

Pryse once even defended Rudyard from his own son Harry, though the incident shows the captain cannot properly have understood Rudyard's predicament, which is explained in 'Baa Baa Black Sheep'. Harry had taken Rudyard's paintbox. Pryse found out and struck Harry across the shoulders with a stick 'till he wept and yelled, and Aunty Rosa came in and abused Uncle Harry for cruelty to his own flesh and blood, and Punch shuddered to the tips of his shoes', knowing that Harry would take it out on him next.

There was something distinctly mournful about Pryse Holloway. He told Kipling stories of the great sea battles he had fought, including the fateful one, Navarino, that left him with his limp. Pryse said the booming of the guns left the sailors deaf for three days. The captain also had a model of HMS *Brisk*, the ship he sailed in, that Rudyard could look at but not touch. But if the note of regretfulness in all these old stories was buried, it surfaced when Pryse took Rudyard to the cemetery, sat down, and told the boy that soon he, Pryse, would be lying under that very gravestone.

Three years after the Kiplings arrived in Southsea, in December of 1874, Pryse Holloway died. The closest thing Rudyard knew to a protector was gone. He and Trix were now alone with Sarah and Harry. Their miseries worsened.

When the time came for schooling, Rudyard was sent to Harry's school. Rudyard's 'reputation' preceded him. Harry had spread about the school that Kipling was a habitual liar. He was shunned by the other boys. 'It isn't every school that takes little liars,' Sarah told him.

Now came his descent to rock bottom. Rudyard's world began, quite literally, to dim before his eyes. For a young boy with little sense of what was happening, this was terrifying. In 'Baa Baa Black Sheep' he writes that Punch, now known as 'Black Sheep', became more and more clumsy, knocking and spilling things, bumping into doors. 'There was a grey haze on all his world, and it narrowed month by month, until at last it left Black Sheep almost alone with the flapping curtains that were so like ghosts, and the nameless terrors of broad daylight that were only coats on pegs after all.'

Not only was his world becoming a frightening blur, but his chief pleasure, reading, was now threatened. Rudyard's schoolwork began to suffer. When Sarah heard about it, she punished him: 'The loss of "reading-time" was the worst of my "home" punishments for bad school-work,' he wrote in *Something of Myself*. He was only ten. He had been abused and degraded as a liar for years, divided from his sister, and made to feel, as in the title of his short story, like a black sheep. Now his only escape was being closed off.

Something within this child broke. He couldn't face showing his school report to Aunty. He binned it and told her he'd lost it. She apparently believed him. Black Sheep had (he wrote later)

conceived a large contempt for Aunty Rosa as he saw how easy it was to deceive her. 'She says I'm a little liar when I don't tell lies, and now I do, she doesn't know,' thought Black Sheep. Aunty Rosa could penetrate certain kinds of hypocrisy, but not all. He set his child's wits against hers and was no more beaten.

He lies and he liberates himself. For Kipling – and for Punch – the lesson was clear. He could avoid punishment by deception. Unfortunately, he could not deceive Aunty Rosa forever: 'Then the crash came and the cobwebs were broken. It was impossible to foresee everything.' She discovered the truth about his failing performance in school.

The gleeful Harry and retributive Sarah beat him and forced Rudyard to don a placard bearing the word 'Liar'. He was marched through the streets of Southsea with this on his back. In *Something of Myself* he drily notes 'In the long run these things, and many more of the like, drained me of any capacity for real, personal hate for the rest of my days.' The reaction in 'Baa Baa Black Sheep' was much more vitriolic. Punch has three days in his room to prepare for the rigours of his punishment – not unlike the old practice of Christian martyrs who would fast before a trial by fire. But that is not the only point where fiction and autobiography diverge.

There are three deeply troubling episodes in 'Baa Baa Black Sheep' that might be brushed aside as dramatic licence, but given the other similarities between the story and Rudyard's own life (and Trix's evident reading of his fiction as autobiographical) they must be an indication of his inner world, even if fantastical. All three involve violence, death and terrifying threats.

In one, Punch, transformed into Black Sheep, cracks when Harry pushes him too far.

> 'All right,' said Black Sheep, possessing himself of the table-knife. 'Then I'll kill you now. You say things and do things and … and *I* don't know how things happen, and you never leave me alone – and I don't care *what* happens!'

Then he fails, he fears punishment and alights on suicide as the only way out: 'A knife would hurt, but Aunty Rosa had told him, a year ago, that if he sucked paint he would die. He went into the nursery, unearthed the now disused Noah's Ark and sucked the paint off as many animals as remained.'

The final fury in this occurs when Aunty Rosa ties the 'Liar' sign to Black Sheep and tries to make him walk through town. '"If you make me do that," said Black Sheep very quietly, "I shall burn this house down, and perhaps I'll kill you. I don't know whether I can kill you – you're so bony – but I'll try."'

The 'Liar' story we must suppose to be true: Rudyard certainly claimed it. The three threats to kill Harry, Aunty, and himself are probably fictional, but offer a glimpse of his mental horrors.

His woes came to a head with what the adult man refers to as 'something of a nervous breakdown'. He and Trix had gone to the Burne-Joneses for Christmas in 1876, as had become their custom. But by this stage Rudyard's eyesight had deteriorated severely. The years of abuse, too, took their toll. He was spotted by his Aunt Georgie hitting a tree at the bottom of the garden. His cousin – later Prime Minister Stanley Baldwin – would write 'The boy was half-blind, and crazed to the point of suffering delusions.'

The doctor was called. His diagnosis was swift, the solution effective. Rudyard was indeed 'half-blind' and was given spectacles. Clearly distressed, Georgie summoned her sister Alice to come home from India and see to her child.

At last. But even at this happy turn of events there was a pitiful note, showing how deeply Kipling's sufferings wove themselves into his reflexive behaviour. When his mother went upstairs to wish her son goodnight, 'I flung up an arm to guard off the cuff that I had been trained to expect,' he writes in *Something of Myself.* To the end he was fearful, but, thankfully, that was indeed the end. 'I was taken at once from the House of Desolation, and for months ran wild in a little farm-house on the edge of Epping Forest.' This running wild was evidently a release.

But was he the same boy who had entered that house six years previously? His writings say he was not. In *Something of Myself* he talks of learning to lie. He also describes how his experiences dulled rather than sharpened his capacity for hate. But in 'Baa Baa Black Sheep' he strikes a different note: '[W]hen young lips have drunk deep of the bitter waters of Hate, Suspicion and Despair, all the Love in the world will not wholly take away that knowledge; though it may turn darkened eyes for a while to the light and teach Faith where no Faith was.'

In his sister Trix's words, 'there could hardly have been a more miserable childhood'. However, she told the BBC in the same 1947 interview that she doubted psychologists who claimed that such influences could 'poison or overshadow' later life – though she herself was to suffer prolonged bouts of mental illness.

I think Trix was at least half-right. Her brother was neither embittered nor diminished by the Portsmouth years and his soul was not pinched. But he was, as it were, broken and born again. Rudyard's hell in Southsea may have shattered the boy, but he put the pieces together in a new way, and sang new songs.

The Epping Forest summer when Trix and Rudyard were liberated from Lorne Lodge by their mother was spent in the company of their cousin, Stanley Baldwin.

Kipling's writing about this period of his life in *Something of Myself* is a narrative at whose heart is liberation. He revelled in not having to apologise for his 'guilty past'. He and Baldwin hared about waging war on wasps' nests and making off with giant, foot-long roly-polys. Trix later wrote that their mother took them there so that they might forget Southsea. Her plan worked.

But as every summer ends, so did this one. As we know, Trix was sent back to Southsea and Lorne Lodge. The reason for this apparently inexplicable decision? Alice and Lockwood can have had only vague notions of what their children had endured. Perhaps they were persuaded that Rudyard had not fitted in, whereas Trix had been fine. Not only did the two say little, but as we've seen, they had learnt the art of deception. It was not until the publication of 'Baa Baa Black Sheep' in 1888 that the Kiplings realised the extent of what had transpired. They were devastated.

Rudyard, who turned twelve in 1877, now needed a secondary school. From India, Alice had found him a prospective school much earlier: a school still being formed, the United Services College, promising an education suitable for boys preparing to take the new army entrance exams – and for a much lower fee than schools like Wellington College. Alice had written to the headmaster, whom she'd once known personally (through family). By the summer of 1877 Rudyard's place at the new school, known as USC, was secured.

*

In January 1878 Rudyard was packed off to Devon; USC

was sited in a small village with a big name, Westward Ho!. At first his dreams were dashed by the cruelty and violence of the older boys. After the terrors of Southsea, USC must have seemed a fresh hell. His first term, he says in his autobiography, was 'horrible'. At the time he was less reticent. He sent a barrage of letters to his mother and his sister, telling them how awful it was and how much he hated it.

But more can be gleaned by what Alice said when she wrote to her friend the headmaster, Cormell Price. 'It is the roughness of the lads he seems to feel most. He doesn't grumble to me – but he is lonely and down.' She added that '[t]he lad has a great deal that is feminine in his nature and a little sympathy – from any quarter – will reconcile him to his changed life more than anything'.

Things had changed, whatever Rudyard's early misery. His mother was properly in touch, and knew what he had been through. Cormell Price was not an unsympathetic man, and Alice's personal links made the difference. Though Rudyard continued to struggle, his father, hearing of this from Alice, hastened home from India. His mother got Mr Price on side and the boy saw his father for the first time in seven years.

Lockwood took Rudyard to Paris for the summer of 1878, where the two enjoyed the Paris Exhibition. Lockwood later said, rather ruefully, that Rudyard was 'the best companion I ever had'. But for young Kipling the wounds of Southsea were scarring over only gradually. As Lockwood told Price:

I find Ruddy a delightfully amiable chap, but the way

in which he only half apprehends the common facts and necessities of daily life is surprising. Vagueness and inaccuracy I fear will always bother him and they take curious forms. He couldn't give me a straightforward and detailed account of school routine for a day, breaking down under a most gentle questioning like a hysterical woman under cross-examination by an Old Bailey barrister.

Little wonder. Lockwood still had only vague notions of what his son had suffered in Southsea.

Time passed and as the autumn term started Rudyard began to acclimatise. He wrote in *Something of Myself*:

My first year and a half was not pleasant. The most persistent bullying comes not less from the bigger boys, who merely kick and pass on, than from young devils of fourteen acting in concert against one butt. Luckily for me I was physically some years in advance of my age, and swimming in the big open sea baths, or off the Pebble Ridge, was the one accomplishment that brought me any credit.

He gained the protection of friends, allied to a new physical confidence. This is the stuff of boarding school life. Hard, in some places painful, but of a different cast to his earlier sufferings. He got through this period; and after his second year of school 'the tide of writing set in'. In the summer of 1882 Rudyard was told he was not going back to school because his parents did not have the money to send him to Oxford. Instead, through his father, he had been offered a job in Lahore on the *Civil and Military Gazette*. Kipling accepted the post. On 20 September 1882, he set foot on the *Brindisi* to sail back to India, the land of his birth.

His time at USC had turned from torment to triumph and the man was beginning to emerge from the boy. But the tide of writing would not have surged if, in Kipling's own words, he had not learnt at Lorne Lodge. As he himself said, his life there 'demanded constant wariness, the habit of observation, and attendance on moods and tempers; the noting of discrepancies between speech and action; a certain reserve of demeanour; and automatic suspicion of sudden favours'. Making things up – or lying – was the final piece in this puzzle.

His life before Southsea in India was princely. His life afterwards at boarding school tough. Both were important in the formation of his character, but all things told, not remarkably different to the experiences of others his age. The period of six years at Lorne Lodge, however, with Pryse Holloway, Sarah and Harry, was unlike anything else. Brutal and cruel, it irrevocably changed the boy. On the surface, later in his life, he may have seemed the same confident adult as he was the boisterous toddler. But that surface masked a dark underside, a subterranean landscape conjured into being in Southsea, a place into which his roots now reached, and which drew up into his character the peculiar, ineffable mixture that made him Rudyard Kipling, the great English author.

Louise Bourgeois

That is the most important thing I have said: Art is a
guarantee of sanity.

Looming overhead at more than nine metres tall, a spider
cast in bronze and stainless steel makes an imposing sight.
If you are directly beneath the abdomen, the legs stand
around you like the bars of a prison. Looking up, you can
see the spider is carrying a sack of eggs, made of marble.
You can see them but they are out of your reach, a safe distance from any harm you might threaten. Should you try
to harm them, the spider will devour you. She is at once
a doting guardian and a ferocious predator. This sculpture, *Maman*, is perhaps the most recognisable creation of
the artist Louise Joséphine Bourgeois. Like so much in her
prolific body of work it references her childhood and is
her vision of her own mother and motherhood. She was
an artist and woman possessed by the magic and monsters
that lived on in her memories of her early life.

Bourgeois was born in Paris on Christmas Day, 1911.
Her circumstances held promise of an idyllic childhood. She was the third child of Louis Bourgeois and
Joséphine Fauriaux, who owned a gallery in town. Soon
after her birth they moved to the comfortable suburbs and
set up a business restoring worn and damaged tapestries.
As a young (and small) girl she would help her parents by
mending the lowest parts of the tapestries, which often
depicted the feet of the subjects and small animals. This
was her first brush with artistic creativity and she was
pleased her parents trusted in her ability. Their validation
was something she treasured.

However, though she was born just a few years before the outbreak of the First World War, the conflict that made the biggest impact Bourgeois experienced was at home. Her father, Louis, had longed for a son and made no attempt to hide his disappointment at the arrival of a third daughter. He teased her mercilessly and publicly throughout her young life about what he saw as her many inadequacies.

His bullying was coupled with a volatile temper so severe that her mother took to leaving a small stack of saucers on the dinner table so that, if she saw his anger starting to rise during a family meal, she could hand him a saucer which he would smash on the floor to release his rage. This was a proxy for his inflicting it on the children. This memory haunted Bourgeois, and the installation *Deconstruction of the Father* is a violent imagining of her revenge on Louis. It depicts a nightmarish fantasy she had in which, one evening at the dinner table, she and her siblings reach a breaking point of their own. Under the pressure of his relentless bullying, they pull him onto the table, dismember him and then eat him.

Though violent and cruel, Louis was a handsome man and an inveterate flirt. Attractive to young women, he revelled in their company in the plain sight of his wife and young Louise. This behaviour peaked with the arrival of an English governess, Sadie Richmond. Sadie and Bourgeois's father began an affair while she lived in the family home. She then stayed as his mistress in residence for ten years. Bourgeois spoke about how at first she had wanted to bond with Sadie and form a loving, familial relationship of her own. Deeply hurt by the betrayal, not only by her father but also the young governess, she was tormented by what she saw as rejection. She felt abandoned by both and, worse, forced to revisit it every day for a decade while the affair continued before the family's eyes. The anxiety this abandonment triggered stayed with her and grew, becoming her greatest fear. She saw her mother as a tender presence, though she recognised her strength, too, in her resilience. She worshipped her mother and never forgot her maternal protection.

Having suffered her father's oppressive taunting for years, and still wounded by his affair with her governess, Bourgeois returned to Paris to study mathematics and geometry at the Sorbonne: an unexpected choice for someone creatively gifted, but Bourgeois found sanctuary in the structure and stability of this field. Later in life she said: 'I got peace of mind only through the study of rules nobody could change.' She felt in control.

Her expressive and deeply personal sculptures, drawings and paintings might never have been created had it not been for a tragedy that nearly destroyed her. After lifelong ill-health, Bourgeois's mother died in 1932. Joséphine had been the only figure in her life who had offered Louise the love and security she craved. Her widowed father mocked her grief. Feeling lost, unprotected and alone, Bourgeois attempted suicide, throwing herself into the Seine. She was rescued by her father who pulled her from the water.

You might at this point expect the fragile, fearful and damaged young woman, now robbed of her mother too, to retreat further into herself. Instead, some switch within Louise Bourgeois seems to have been thrown. There arrived a dramatic shift in her focus. Bourgeois decided to pursue art. She enrolled in a series of Paris art schools including the

École des Beaux Arts and the École du Louvre. Her mother's death seems to have awoken a freedom within her: not least a freedom to expose and acknowledge her fears and resentments. Hesitation and uncertainty appeared to depart. She began allowing herself to be confrontational, even aggressive, in the way she communicated feelings she had previously repressed.

Bourgeois confronted the events of her youth endlessly in her works, which flick back and forth between themes of vulnerability and aggression, sometimes within the same piece. But it wasn't her work alone that changed. Bourgeois herself developed a notoriously difficult character and could become angry if she felt afraid. It can be seen as a defence mechanism, but an aggressive rather than defensive one. 'Quand les chiens ont peur,' she said, 'ils mordent.' When dogs are afraid, they bite.

She curated her life like the design of her sculptures. A living, breathing tableau that featured her as the dominant figure, particularly when she was with men. Probably because of her early experience of her father she developed a tendency to undermine men: an irony, as this is how he had treated her and Joséphine. When she was eighty-six the former French president, Nicolas Sarkozy, visited her home, then in New York. He was there to award her the French Legion of Honour, the highest French decoration. She seated him (a short man) on the lowest chair in the room.

It may be said that Louise Bourgeois never truly exorcised the demons of her childhood; but after her fracture as a young woman she found ways to fight them on open ground – both in her life and her work. Who is to say whether, without the humiliation and death of her mother, the humiliation by her father and the complete and devastating breakdown that followed, she might not still have grown into the artist she became. It's possible. But I doubt it.

Rudolf Nureyev

I was possessed. I felt a calling … I had the absolute certainty that I was born to dance.

Legend has it that Rudolf Nureyev was born in a third-class carriage in a wagon on the Trans-Siberian Express. True or otherwise, the story does not exaggerate the desperate circumstances of the great Russian dancer's boyhood. He was poor to the point of destitution. He was cold. He was hungry. He was gay, in an era when to be so was unthinkable and dangerous. And his family tried to impose absolute obedience and conformity on the ragged, wayward, mutinous son.

For young Rudolf there was no single moment of fracture, but instead a long grinding down of the spirit, and then a moment of epiphany. Nureyev's family were not unusual examples, but they were sharp ones, of the desperate poverty and daily fear in which millions in Stalinist Russia led their lives. The boy was born two days after the end of the Great Terror on 15 March 1938. His mother and elder sisters had almost frozen to death on a trans-Siberian railway journey. In just two years, 700,000 people had been killed. Many had starved. The slightest deviation from official tyranny in thought or deed was punishable by death or imprisonment.

Little wonder that Rudolf's parents had fully aligned themselves with the Stalinist cause. They had been

Muslims. His father, Hamet Nuriakhmetovich Fasliyev, was a model of conformity, and served as a political officer in the Red Army, charged with 'educating' the military on the benefits of Stalinism. The family lived in Ufa, a Muslim-dominated city, but as a means of survival both parents had abandoned religious practice. Just as Hamet had obeyed the orders of the state, he expected absolute obedience from his son.

Rudolf was a rebel from the start. He attended school wearing his sisters' dirty clothes, and was branded a beggar by his classmates. He responded with the aggression he was to show all his life.

But on 1 January 1945 his mother smuggled her four children into Ufa's theatre, where a patriotic ballet, *Le chant des cigognes*, was due to be performed. Rudolf was seven. As he recalled, the theatre was 'a place that transported me so far from the sordid universe that I had known … I was possessed. I felt a calling. As I saw the dancers that evening, defying gravity and flying, I had the absolute certainty that I was born to dance.'

Nureyev sensed already that he did not fit into Soviet society. The youth and man he became longed to be different. His individuality expressed itself in his determination to escape a grey and confining childhood, his pioneering and controversial approach to ballet, his demanding, arrogant and tempestuous personality, his homosexuality in a society that considered it the ultimate taboo and, of course, his famed 1961 defection from the Soviet Union to France. His rebelliousness served one desire: to dance where he wanted, when he wanted and how he wanted. By fulfilling that desire, he revolutionised the world of ballet.

After that glorious night at the ballet, the young Rudolf set out to achieve his dream. His ambitions took a difficult turn, however, when his father beat him severely for coming home late with a loaf of bread and claiming he'd been looking for food. In fact, the boy was taking free classes at the weekends. But if anything, his father's anger reinforced his individuality.

At ballet class Rudolf immediately stood out as a prodigious talent. His bestial energy and athleticism were unparalleled. But small-town Ufa was no place for a great dancer. Rudolf had to go to St Petersburg. He managed it at twenty, when he entered the Kirov Ballet. He was already five years behind his peers and, from the start, different: his regional accent and his Eastern appearance were mocked by Russia's upper class. He considered himself an outsider – not Russian but a Tartar, a race he described as 'a complex beast, just like me'. Trained under the legendary Alexander Pushkin, the young dancer was encouraged to curb his tempestuousness but maintain his individuality. Steps that deviated from the choreography were not punished but incorporated into the routine. It was a revelation for Nureyev. He excelled and, on finishing his training in 1958, was immediately welcomed into the Kirov Ballet as a soloist, one of very few dancers ever to have done this. By accepting his place, he turned down offers from the Bolshoi and Moscow's Stanislavski Ballet: he wanted to be a soloist and did not want to wait.

Throughout his career, Nureyev would go on to do exactly as he wished, and make waves by doing so. He found the stocky male dancers of the period ugly, and so he fashioned the elongated, sometimes androgynous look that we often see in male ballet dancers today. He also adopted a high demi-pointe and a highly pulled-up torso, gracefully elongating his body. The effect was immediately adopted by his rivals. On another occasion, he shunned the heavy, baggy trousers for the role of Basilio in *Don Quixote* and chose to dance in tights. Unheard of at the time, the decision accentuated his long, powerful legs and suited his explosive style. Today, it is the norm.

The same showed through in his personal life; his decision to defect to Paris in 1961, when the Kirov visited Europe for the first time, was by no means a political statement. Rather, he had taken full advantage of Parisian nightlife and decided that hedonism suited his personality much better than communism. Once settled in Europe, he sought out the graceful Danish dancer Erik Bruhn, whose technique he admired. They began to train together and Nureyev promptly made him his lover.

Nureyev's tendency to demand his own way was rarely popular. Like the boy in Ufa, the adult Rudolf struggled to make friends. He struggled even harder to keep them. His partnership with the great British ballerina Margot Fonteyn led to a dance boom in sixties and seventies London, but the pair's relationship became strained due to Nureyev's relentless demands on the older dancer. When she made mistakes in rehearsal, he screamed: 'Shit, shit, you dance like shit.' He would rage at the media, theatre directors and choreographers who disagreed with him. Likeable he may not have been, but his impact on the world of dance was unforgettable. There is, in the end, no arguing with genius.

With the knowledge we have now of the beauties and grace of Nureyev's conception of a male ballet dancer, we may ask this: why had no other man before him – and there had been tens of thousands of wonderful dancers – been able to make this imaginative leap?

In particular, why did a boy from the sticks with no family or (at first) friends to encourage him, no early cultural grounding and no independent financial resources, prove so careless of the conventions, so unafraid to risk advancement in the world of ballet, so ready to defy what was expected of him and take male dancing to a new and unexplored level? The question answers itself. It is not despite the chains that seemed at first to bind but because of them that, once he had burst through, he felt himself so free. Those few hours with his sisters and mother watching *Le chant des cigognes*, the unkind, constricting world he knew outside the theatre, and that moment of bliss inside it, was his taking imaginative wing. The courage, resolve and internal liberation that followed – the creative alloy of freedom and discipline – could only come from revolution: not Lenin's or Stalin's, but his own.

The Brontë sisters

The pictures, ideas and conceptions of character received into the mind of the child of eight years old, were destined to be reproduced in fiery words a quarter of a century later.

Kate Bush's huge 1978 hit, 'Wuthering Heights', beautifully captures the feeling of excited abandon that, in that novel's day, would have been little short of shocking. Bush was more than referencing Emily Brontë's novel, published 131 years earlier: she was channelling Brontë herself.

Most respectable British women in the first part of the nineteenth century led lives centred around the houses of their husbands or families. But this, although the social norm, did not go unchallenged as the century proceeded. Florence Nightingale, Mary Carpenter, Angela Burdett, to name but a few, broke new ground in thought and action.

Charlotte, Emily and Anne Brontë were among this number. Their work was always implicitly and sometimes explicitly revolutionary. As writers they created brave new imaginative 'possibilities'[17] for women, using their prose and poetry to test male authority. In its sometimes wild romanticism, the Brontës' work is innovative in style as well as message. We can admire the imaginative leap the Brontës took for its literary genius alone, quite apart from its courage.

The Brontë novels – from *Wuthering Heights* to *Jane Eyre* to *The Tenant of Wildfell Hall* – breathe a remarkable independence for their time. Take Jane Eyre's complaint: 'it is narrow-minded in their more privileged fellow-creatures to say that [women] ought to confine themselves to making puddings and knitting stockings, to playing on the piano and embroidering bags'. Who are men to limit women to a life of domestic chores? Nothing but 'fellow-creatures', just like us, Jane seems to scowl. As for Cathy in *Wuthering Heights*, her famous 'I am Heathcliff!' lays bare the devotion men demand of women: all-consuming and controlling. Simone de Beauvoir would call it the cry of every woman in love. If feminism hadn't quite reached de Beauvoir's heights in the early 1800s, the Brontës were a British precursor; proto-feminists, challenging what was accepted and expected in women.

The Brontës had always been independent. Elizabeth Gaskell's description of their Yorkshire surroundings in her 1857 biography of Charlotte was forthright. Yorkshiremen were painted as rough, greedy and irreligious. The Brontë family home, and its 'exquisite cleanliness', was a haven from the 'peculiar forms of population and society' in the dark North. Here, the six Brontë children – Maria, Elizabeth, Charlotte, Branwell, Emily and Anne – lived and played with no need for outside company. They created breathtakingly detailed stories and plays, concocting fantasy worlds to avoid the boredom of their own. They had lost their mother to cancer when Charlotte was five; and Patrick, their father, was dutiful but distant, busy with his work as a local clergyman. He would outlive all six of his children.

The calm isolation of their childhood was broken cruelly in 1824 when the four oldest girls were sent to a school for the lower clergy. Any child would have found these new circumstances a challenge, but for these sheltered girls the rupture was shocking.

The Brontës' stay at Cowan Bridge is now infamous. Conditions at the school were unspeakable. The cook was careless, using dirty cooking equipment and frequently serving up spoilt food to the children. Meat and milk often went off but were served up regardless. The dormitories were bitterly cold and the school doctor cared little for the girls' complaints. Sundays were particularly gruelling. The children were supplied with cold scraps of leftover meat and potatoes and sent off on a two-mile long walk from the school to Tunstall church, where the headmaster preached. Come rain, hail or shine, the weak, malnourished girls would set out, taking their cold dinner with them to eat between services at the back of the unheated church.

Entirely unused to these brute circumstances, the sisters found it almost impossible to cope. Maria, an intelligent but careless, untidy child, was disliked by the housekeepers. When she struggled to get up one morning, she was declared lazy, forced to dress and dragged from her dorm. Her complaints were genuine; she had contracted typhoid. The filthy environment meant that a dozen or more of the girls were struck down with the disease, Elizabeth as well as Maria. At this point, the cook was dismissed and Maria sent home to her father. It was too late. Maria died, then Elizabeth, sent home next, died just a few months later. Patrick Brontë withdrew the rest of his children from the school.

The wounds ran deep. Gaskell writes: 'the pictures, ideas and conceptions of character received into the mind of the child of eight years old, were destined to be reproduced in fiery words a quarter of a century later.'

And that was true. Emily's metaphors are often almost sadistic, describing *Wuthering Heights*'s Isabella 'shrieking as if witches were running red-hot needles into her'. Scarred by the loss of her older sisters and her nightmarish school, she took refuge at home, now desperately shy and agoraphobic, leaving home only four times more in her short life. But in *Wuthering Heights* she created an extraordinary work of moral ambivalence. She had had an experience which fundamentally shook her belief in the justice of the world.

Charlotte also drew on the experiences in her vivid description of Lowood, *Jane Eyre*'s orphan school. The injustice haunted the surviving sisters. Outwardly demure, they shouted their pain and lamented their feelings of enclosure in novels that were to become classics. Nor was it all about trauma. Just as central was defiance. Their sister, Anne, in *The Tenant of Wildfell Hall*, challenges preconceptions about male/female relationships and the role of women. Her heroine is (remarkable in women's writing of the era) an artist who makes an independent living with her work.

Gaskell's biography, published shortly after Charlotte's death, sold as well as *Jane Eyre*. British society was 'intrigued to discover how and why a woman as retiring as Charlotte Brontë had produced some of the most passionate and explosive fiction the world had yet seen.'[18] The answer could be found in that hellish time at Cowan Bridge.

Frederick Douglass

After one particularly violent incident, something within the youth snapped.

Once the rising sun has touched the visible sky and light begins to flood across the plain, people know the day has arrived. In the dark before dawn, though, it is different. When hardly a glimmer tints the hilltop it takes a leap of the imagination to see and know what must come. Men and women who are very early to the understanding that change is on its way, early to the confidence that it must be, are often overlooked by later generations because their vision seems unremarkable against the noontide glare of what we take for granted now. But their audacity is the greater because the light they worked in was so dim.

In the history of the evolution of black consciousness, Frederick Douglass was one of these. His name may not today be quite as familiar to many readers, as, say Martin Luther King, but for these more modern heroes, slaves like Douglass had already laid foundations. His sheer audacity is thrown into relief when seen against the background of the general, uniform and crushing repression which, through some extraordinary flash of imaginative strength, Douglass managed to cast off.

This man is arguably the most influential African American of the nineteenth century and his story is a legend we must not forget: from slave to statesman, abolitionist and orator. During his life he was internationally recognised, becoming one of the most widely travelled and photographed Americans of his generation. He possessed an uncommon strength of mind and was a literary genius whose writing is still read today across the world. Dedicated to natural human rights and equality, he reached beyond colour: he worked for women's freedoms long before they were even conceived of by most. He struggled publicly with Abraham Lincoln's failure to endorse black suffrage.

Douglass was born Frederick Augustus Washington Bailey, in February 1818, Maryland. His father was likely the white owner of his slave mother. He spent the first few years of his life with his maternal grandparents, seeing his mother only infrequently, until, aged six, he was sent away to a plantation in 1824. From this point onward, Frederick – like almost all slaves – endured relentless hardship. His three autobiographies detail routine violence and emotional anxiety, experiencing as well as witnessing extreme cruelty. In constant danger, Douglass began to realise that while he could not protect his body, he could protect and develop his mind.

There were two key moments of personal revelation. Aged eight he was sent to join the household of Hugh and Sophia Auld. In Sophia he met kindness beyond anything he had ever experienced before – it was so unusual, he didn't know how to act around her. On the plantation, he'd been treated like an animal, but for the first two years, Sophia saw him as a child, and became more a mother than a master.

Her most radical act was starting to teach him how to read. But here the story takes a strange turn. At first she took pride in his abilities, but when her husband Hugh found out, he was furious, and at once banned her lessons. He impressed upon his wife with such passion the danger of teaching slaves to read – they might one day begin to desire freedom, and literacy would make slaves unmanageable – that she stopped completely. That was perhaps forseeable. But then she seems to have undergone some kind of counter-reaction. She became even more violently opposed to Frederick's dawning literacy than her husband. Her attitude towards the boy changed quite suddenly. Upon seeing Douglass with a newspaper she would furiously rush at him, and snatch it from his hands. No longer her star pupil, her slave pet, Douglass was now under close surveillance lest he came into contact with books.

The lurch was shocking, traumatic. But it was not just Sophia who had changed. His master's rage and his mistress's betrayal were transformative for the boy: he must learn, at whatever cost, how to read. He had tasted knowledge then had it cruelly swept beyond his grasp; and to seize more knowledge became a new form of defiance against slavery's grip. He began trading his food with white street urchins in the neighbourhood in return for reading lessons. When his masters were out of the house, he would teach himself to write using their son's books.

Acquiring knowledge became at the same time his reason for living, and a terrible blight. The more Douglass learned, the more intolerable his position became. At times he wrote that he wished himself dead, and could no longer feel happiness. He wrote: 'and but for the hope of being free, I have no doubt but that I should have killed myself, or done something for which I should have been killed'. He was no longer the same 'light-hearted' boy who had arrived at the Aulds.

Douglass was now determined to spread the skills he had come to see as the foundation of freedom, and began teaching other slaves – first on his own, and later in a Sunday school. But the school was banned; and not long after that, Douglass was sent, as punishment for his insubordination, to 'slave-breaker' Edward Covey, famous for his cruelty. Now sixteen, Douglass was brutalised for six months. After one particularly violent incident, something within the youth snapped. Douglass had run into the woods after a beating and when he returned, was promptly beaten again. But he fought back hard (he was fighting for his life: a slave who resisted was liable to be killed) and bested Covey. For the remaining six months, the master left him alone.

The risk had paid off. Douglass saw the power of resistance. The shock of success changed him: it had 'revived [his] sense of manhood' and renewed his determination to escape his situation and fight for the liberty of slaves.

It would be four years before Douglass escaped, and another nine years before he was able to stop living as a fugitive. But these fractures not only set him on the course to freedom but shaped how he used that freedom. He had learned to define himself against his opponents, to make their fear and anger his spur. He used the power of the written word and his astonishing oratory to fight for abolition, becoming the voice of black America and revealing to the world in unflinching detail the horror of slavery. The greats of the American civil rights movement stand on Frederick Douglass's shoulders.

Anthony Ashley Cooper, 7th Earl of Shaftesbury

It would often be better if children had no parents at all.

It would be easy to make assumptions about the character of a person born into the gilded world of the British aristocracy in the early nineteenth century. Personal wealth and privilege combined with very little exposure to the abject poverty of the day could – and in most cases did – yield a sense of entitlement in later life. It is this that makes the revolutionary social reforms, tireless parliamentary campaigning and vast personal philanthropy of Anthony Ashley Cooper, 7th Earl of Shaftesbury, quite so remarkable.

Anthony Ashley Cooper was born in 1801 to Cropley Ashley Cooper, the 6th Earl of Shaftesbury and chairman of committees in the House of Lords, and Anne Spencer-Churchill, the daughter of the 4th Duke of Marlborough. The parentage and background look auspicious. The reality was anything but: his childhood was quite extraordinarily wretched.

While it was not unusual for parents within his social class to maintain a certain emotional and physical distance from their children, young Anthony's took this to extremes. The 6th earl and his wife were almost entirely absent, leaving their children to be raised by servants and school teachers. When social events or convention demanded they see their children, they behaved in a haughty and callous manner – only interested in whether or not the children were 'representable' upon inspection. Ashley Cooper's own description of them paints a picture of Dickensian villains. He saw his father as a bully and described his mother as 'a devil' according to biographer G. F. A. Best. He wrote about her later in life: 'Away with her memory! The idea of such fiend-warmed hearts is bad for a Christian soul.' He never forgave or forgot their appalling behaviour towards him.

Any hope the young boy might have held of finding sanctuary at school was misplaced. He attended Manor House School in Chiswick, an institution he remembered with as much bitter resentment as his childhood home. 'I think there never was such a wicked school before or since,' he once wrote. 'The place was bad, wicked, filthy; and the treatment was starvation and cruelty.' His experience at Manor House gave him an insight into the oppression and brutality many less fortunate children faced without the prospect of any means of escape.

Lonely and otherwise unloved, the young Ashley Cooper knew only one source of kindness. The family's housekeeper, Maria Millis, showed affection. She was a staunch evangelical Christian and would tell him stories from the Bible and school him in prayer. Though he was raised with religion at school and attended church on Sundays, it was her teachings and the visible, practical application of her Christian values that most shaped his outlook. She died shortly after he started school, and among what little she had to bequeath she left him her gold watch. He wore it until the end of his own life some three-quarters of a century later. Though it would be decades before he committed himself completely to evangelical Christianity there can be no doubt that what affection he received from Maria resonated deeply.

Ashley Cooper's early adulthood was fairly typical of a young aristocrat of his day. He was at Oxford, but set apart from his peers by his 'withdrawals into introspection' when he would become 'alternatively moody and rapturous'.[19] His character had been marked by his childhood and he was said to have had a 'melancholic air'.[20] It was perhaps this that encouraged him to look beyond his own circumstances.

Aged just twenty-five Ashley Cooper was elected the Tory Member of Parliament for Woodstock. This platform enabled him to apply his own experience: not only to seek out those who might be in need of his help personally, but to work politically towards real (and tremendous) social reform.

Perhaps unsurprisingly his main mission, permeating almost all his most significant reforms, was the protection of children. He worked tirelessly to abolish the cruelty and neglect in employment that endangered countless lives. Through his efforts, young boys could no longer be used as chimney sweeps, a job that usually led to serious injury, respiratory problems and premature death. His Chimney Sweepers Act of 1875 prevented helpless children from being forced into this perilous work. This Act – only passed after the extensive research and crusading within and outside parliament characteristic of all his reform work, was just the beginning. After years of campaigning he persuaded parliament to pass the Factory Act, banning anyone under the age of eighteen from working more than ten hours a day. By the standards of the era, both in Britain and abroad, this was revolutionary in its protection of the young employed as manual labour in mills and factories. His campaigns were too numerous for elaboration here – and, in fact, my own parliamentary experience tells me that he will have acquired a reputation in the Lords and Commons Smoking Rooms for being something of a bore on his chosen subjects. There will have been groans when he stood to speak. Phrases like 'bee in his bonnet' will have been muttered. Ashley Cooper didn't care.

Beyond health and welfare, intellectual and spiritual development stayed close to his heart. In 1844 he became president of the Ragged Schools Union, an organisation that promoted free education for destitute children.

Few would dispute that Shaftesbury's own early misery helped awake in him a lifelong dedication to helping children. A different man, though, might have turned his back on a lonely childhood, walked away from the past, pulled over his head the blanket of wealth and privilege, and headed for an easy life. He didn't, and this distinction in Ashley Cooper's story is partly the moral legacy of Maria Millis.

But I believe his dreadful parents too could claim authorship – of a kind – of Shaftesbury's driven, and unceasing mission to reform. It was little short of obsessive. He badgered his parliamentary colleagues, badgered the newspapers, badgered church congregations, badgered his country. Ashley Cooper's parenting, I'd argue, damaged him – killing the incurious, entitled, complacent young aristocrat Anthony might have become, and leaving him permanently unsatisfied. I cannot read his story without detecting something unbalanced about the man – but it is indisputable that he changed his age for the better. When Shaftesbury told his listeners in a speech on the neglect of children that 'it would often be better if children had no parents at all', he spoke more personally than his audience knew.

Chapter Six

SHOCK

To confront ourselves we may first have to be confronted. Something must pull us up short. A life may otherwise jog along more (or less) contentedly, the individual half-aware that things are not ideal – perhaps even aware that things are pretty wretched – but unable to get to grips with what's wrong.

Often it is a death that galvanises: whether to a father, mother or sibling. In despair (or in Genghis Khan's case, triumph) a spark flies. Sometimes the fire is destructive. 'I do not believe in this world and I do not accept the past, the present, or the future,' says an angry voice within. Something has started a clock ticking in the child's head: life is short and this is not a rehearsal. Time to act.

That may all sound as if those who have achieved greatness wouldn't have bothered without a kick in the pants from Fate. But it's not so simple. Whether the child is left an orphan or robbed of a sibling or a best friend, the shock does not just sadden, toughen or scar: it fundamentally changes the child.

Sometimes a sharp kick can bring a sophisticated piece of electronic equipment to life. To Simón Bolívar the death of his young sweetheart was that kick. To Machado de Assis it was his own near-death. To Muhammad Ali it was the lynching of an innocent fourteen-year-old. People who change the world may first need to be changed themselves. Shock can do it.

A Polish patriot

She would often sit in some corner and cry bitterly. Her tears could not be stopped by anybody.

> This catastrophe was the first great sorrow of my life. My mother had an exceptional personality. With all her intellectuality she had a big heart and a very high sense of duty. And, though possessing infinite indulgence and good nature, she still held in the family a remarkable moral authority. Her influence over me was extraordinary, for in me the natural love of the little girl for her mother was united with a passionate admiration. For many years we all felt weighing on us the loss of the one who had been the soul of the house.

If the death of the girl's mother was 'the first great sorrow', it is also true that vices had been tightening steadily on this little girl during the ten years she had been alive. Her mother, wracked by coughs over many years, had succumbed to tuberculosis. Less than three years earlier her eldest sister had contracted typhus and died. Her family had faced financial ruin: the father had been dismissed from his job at a state-run school, losing not just his income but the home that came with the position. They'd moved lodgings and had to open their doors to boarders. A committed patriot, the father's love for his nation had angered the authorities and so spelt disaster for his family and his youngest daughter. Her suffering and her anger, which the young girl experienced most keenly, stemmed not just from personal tragedies, but from the subjugation of her people.

In 1797, seventy years before that girl was born, Poland had been invaded and divvied up by its Russian and Prussian conquerors. The oppressors had excised the native language from public life as much as possible: street signs and shopfronts were all rewritten. Children in schools were not taught their alphabet, so could not read the tongue in which they spoke. Loyalty to the new great ruler, their faraway lord, was demanded; history books revised. The people rebelled; their rebellions were crushed: retribution, especially in the area of the country the young girl would grow up in, was brutal. Reigns of terror began across the country, the rule of law weakened. Many were exiled, or fled of their own accord. In the words of historian Adam Zamoyski, 'the whole reckless enterprise had been a costly catastrophe'.

Such were the times at the birth of this child. The growing girl's sense of national pride was – like many of her compatriots – profound: deepened and romanticised by the legion of disasters that littered their history. Years later she would recall her father reading poetry and prose to her and her siblings in their native language, an act with a long, resonant history in their culture that was forced so often to hide itself: 'These evenings were for us a great pleasure and a source of renewed patriotic feelings.' There was certainly reason enough to be proud.

When the life we're examining became great through its contribution to the advance of scientific knowledge, you may ask why I open this story with a reprise of a section of Polish history. It is because rebellion, self-reliance, and a rejection of the norms of her male-dominated discipline are what distinguish her from so many other scientists who have contributed to human knowledge. Her findings were an important breakthrough, but *she* broke through, too, in an equally important way. Arguably the greatest scientist of her age, this was a little girl who fought out of – and was moulded by – a childhood that would have crushed most. She was not born Marie Curie but Maria Skłodowska.

*

When Marie and her husband Pierre Curie isolated radium in her laboratory in France in the early twentieth century after years of backbreaking, health-destroying work, she felt an intense pride. But even though they were the authors of this discovery, they could have little inkling of the way their life – and the world – was about to change. Marie's isolation of radium in 1902 was viewed by one member of the Nobel prize committee as 'the most important new chemical element discovered in recent times' and was 'likely to change chemists' notions of the basic and invariable nature of the elements'. In 1903 the first Nobel Prize for Physics arrived, which Marie shared with Pierre and the French physicist Henri Becquerel. It was the first time a woman had ever won a Nobel prize. Such became the renown of their remarkable discovery that the Curies ended up boosting the reputation of the Nobel Prize for sciences, rather than the other way round. In 1911 Curie won the Nobel Prize for Chemistry, becoming a member of the club, currently numbering four, of those who have won two Nobel prizes. She was the first. She remains the only person ever to win two awards in two different scientific fields.

The discovery of radioactivity – it was Marie who coined the word in 1898 – was an epoch-defining moment. It paved the way for a revolution in our understanding of energy; it broke new ground in the medical sciences; it led to the creation of nuclear physics, nuclear power, and, far more terribly, nuclear warfare. It led to what for at least a century was to become one of the principal treatments of cancer. At the heart of this, occupying as important a position as any individuals can within the world of science, stood Marie Curie and Pierre. Among a number of famous scientists working in the field, such as Ernest Rutherford, Frederick Soddy and Stephan Mayer, the Curies stood out. Marie in particular captured the world's imagination. For, like her discoveries, she herself was pioneering. She broke into a man's world.

In this the Curie effect has long survived her death. In 1995 the French president, François Mitterrand, had her and Pierre's remains moved from where they were buried in Sceaux, outside Paris, to the Panthéon, the resting place of France's most distinguished children. She was the first woman to be there in her own right. Mitterrand was clear that this had been done 'in order finally to respect the equality of women and men before the law and in reality'.

There is an obvious question that must be answered. Her achievements seem to go hand-in-hand with those of Pierre, her husband. And anyway, in the world of science, it's often easy to overstate the importance of a single person. Was she great in her own right? On the merit of her work the answer is a clear yes. And in terms of her struggle as a woman the answer is also yes.

In 1906 Pierre slipped while crossing the Rue Dauphine in Paris and his head went under the wheel of a passing carriage. His untimely death left Marie bereft – she lived in mourning for the rest of her life. But she continued to work. The year she won her second Nobel prize, in 1911, she also, unsuccessfully, applied to become a member of the illustrious Académie des Sciences. Making the case for her membership was one Gaston Darboux, a permanent secretary of the Académie. He pointed to her isolation of pure radium, her two volumes, published the year before, on radioactivity, her membership of sundry learned societies, all as evidence for her achievements as an individual.

She would have been the first woman admitted to the Académie. Yet it was not to admit a woman until 1979. Few doubt that much of the reason for her rejection was due to her sex. No other woman, after all, had ever won a Nobel prize.

Nor must we accept her image – though she was happy to present it to the world – as the model determined, devoted scientist, whose brainpower was subordinate to their willpower. It was not just the hours she put in and the huge workload that became famous. Her mind was razor-sharp, and her own insight pivotal to her discoveries. The remarkable collection of accolades she piled up over her career give an indication of this.

We may speculate – I do – that her self-presentation was perhaps unconsciously shaped by the difficulty in that era of presenting a woman as an intellectual giant. In a woman, the picture of a diligent, conscientious, persistent, self-sacrificing, devoted servant of science was easier for a male world to accept than that of a female pusher of the boundaries.

Curie was also admirably lacking in any kind of avarice or arrogance: she and Pierre refused to patent their techniques for isolating radium. Her justification for this liberality illustrates much of the quasi-spiritual, ascetic approach she took to science:

> Humanity, surely, needs practical men who make the best of their work for the sake of their own interests, without forgetting the general interest. But it also needs dreamers, for whom the unselfish following of a purpose is so imperative that it becomes impossible for them to devote much attention to their own material benefit.

It may be, as Eva Hemmungs Wirtén has argued, that this lofty position was not the whole story; but the picture that emerges of Marie Curie over the course of her life is of a remarkably good, remarkably simple (in the best sense) person, unconcerned with worldly things.

The material benefit to the world from her discoveries was sharp. Cancer, which had stumped doctors and left patients and relatives distraught, could now be attacked through the new process of 'Curie therapy'. Marie Curie herself would go on to create new, portable X-ray machines, which were invaluable in the First World War for doctors treating soldiers' injuries. New methods of energy creation could help humanity move away from its destructive relationship with coal.

Marie's familial legacy is remarkable, too. She had two daughters with Pierre: Irène and Ève. Ève would go on to write the first biography of her mother, published in 1938. She also gave permission to the British Hospice Foundation to use her mother's name in 1948. Today Marie Curie hospices provide care for over 50,000 terminally ill people in the UK. Ève was instrumental in charity work throughout the world and her husband, Henry Labouisse, accepted the Nobel Peace Prize of 1965 on behalf of UNICEF.

Marie's first daughter, Irène, would, in many ways, imitate her mother. She became a scientist herself, married a scientist, Frédéric Joliot, and in 1935 won a Nobel prize with him for discovering artificial radioactivity. With five wins (two for Marie, one for Pierre, and one each for Irène and Frédéric), the Curies are the most successful family in the history of the Nobel prize.

Marie Curie is a byword for scientific endeavour, diligent hard work, and female excellence. But how did she transform, like Coco Chanel, from a distraught, motherless girl, into one of the women who shaped the twentieth century?

*

If you mention Marie Curie to a Polish native, you will find yourself politely but instantaneously corrected. Maria (the Marie is Frenchification) Skłodowska was her family name, before she met and married Pierre Curie in Paris. She herself (not that the world took much notice) never let go of her surname, calling herself Marie Skłodowska Curie.

She was born in Warsaw in 1867. Poland existed as a nation but not a state, having been carved up by its enemies in the century before her birth. But if Poland was untethered to the geopolitical reality of Europe, it was rooted in the hearts of the Poles strewn across the territories of Russia, Prussia, and Austria-Hungary and living as a diaspora in other countries and capitals, most notably Paris. Theirs was a constant struggle, a continuous fight to revive and re-found the state that they loved and that was their home. By the time Maria was born the battle had a long history. By the time she died an independent Polish state existed – but was about to be snuffed out yet again.

The currents and conflicts swirling around the year Maria Skłodowska was born can be traced back to the infamous Partitions of Poland of the eighteenth century, which culminated in the final, brutal, Third Partition that split the country asunder in 1795. Austria-Hungary, Prussia, and Russia were responsible, combining specious and real claims of Polish aggression to carve up the country as they saw fit. The injustice took many forms. The best sense one can get of the prevailing atmosphere, over two hundred years later, is captured in the almost cartoonishly evil 'secret article' of the treaty of partition:

> In view of the necessity to abolish everything which could revive the memory of the existence of the

Kingdom of Poland, now that the annulment of this
body politic has been effected ... the high contract-
ing parties are agreed and undertake never to include
their titles ... the name or designation of the Kingdom
of Poland, which shall remain suppressed as from the
present and forever ...

A failed Polish rising was followed by a second in 1862,
the January Rising, which also failed, and affected Maria's
family directly. After this, Russian oppression became far
worse. It was the Polish nobility, the *szlachta*, who had
been a driving force behind the risings: not for the most
part wealthy or entitled, and whose incomes and estates
had faded over time, though their titles had not. This is
where Maria's family had its roots. Flames of resistance
were fanned by the ideas of men like the poet Adam
Mickiewicz and his contemporaries Juliusz Słowacki and
Zygmunt Krasiński. Maria described all three as among
her favourites, learning whole long passages of their writing 'willingly ... by heart.'

Maria Skłodowska had been born just a few years after
the Russian occupation had done its brutal worst. The fifth
child of Bronisława Boguska and Władysław Skłodowski,
she was the newest in a rambunctious, remarkable family.
As members of the *szlachta* minor nobility, the family's
origins were distinguished, and born a hundred years
earlier Władysław might have expected to manage the
family estates or join the army. But, like most *szlachta*,
their family wealth had drained away and they were noble
in little more than name and tradition – and in their fervent
advocacy of Polish nationalism and (as it seemed) hopeless

romanticism. It is fair to say that for their children, not least the young Maria, this cultural inheritance would prove electrifying.

Both Maria's parents were immersed in learning and teaching. Bronisława became headmistress of a girls' school in Warsaw, on Freta Street. It was there, in the family apartment, that Maria was born. Władysław's experience of university was typically Polish. The Russians had officially closed Warsaw University, but unofficially he obtained a degree from the biology department. His degree had no status. He too became a teacher, working at a number of schools across Warsaw.

His children, Maria's older brothers and sisters, were all precocious. Maria, the baby of the five, (writes her daughter) was showered with endearing nicknames. Accounts point to a puffball of a young girl, a bundle of energy and sweetness, with a planet-sized brain. All the Skłodowski children were top in their class. To her son Józef on his birthday his mother wrote: 'always be good and helpful to your friends, that's your duty. But don't let them beat you in your studies – I would be very ashamed if my son were at the bottom of his class'.

Yet even in a family of whip-smart parents and children, Maria stood out. Once, when her elder sister Bronia was reading aloud to their parents – and making slow, faltering progress, young Maria, aged only four, impulsively reached for the book, bored by the umming and ahhing, and promptly read the first sentence to stunned silence. Undeterred by the wide eyes of her mother, father and sister (no doubt at that moment subject to a powerful access of jealousy), Maria continued until, like a cartoon character whose legs continue to whir as they career off a cliff, she noticed the silence, panicked, and burst into tears: 'Beg – pardon! Pardon! I didn't do it on purpose. It's not my fault – it's not Bronia's fault! It's only because it was so easy!'

A photo exists of the five children, taken in the early 1870s. To the left of the image is Zosia, the eldest child, aloof, one hand holding the other, standing balanced on her left leg, with her right foot relaxed at a jaunty, confident angle; on the far right of the frame stands Bronia, looking just past the camera somewhat distractedly, less sure of herself, also holding one hand in the other; on the table Bronia leans on is sat Józef, a small boy of about six, holding a boater-type hat in his hands, with an impish, questioning glance; in the middle of the shot, on a single chair, sit two little girls, Helena on the left, Maria on the right. Helena's legs are crossed easily on the footstool in front of her, her arms at gentle right angles. Her face is tilted slightly upwards, her eyes just to the right of the camera. Next to her, her right shoulder hidden behind her sister's, is a sweet, round-faced, nervous-looking, plump girl, staring straight at the camera. One tiny boot is held above the other as her feet dangle from the chair into the uncertain space below.

*

Maria was sent to Madame Sikorska's school in Warsaw – one of the best. Unfortunately Maria's easy intelligence would bring her grief here too. At Sikorska's, students and staff led that double life so typical of Poles after 1864. A secret code told students that German Language, on the timetable, really meant Botany, Home Economics meant Polish history, and so on. The students had special textbooks as well as the real ones in their desk. The school was of course subject to inspections.

Once the school had submitted the timetable to the authorities the waiting game for the inspection began. Madame Sikorska said, 'the tension rose and we were on constant alert'. When the inspectors were abroad, some signal would be given in the school to alert teachers and students – such as the ringing of a bell. And, like a speakeasy bar in Prohibition America, everything would flip, textbooks would be switched, lessons and languages changed and the passing inspector would see nothing untoward, just a typical school in russified Poland, speaking Russian, reading Russian textbooks, studying Russian subjects.

Still, the inspectors wouldn't just glide by. They'd seek concrete proof and ask questions in Russian. As the ablest student, Maria was often picked to give the answers in her near-perfect Russian. Once, having made her perform in front of the whole class, an inspector asked a final, barbed question – 'who is our beloved Tsar?' to which Maria had to respond 'Tsar Alexander II'. The door closed and she burst into tears, aghast at her betrayal of her country and her heritage.

Maria's daily life was one of oppression, and the hopeless yearnings sparked by Polish romanticism. She was learning not only the spirit of rebellion, but the moral and intellectual confidence felt by her peers and family that the weak may be right, and the strong wrong. In later life, she wrote 'I feel everything very violently, with a physical violence.'

But to this ongoing, patriotic struggle and sense of lost personal autonomy that Maria began to experience as she grew into youthful consciousness were added two very sharp personal woes. I contend that with the flint of these two terrible losses came the critical spark that lit a fire within her. She would dare to be different. Rejection as well as affirmation may prove the foundation of genius. The deaths of two who to her were most dear turned her away from God, away – finally – from home and domesticity, away from perhaps a career as a brilliant schoolmistress before marriage, and towards what was then the unknown, fraught with risk.

When exactly Bronisława Skłodowska contracted tuberculosis is unknown. One of Maria's sisters dates it to the year of Maria's birth. And for almost all of Maria's remembered life, her mother had been ill with TB. Aware of the risks she posed her own children, Bronisława kept her own cutlery and crockery and would not allow Maria to touch, hug or kiss her mother. Maria was forever kept at a physical distance.

This was an age before the discovery of penicillin, and the most effective cure for TB was thought to be rest at certain locations with purifying, health-giving air. So Bronisława set off first for Hall, near Innsbruck, in what today is the Austrian Alps. A year later, no better, she went to Nice. She didn't go alone. With her, acting as companion and carer, was her eldest child, eleven-year-old Zosia, who wrote to her godmother Eleonora Kurchanowicz:

I help her get dressed, and undressed, I boil water for her herbs and tea morning and evening. She often says that she is pleased with her Małgosia (that's what she calls me now), but I have a feeling that she needs more than just me, and I often worry, seeing her sad and not being able to cheer her up. Each day we count, several times, how many months we will have to stay here, and we are frustrated with time for passing so slowly. In Warsaw a year went by quicker than a month here.

The emotional cost to the rest of the family is hard to fathom even if its broad contours are easy to imagine. The financial cost was significant too. Paying for travel, living costs and healthcare was not cheap and Władysław's government salary was modest.

While away, Zosia and Bronisława put on a brave face, sometimes at great emotional cost. The nadir of their loneliness together came at Christmas 1873, as illustrated by Bronisława's doleful letter to Eleonora Kurchanowicz.

How empty and silent it seemed, compared to all the previous years! We missed the excited buzz of children waiting to see the Christmas tree ... we missed the presence and embrace of everyone dear to us ... At the time when our family in Poland was sitting down to Christmas supper, Zosia and I broke our wafer with tears in our eyes.

Such sadness transmitted itself to those at home.

They also kept up appearances. In Nice Zosia attended school and, like a true Skłodowski, was soon top of her class despite the lessons being in French. Bronisława could not hide her pride. 'I told Zosia that we could stay here longer, so that she wouldn't lose all the prizes, but she won't hear of it,' she wrote. Her love of family success and hard work, so clear here, even when she was ill and desperate to see the rest of her children, would leave a deep imprint on Maria.

Back home in Warsaw, Władysław was caring for the others. Enormous pressure was upon him: a stern, serious man, but a loving father too. Some of Maria's strongest, happiest memories are of Władysław reading poetry – both his own and that of the Polish greats like Mickiewicz – by the hearth on a Saturday night. These readings stirred within her a love not just for Poland, but for the condition of man. Only later did she decide upon science as her career, but public spirit had been born much earlier. She wrote, years later, in her *Autobiographical Notes*, of the effect of her father's readings: 'On Saturday evenings he used to recite or read to us the masterpieces of Polish prose and poetry.' Such moments were doubtless comforting in the bleak months that would blight her life.

While her mother was away, her father suffered two severe blows. In 1873, Władysław had been fired from his job as assistant director at the Nowolipki gymnasium: he lost not just his income, but the flat that came with the job. It was around this time, Maria's biographers agree, that Władysław lost 30,000 roubles in a failed investment. For practically all his life, save this one moment, he'd been a sober, judicious man. But when his brother Henryk asked him to invest in the wonderful steam mill he'd found in the country, Władysław assented. It was only towards the end of his life, Maria's brother Józef says, that Władysław began to forgive himself for squandering the money he had saved to educate his daughters. Labouring under the burdens of his wife's illness, his bad investment, and his lost job, Władysław moved lodgings and was forced to bring in boarders to stay afloat financially.

'When I think about that time,' wrote Józef, 'the impression I have is of some kind of beehive where the noise and commotion never ended. When we [the Skłodowski children] returned from school each day, we ate lunch all together – about twenty people – and then we would all sit down to study. Every corner of our apartment was then filled with students – not only those who lived with us, but also those who just came along to study.'

Worse was to come. In 1876, when Maria was nine, two of her sisters, Zosia and Bronia, caught typhus. Bronia survived. But Zosia, aged just fourteen, and her mother's carer for the past few years, did not.

Typhus of the kind that most likely killed Zosia is spread by lice. The Skłodowskis were assiduous and clean, but were compelled to admit up to twenty boarders to their house. It is likely these boarders were the source of the infection, and, indirectly, the Russian authorities whose sacking of Władysław had caused the whole situation. The effect was seismic and (her children suggest) for Maria's mother it was the beginning of the end.

In 1878 Bronisława Skłodowska succumbed to the TB that had been working its way through her body for years. Her children blame a more proximate cause: the loss of her principal carer. 'Our sister's death literally crushed our mother; she could never accept the loss of her oldest child,' wrote Helena; Zosia's death was 'the final blow', wrote Jozef; Maria says her mother was 'cruelly struck by the loss of her daughter and worn away by grave illness'.

The blow fell perhaps hardest on Maria. In her *Autobiographical Notes*, usually sparing in emotional detail, Maria wrote the sentences with which this account started:

> This catastrophe was the first great sorrow of my life and threw me into a profound depression ... Her influence over me was extraordinary, for in me the natural love of the little girl for her mother was united with a passionate admiration ... For many years we all felt weighing on us the loss of the one who had been the soul of the house.

The change wrought in the once infectiously merry girl was conspicuous. Her sister Helena said, 'She would often sit in some corner and cry bitterly. Her tears could not be stopped by anybody.' Her teacher, Madame Sikorska, recommended she wait a year before entering the next year at school (she was already a year ahead).

Instead her father did something unexpected. He removed her from the Sikorska school and sent her to a state-run gymnasium. This was much tougher for the grieving Maria than the pleasant, sympathetic environment of Sikorska's. The prohibition from speaking Polish was viciously policed. She wrote later, 'Constantly held in suspicion and spied upon, the children knew that a single conversation in Polish, or an imprudent word, might seriously harm, not only themselves, but also their families. Amid these hostilities, they lost all the joy of life, and precocious feelings of distrust and indignation weighed upon their childhood.'

There was another consequence of her mother's death. Maria's commitment to prayer wavered. Her daughter Ève wrote that in church 'she no longer invoked with the same love that God who had unjustly inflicted such terrible blows'. Ève does tend to over-dramatise Maria, but, reeling from the deaths of her sister and mother, it seems that the path to an atheism of some kind grew more clear for her.

In fact this was entwined with Polish Positivism, the movement her father had anticipated, and one that would greatly influence Maria. It was Positivism that helped Maria study when she could not afford to, and led her to join underground groups of like-minded learners in Warsaw in her twenties. Positivism prepared her for the road to Paris. It had been her mother's death, and a kind of disillusionment, that began to point Maria in these directions.

*

But first – and in a strange interval in her life that I'd contend was not unrelated to this moment of moral despair – comes an episode with which biographers have struggled but which, for those persuaded by my argument, is easily explained.

Maria had been fifteen when she finished her studies in 1883, 'always having held first rank in my class'. The adult Marie Curie then becomes studiedly vague about what happened next – or, more precisely, what caused it. In a kind of absconsion, she took herself into the country for a year. Why? In her *Notes* she says only that 'the fatigue of growth and study compelled me to take almost a year's rest in the country'. By the next sentence she has returned to her father in Warsaw and is getting on with her life. What's behind that mysteriously perfunctory sentence? One of her biographers saw it quite plainly as a 'total nervous collapse'[21] in which the teenage Maria took to bed for days and would barely admit food. Another notes that 'in her lexicon, however, fatigue can mean many things. Later, when she suffered depression, she and others always described it as a fatigue or "exhaustion".'[22] Her daughter Ève maintains a somewhat less plausible reason – that 'Manya suddenly became lazy'. Ève Curie quotes a letter from her mother to one of her school friends that seems to support her assertion: 'I read no serious books, only harmless and absurd little novels ... Sometimes I laugh all by myself, and I contemplate my state of total stupidity with genuine satisfaction.'

Given what she had just gone through – financial break-down, the death of her eldest sister, the death of her mother, depression, then a move to a brutal school – all under the continuing weight of political and cultural oppression and yet still managing to come top of her class, it seems very plausible that she had a breakdown of some kind.

The picture, though, is more complicated than simple collapse. She let go, and it is certain that during that year, Maria loved the countryside. She writes in her *Notes*:

There we found the free life of the old-fashioned family estate; races in the woods and joyous participation in work in the far-stretching, level grain-fields. At

other times ... we went southwards into the mountain country of Galicia, where the Austrian political
control was less oppressive than that which we suffered. There we could speak Polish in all freedom and
sing patriotic songs without going to prison.

A kind-hearted, modest person to the end of her life,
Madame Curie rarely missed a chance to kick out at
Russian oppression in her *Notes*. But in her year of bucolic
rejuvenation she enjoyed herself greatly, attending dances
that went on till the early hours. She experienced that
'Poland profonde' she had dreamed of from Warsaw. Years
later her daughter wrote that she 'thanked the destiny
which, before it dictated this woman's austere and inexo-
rable summons, had allowed her to follow by sleigh after
the wildest *kuligs* [sleigh rides], and to use up her shoes of
russet leather in one night of dancing'. Shock, breakdown,
pause, and a resetting of a life's compass. The sequence
should not surprise those following this book's hypothesis.

On her return Maria had to face the consequences of
her father's bad investment, and of her gender. What family
money remained had gone on sending Józef, the only son,
to medical school. Money was becoming increasingly
difficult to scrabble together as Władysław approached
retirement, which would mean a further drop in their
income. So Maria could not teach in the free schools as
she had wished. Instead she took up a position as a governess, to fund her sister Bronia's study in Paris. Maria would
save for her own study, and then come herself to the City
of Light, a city of deep learning, and one so resonant for
like-minded Poles ever since the 1830s.

*

Before Paris, though, came the money. It was no easy thing to become a governess and sign away prime years of your life at the age of just seventeen. The job with her first family, based in Warsaw, was not a success. She described her existence as that of a prisoner. Luckily, she was able to free herself and move elsewhere, but at significant emotional cost. The new family, the Zorawskis, lived in the country outside of Warsaw. She'd grown closer to her father over the years and hated to be away from him. She writes of this period in her life with her typical understatement, but it's clear what a great effect it had on her:

> Thus, when scarcely seventeen, I left my father's house to begin an independent life. That going away remains one of the most vivid memories of my youth. My heart was heavy as I climbed into the railway car. It was to carry me for several hours, away from those I loved. And after the railway journey I must drive for five hours longer. What experience was awaiting me? So I questioned as I sat close to the car window looking out across the wide plains.

In her early twenties, living and studying in Paris, she suffered a great deal more: sleeping with all her clothes on top of her during a particularly 'rigorous' winter, lugging what coal she could carry up the stairs on her own in a bid to keep her little room in the freezing garret warm; subsisting on a diet of 'bread with a cup of chocolate, eggs, and fruit'.

She recounts that hardship breezily later, but lingers here over her departure from her family home, describing her outward journey at greater length than she devotes to describing the people she went to serve. Her sadness at this moment of loss rises from her clipped language like mist from a river. Then, she knew where she did not want to go. Later, in Paris, a university student rather than a governess, she knew she was where she wanted to be.

After patriotic rage, after family tragedy, after rejecting God, after the nervous breakdown, after subjection to circumstances she hated – after fracture – comes a liberation, a new direction. The destination was unknown but the path was set, and Maria was no longer a sweet puffball of a child, but, in 1891, on the road to Paris, Pierre, 'Marie', scientific discovery, and a new branch of science.

Machado de Assis

To the worm who first gnawed on the cold flesh of my corpse.

There are two good reasons for omitting one of the finest authors in the Portuguese language, and the greatest writer that Brazil has ever produced. The first is that many English-speaking readers will not have heard of him. The second is that the fracture in the life of this nineteenth-century novelist, poet, playwright and short-story writer came not in childhood at all, but halfway through his career. Yet the break was so clear, so sudden, and so explosive in the unlocking of his genius that some brief account of the event should reach these pages.

I would speculate that this unlocking of genius through

fracture may have been an unlocking, too, of childhood trauma: an upbringing that he may have supposed he had put behind him as he translated himself from sickly pauper into a supplier of literary pap to the Brazilian middle classes. Joaquim Maria Machado de Assis's childhood was by no means conventional. He was born in Rio de Janeiro in 1839, the city in which he would spend his entire life. Joaquim grew up in Rio's slums, the son of an Azorean washerwoman and a mulatto house painter whose parents had been slaves. His mother died from tuberculosis when he was ten and he had little formal education, attending some classes at a girls' school where his stepmother worked. A sickly, shy and small boy, he suffered from epilepsy and other disabling conditions throughout his life. But he possessed a relentless work ethic. At his stepmother's insistence, young Joaquim was taught classical Latin by his local priest, a certain Padre Silveira Sarmento, and French by Madame Guillot, a French baker, and her 'master of the ovens'. He began writing and, at fifteen, his first poem was published in a local newspaper. From here, the boy embarked on a literary career, working as a typesetter's apprentice and journalist, before going on to greater literary feats. From an unconventional upbringing would emerge a man Susan Sontag declared 'the greatest writer ever produced in Latin America' and a Brazilian national hero. He was known simply as Machado de Assis.

All the challenges of Machado's upbringing may have armed, but never detonated, the explosion of his genius. They are hard even to relate to his later work. His early novels garnered significant fame in Brazil but were hardly innovative. He was simply an accomplished producer of romantic novels destined to be read by high society. Ironides Rodrigues, an early biographer, wrote that 'Machado expresses himself as a white writer who did not feel the least bit of black blood coursing through his heart ... [he] worried himself very little with the social movements of his time, such as Abolition and the Republic.' Machado – a mixed-race, working-class man, seemed content to ignore these huge themes. By dint of his remarkable intellect and diligence he was in time assimilated into Brazil's journalistic, governmental and literary establishments and obtained a well-paid post in the Ministry of Agriculture; and another establishing the Academia Brasileira de Letras, Brazil's literary body.

So far, so good. A poor boy from the slums, making it as an accomplished hack writer. He had broken one ceiling but was constrained by the next. Real originality still eluded him. If there was anything left to give, something would have to break.

As he approached forty he had become a local celebrity, with four novels published and two collections of magazine stories. His position in the civil service was secure and he was happily married.

Then, at the end of 1878, Machado suffered a crippling epileptic attack. It was so strong that it almost blinded him. He would only recover thanks to months of complete inactivity. And it seems this brush with death led to an entire rethink of his creative output. He began to complain to friends of his 'illness' and 'the evil that accompanies me'. The attack seemed to coincide with the 'exhaustion of the fictional vein he had been working since his teens'.

Very rapidly, Machado's writing darkened and deepened – barely recognisable from his early work.

He went on to produce some of the most brilliant satire Latin America had ever read. And it is for his biting, macabre vision of Brazilian society – and only this – that Machado is remembered today. The Brazilian critic Roberto Schwartz has discussed Machado de Assis's work in detail. His belief is that Brazil is a country of 'misplaced ideas': following the latest trends from Europe without ever managing to express its own reality. In Machado's time this caused writers living under monarchical rule, in a country where slavery was a norm, to pen the sort of romantic novels pioneered by liberal France. Brazil was also a country whose economy was not prepared for capitalism but which embraced it eagerly – perhaps too eagerly – in the ruling class's hunger for foreign products. The ideas didn't quite mesh with reality. Machado has become Schwarz's idol because he is 'the only Brazilian novelist capable of understanding the Brazilian condition', and pointing out its hypocrisy.

Galvanised by his brush with death, Machado's next work, and his first post-seizure, was *The Posthumous Memoirs of Brás Cubas*. It featured, as the title suggests, a narrator telling the tale of his life from beyond the grave. The tone was *Tristram Shandy*-esque but leagues darker. Whereas Machado's previous works were largely read by upper-class, well-to-do Brazilian women, *Brás Cubas* set out to offend those readers. The novel begins with a dedication to the '*worm* who *first gnawed* on the cold *flesh* of *my* corpse', and the opening chapter is an exhilarating account of Brás's delirious visions before death, in a fantastical style of which Gabriel García Márquez would be proud. Social questions, consciously eschewed in Machado's previous literature, are dealt with satirically. The deplorable treatment of slaves is narrated in an off-hand manner – tilting at the upper class to which Brás belongs – and the 'misplaced ideas' of Brazil's high society are called into question on every page. As the American academic Dudley Fitts commented, 'no satirist, not even Swift, is less merciful'.

The *Posthumous Memoirs of Brás Cubas* was followed by *Dom Casmurro, Casa Velha, Quincas Borba* and *Esaú e Jacó*, the whole outpouring created within in the space of a few years, all exposing the insanity of the apparently respectable. It is as though the second half of his life and work is an attack on the first. Although full of Brazilian references, these stories are impressively universal for a writer who barely left his hometown during his life.

Today his work finds fame worldwide; a revival of English translations in the 1960s created a fan base which includes Salman Rushdie, Woody Allen, Susan Sontag and Harold Bloom. All agree that Machado is one of literature's greats. How little inkling of this Machado could have had, as that blinding, devastating mid-life epileptic seizure struck him down.

Genghis Khan

He cried easily and was afraid of dogs.

In twenty-five years (as Genghis Khan's modern biographer, Jack Weatherford, writes) Genghis Khan's army managed to subjugate more people than the Romans had done over a period of four hundred years. By whatever metric – measured in land, people, countries – he conquered more than any other man in history. At its height, the Mongol Empire spread over roughly 12 million contiguous square miles, and, if calculated today, would contain about three billion people. Khan managed this with an army of just 100,000. He 'redrew the boundaries of the world', and 'transformed warfare into an intercontinental affair fought on multiple fronts across thousands of miles', spreading the knowledge of technology, arts, literature and commerce as he went. All this was achieved through a combination of speed, accuracy and extreme brutality – by one of the most renowned and ferocious warriors in history.

It's probably impossible to separate myth from reality in any account of a conqueror so distant from us in time and place, and one of whom no comprehensive or objective biography would have been remotely possible. The accounts we rely on in this brutally summarised and unavoidably fragmentary sketch are not the only ones, and all differ. It is possible, however, to conclude that this was a life that started, downtrodden, in chaos and confusion, and went on to achievement of a monumental kind: in imperial terms among the greatest in history.

'Genghis' Khan was born Temüjin in 1162, in a region that is now located in eastern Mongolia. His great-grandfather, Kabul, had united the clans for the first time as a confederation – Temüjin would later forge the Mongolian nation. Following tradition, he was named after the man his father had just captured, which points to the continuous tribal violence of life on the steppes. Murder, kidnapping and enslavement were routine.

As a young child Temüjin showed little signs of what he would become. He cried easily (says Weatherford) and was afraid of dogs, and his young sibling was a more proficient archer and wrestler. As was the tradition, Temüjin's father took him to a neighbouring tribe at the age of eight, to serve the family of his future wife until he reached marriageable age. On the way home, his father was poisoned by Tartars who probably recognised him from previous attacks. By the time the boy got back home his father was dying. Temüjin – still only a child – was summoned back to take his rightful place as chief. But his father's death created room for another clan to bid for power. To eliminate the risk of rivalry from Temüjin, they drove out the entire family (Temüjin's mother, his father's second wife, and their seven children) to die.

For up to four years the family lived a precarious and brutal existence as hunter-gatherers. Vengeance must have been a preoccupying thought for Temüjin, and it was during this disastrous fall from pre-eminence that he began funnelling his personal pain into fury and murder – preoccupations that would only intensify as he grew older and more powerful. The claustrophobic family environment created tension with his older half-brother, Bekter. This was more than just sibling rivalry: it threatened Temüjin's role as head of the family, which would in turn have defined the treatment and position of his mother and full siblings.

When Temüjin was thirteen years old, Bekter stole the spoils of a hunt from him. His mother, Hoelun, was uninterested, reminding Temüjin that critiquing family was not helpful when they had nobody else in the world. But a switch in the boy was thrown. Together with another brother, Temüjin crept up on Bekter with a bow, and, when his bluff was called, killed him in cold blood. The shocked response of Temüjin's mother suggests that this was not an ordinary or expected act of violence. The tectonic plates within Temüjin had shifted.

He was now the clear head of the family but, more than that, he was mustering a steely and ruthless confidence. His slow and resolute path to leadership began in earnest.

Much of the information regarding Temüjin's life is taken from *The Secret History of the Mongols*, a rich yet unreliable source written as a 'foundation epic' two years after Genghis Khan died. One of the key themes throughout *The Secret History* is the sense of heavenly ordination – that Temüjin was destined for greatness, as predicted when he was born with a large blood clot on his hand.

Beyond these predictions, however, we get a clear sense of a child, then a youth, who was willing to do whatever he needed, no matter how violent, in order to survive. This now brutal, unforgiving boy would become a brutal, unforgiving man. When he eventually came to defeat the Tartars, he avenged his father's death by killing every male taller than three foot. He continued to grow in strength – eventually conquering every tribe on the steppe, and uniting them under his banner. Unusually for a conqueror, he lived into his old age, dying in 1227, surrounded by family and friends.

And it had all begun when, in a temper at thirteen, his mother having refused to stick up for him, he decided to kill his half-brother for cheating in a hunting contest. In the flight of that arrow from the hitherto timid boy's bow, a journey of self-discovery as well as world domination had begun. Hoelun has much to answer for.

Martin Luther King

It was the angriest I have ever been in my life.

Between 1955 and 1968, Martin Luther King, Jr became the most popular and effective leader of the American civil rights movement, and has never relinquished that pre-eminence. An eloquent proponent of non-violent protest, he was, by the time he was assassinated, world famous for his moving rhetoric and powerful commitment to civil disobedience as a means of tackling societal injustice. King was awarded the Nobel Peace Prize in 1964, received the Presidential Medal of Freedom posthumously in 1977, and his birthday is celebrated as a federal holiday in America.

Christened Michael, and known throughout his life to his family as Mike, King was born in January 1929, in Atlanta, Georgia. His mother was the daughter of a successful minister, and his father the pastor of the same church. A dynamic and physical man, his father was an indomitable presence in his son's life. King had mixed and powerful emotions towards him: he was whipped by his father until the age of fifteen, but respected his courage and dignity in the face of racial injustice.

King was very close to his grandmother, and her death must be considered the first of two key fractures during his adolescence. On 18 May 1941, King crept out of the house to attend a parade instead of studying. While he was out, she suffered a heart attack and died. He was racked with guilt, and worried that her death was a punishment for sneaking off. Grief-stricken, he leapt out of a second-floor window in a suicide attempt. He struck the ground hard, but survived with only bruises. He continued to cry in his bedroom, unable to bear the pain or to sleep, for days. He was tormented with doubts about God's plan, about heaven and ascension; his sense of helplessness in the face of a cruel world was compounded.

Growing up in segregated Atlanta was another trauma. At home, his mother told her children that they were 'somebodies', but away from home he was daily confronted by a system which told him he was 'less than somebody'. Those years were marked by anger, and the boy had violent mood swings: despite being small, he was a fullback in neighbourhood soccer because he simply charged into anybody in his way. But he was also a precocious and hardworking, skipping two grades at school.

The personal affront that the child felt at the limitations placed on him because of his colour came to a head during his junior year, after he won a speechmaking contest in Dublin, Georgia. He had travelled to take part with some teachers, speaking on 'The Negro and the Constitution'. On their way home the group were ordered to stand on the bus to allow white passengers a seat. The young King refused. His teacher insisted. Smarting, he complied. They all stood for the entire 90-mile journey.

This was hardly the cruellest manifestation of that cruel policy, but for a boy who had just won a prize it was the most stinging experience of segregation. It seems to have cut him to the quick. That night on the bus would never leave his memory: 'it was the angriest I have ever been in my life', he later wrote.

King was born into a family of respected ministers, but as a teenager he at first rejected this path. He began rebelling against his father, critiquing the lessons taught at church. He dismissed the ministry as unintellectual, archaic, and irrelevant to societal issues. The adolescent rebellion against what he was expected to be led him to reject some of his father's values, but he came eventually to accept the overall worth of the ministry. Spending so much time around preachers influenced his vocabulary and speech patterns as well as his leadership style: he honed what was perhaps an inborn skill at unlocking an audience's emotions as a charismatic preacher can do with a congregation. Later, while studying at Crozer Theological Seminary, he fell in love with the white daughter of a staff member. They planned to marry, but were dissuaded by friends led by his implacably opposed mother; an interracial marriage would provoke animosity between black and white communities and would not help King's career in the south. Dedicated to the cause, they parted ways, but pastor J. Pius Barbour later said that King 'never recovered' from the heartbreak.

For King, constant racial segregation was compounded by a series of fractures that pushed him towards the civil rights movement. He was marked by the whippings of his father, the death of his grandmother, the racial abuse he suffered on that bus when he had just been recognised for his talent, and the loss of a forbidden love. Here, then (to a boy, youth or young man with a strong sense of justice) was a range of great injustices. There was only one he could truly do something about. An emotional, angry teenager became a charming, intelligent and hugely respected adult – and began his lifelong campaign for equality. The child's anger and rebellion were not the antithesis of the adult's open-hearted courage: they were what unlocked it.

Muhammad Ali

I couldn't get Emmett out of my mind.

Among the greatest boxers of all time, Muhammad Ali was an outstanding personality of the twentieth century. Many of the fights he was involved in – such as the 'Fight of the Century' and 'The Rumble in the Jungle' – retain their cultural significance today. Confident and provocative, he was famed for his trash talk. But his impact extended beyond the boxing ring: his political activism and religious commitment, including being temporarily banned from the sport for draft evasion (he was a conscientious objector during the Vietnam War), made him an icon to some, a bad influence to others.

He was born Cassius Marcellus Clay Jr in 1942 in Louisville, Kentucky, named after a famed lawyer and abolitionist. In 1964, after winning the world heavyweight championship and joining the Nation of Islam, he rejected this 'slave name' and became Muhammad Ali.

Ali's family life was generally comfortable. He was well loved and looked after, although there were periods of tension. While his mother was a gentle churchgoer, his father – when drunk – could be violent. Ali was precocious and cared little for rules. By the time he was about eight he was the leader of a gang of boys, keen to cause mischief and not particularly interested in sports. He was known for his ability to take punishment on the chin – a trait later crucial in his career, although potentially damaging to his health.

The boy was introduced to boxing by a chance encounter in October 1954, aged twelve. Along with his brother, he attended an 'Exposition' at the town hall, but afterwards found his bike missing. Ali's family were poor – they wore second-hand clothes and used cardboard in their shoes to make them last longer. The bike was perhaps his only status symbol growing up, and he took vast pride in it. He began to cry, distraught at losing the bike and worried about his father's reaction.

To report the crime they were told to visit Joe Elsby Martin, a policeman training boxers in a nearby auditorium. Ali was much struck by Joe Martin. He angrily told the policeman what he would do to the thief when he found him. Martin asked him if he even knew how to fight. He didn't: 'Well, why don't you come down here and start training?' Whoever stole that twelve-year-old boy's bike really started something.

Ali didn't return immediately, but after he saw Joe Martin on TV, he decided to go back. His parents were relieved: it would be a way to keep him out of trouble and control his emotions. Like many African-American children at the time, he found the racial discrimination surrounding him emotionally hard to deal with. He would lie in bed crying about the suffering of African-Americans. This worried his parents.

The lynching of the fourteen-year-old Emmett Till in

1955, a notorious and monstrous injustice, was a point of fracture. Till and Ali were about the same age; Ali felt 'a deep kinship to him', finding the murder profoundly difficult to come to terms with. As he recounts in his autobiography, *The Greatest*, he 'couldn't get Emmett out of [his] mind'. Ali's father 'dramatised' the crime and talked about it 'night and day'. Filled with rage a week after the murder, Ali vandalised a railway station with a group of friends, including the lines, so that a passing train was also damaged. Ali recalls an 'Uncle Sam Wants You' poster nearby, which they threw stones at, but which seemed to watch him as he ran away. He writes: 'I knew that sooner or later [the man in the poster] would confront me, and I would confront him.'

The youth had already decided that the world was shaped to suit white people. As a young boy his focus was not how to change the world, but to earn money and prosper within it: only money, he argued, would give black men a chance at equality and respect. Boxing, he realised, could be his route to success. He didn't at first look like a prodigy but the sport brought about something new in him: ambition. His self-belief was huge – he would canvass the streets to attract a bigger audience for a fight, something his coaches had never seen before.

And boxing transcended race. In the ring Ali had equal status with white boys. His desire to be successful – to be free in his own right, to be known, and able to do what he wanted – was powerful in him. His celebrity grew, based on his lip as well as his skill as a boxer. And his lip sprang at least in part from his sense of injustice. There was a kind of divine insolence within him.

*

I remember as a young man, and over a period of many weeks in 1987, experiencing a mounting rage that became (as I can see, looking back) obsessive. A nurse called Lawrence Newcombe had hit the front page of the *Daily Mail* in the paper's headline story about an 'Aids scare'. It seems that during the terrible fire at King's Cross underground station which killed thirty-one people and injured many more, Newcombe emerged after helping in the rescue, then ran back down into the inferno to help some more. This time smoke killed him. The *Mail* discovered that he had been HIV-positive and gay. The whole focus of their lead story was the fear that firemen who had touched his body might have become infected. His heroism was ignored.

For reasons unknown to me I could not stop thinking about this injustice nor let it drop. More and more furious at the cruelty of such journalism, I almost felt I loved a man I had never met and never would. Finally, I decided to research something of Newcombe's life, worked hard at it, interviewed friends and others who had known him, and wrote an angry tribute to Newcombe which the *Sunday Telegraph* published. I was not then a journalist, but this helped (as things turned out) my entry into the trade.

Something, therefore, in the story of Ali's long and (one might say) disproportionate obsession with the lynching of Emmett Till, whom he did not know, chimes with me. The easy argument is to say that this incident and his furious response were the turning point, the creative fracture for Ali; and in a way that's true. But the more complete truth is that something within the boy was ready for the trip-switch to be tripped; and the shock of Till's lynching tripped it. All his anger spilled out and, in spilling out, changed him. Fracture often works like that.

Simón Bolívar

I feel something has broken in me.

Today the idea that South America could be ruled from Madrid would be laughed off as absurd. But at the turn of the eighteenth century it was different. To imagine that South Americans could govern themselves required an imaginative leap that was beyond most. Simón Bolívar took that leap, acted upon it, and finally brought an entire continent with him.

For eleven years Bolívar ruled over Gran Colombia, a territory that extended across an area as large as modern Europe. His military know-how did much to liberate northern Latin America from Spanish rule. As well as masterminding military victories at Caracas, Boyacá in central Colombia and Junín in northern Peru, Bolívar was renowned for leading soldiers where few others dared tread. His intrepid marches across hundreds of miles of some of the world's most inhospitable terrain – the Peruvian Andes or the Colombian marshlands – are the stuff of South American legend.

He also (and it's this that's of the last importance) laid the philosophical framework for the overthrow of the Spanish Empire and the establishment of an independent continent. This wasn't just a military process; it couldn't even start with a military process. The fighting (though Bolívar was good at it) was merely a consequence. What was needed first and throughout was a new political and cultural idea; an idea that must shake the mental habits of almost three centuries of imperial Spanish predominance; an idea that required a self-belief to lodge itself in the imagination of his fellow Americans, that vast array of races, colours and creeds that Bolívar was determined to unite.

Before all this, though, the idea needed to be born in Bolívar's own imagination.

His 1815 *Letter from Jamaica* envisioned Americans as a 'middle species', somewhere between the Spanish usurpers and indigenous people, who could lead Colombia to glory. The concept was a gross simplification of the huge ethnic and cultural variety that existed in Latin America, but it had imaginative power: a useful tool to unite Colombians under his banner, against Spanish rule.

Today, Bolívar's dream of shaking off the imperial yoke has come true, but his dream of a united Latin American continent lies in tatters. He remains a hero. His statue adorns the squares of thousands of towns across the countries he governed, and he has become a mythical symbol of Latin American identity, evoked in art, film and literature. Gabriel García Márquez's *The General in His Labyrinth* is witness to the enduring fascination this man has for Colombians, for Venezuelans to whose currency he gave his name, and for Bolivians whose nation is named after him.

Bolívar represents glory and liberty, of course, but first self-belief. He once described such values as 'the only object worth the sacrifice of a man's life'. The great Spanish writer, Miguel de Unamuno, thought of him as an American Don Quixote. Although his fantasy of continental unity ended in failure, in Unamuno's words Bolívar's 'idea of America as a great and undying unit, as an exalted and glorious fatherland' was a 'high and noble dream'. It is in the depth and daring of Bolívar's dream as much as – I would say more than – in his battlefield victories that his genius lies.

His youth was marked by large reward and heart-breaking loss. Bolívar described the family slave, Hipólita, as the only mother he ever knew.

Born in 1783, the son of wealthy, aristocratic Venezuelan landowners, he was (like so many of our heroes) orphaned at an early age: he lost his father when he was just three, and his mother when he was nine. The loss of his parents would have an enduring impression on the boy, making him mature beyond his years.

That the family had a slave shows their privilege. Fostered by relatives, Bolívar was afforded the best of educations. Among his teachers was the Chilean poet and diplomat Andrés Bello and he became particularly close to Simón Rodríguez, a mentor who taught him the ideals of the European Enlightenment and the basics of human rights. At sixteen he was sent to Madrid to complete a military education. At this point in his life we could be observing a privileged teenager, attracted by the kind of romantic ideals teenagers often entertain, who was likely to revert to type and join the governing class – whose authority came from Madrid.

But now the young Bolívar first found love. He met

María Teresa Rodríguez del Toro y Alayza, a Spanish aristocrat two years older than him. He was only sixteen and fell head over heels in love. They married two years later, on 18 May 1802. Bolívar brought his wife back to his hometown, San Mateo, and seemed settled at last: a contented landowner.

But Bolívar's love, if what he said about himself later is to be believed, verged on obsession. Describing his wife as a 'jewel', he wrote that 'back then my head was filled by a steamy, violent love, and not by political ideas'. His happiness was not to last. María Teresa contracted yellow fever shortly after arriving in Venezuela. The couple returned to Caracas and María Teresa remained bed-bound, growing weaker by the day and dying from her illness in 1803. Just eight months after his marriage, Bolívar was a widower.

For the young man, María Teresa's death seems to have meshed with the earlier loss of his parents. Friends and relatives noticed a change in his temperament. The free-spirited and joyous youth sank into melancholy. Her death was described by the Spanish historian Santiago de Madariaga as 'one of the key events in the history of the New World'. After it, Bolívar swore never to marry again. 'I feel something has broken in me,' he said. His destiny must lie elsewhere.

In later life he would recognise the significance of this fracture as the moment when death separated him from what and whom he had loved most: the turning point in his life. 'If I had not been widowed, perhaps my life would have been different; I would not be General Bolívar or The Liberator,' he wrote.

And María Teresa's death led to a second, formative trip to Europe. Bolívar visited Paris and Italy with his mentor,

Simón Rodríguez. In the French capital he saw Napoleon's coronation. Disgusted by the gothic crown, Bolívar was impressed by the spectacle. The idea that one man could change the course of history fascinated him.

With Rodríguez he visited Mount Sacro, a hill outside Rome. Inspired by enlightened idealism, hatred of Spanish tyranny and the pain of María Teresa's death, he made an oath: 'I swear before you, I swear by my parent's God, by them, by my honour and by my country, that my arm will not rest, that my soul will not be calmed, until I have broken the Spanish chains that oppress us.' And on this oath, born in despair, he never relented.

Vladimir Ilyich Ulyanov – aka V. I. Lenin

[The execution was] the key to understanding how Lenin became a revolutionary.

I could argue that the creation of world communism, the story of the Union of Soviet Socialist Republics, the whole course of twentieth-century international relations, and the dysfunctionality of the post-communist Russian Federation can be traced to a single individual. No, not Lenin, but his father.

Ilya Nikolayevich Ulyanov was by all accounts a dominating, driven and hard-driving, achieving, deeply religious, idealistic, socially conservative and in some ways narrow man: a man of conviction both severe and yet inspiring to two of his eight children, Vladimir and (the elder of the two) Alexander. The young Vladimir's background was as middle class as they came in tsarist Russia. His father was a well-to-do councillor of state whose aim was to bring literacy to the Russian people. He was also a strictly religious man, who forbade criticism of Christianity or talk of politics in the house. Vladimir didn't seem to mind this restriction and scorned his brother Alexander's interest in socialism. He later said 'we lived in easy circumstances ... we did not know hunger or cold; we were surrounded by all sorts of cultural opportunities and stimuli, books, music and diversions'.

So when and how was the revolutionary spark lit?

Nikolai Valentinov, Lenin's acquaintance and biographer, writes that as a student Vladimir was addicted to coming out on top: 'He simply had to succeed constantly. He always had to be the best student ... it was only a question of will.' He was prone to arrogance, but kept in check by his disciplinarian father and the strict, conservative gymnasium he attended, where 'the future revolutionary did not in the smallest way violate the rules of conduct'.

Vladimir was sixteen when his father died. This was not the fracture that broke him, but it set the stage. His sister wrote that something changed, and soon after, he 'was not disinclined to maliciously tease his teachers ... to throw out mocking and sharp remarks concerning religion'. He became rude and cruel towards his mother and sisters, and grew increasingly arrogant – focusing relentlessly on his studies following his father's death. It seems as though Vladimir was having some kind of slow-motion mental breakdown.

But it was with the death of his brother Alexander that Vladimir's behaviour took its final lurch. If Vladimir had been hit hard by his father's death, his older brother had been 'inconsolable'. In the words of their sister, Alexander began to see revolutionary activity as 'a categorical imperative for each morally honest citizen of his country'. He became engaged in a revolutionary cell at the University of St Petersburg and, as a talented chemist, was charged with designing a bomb capable of killing Tsar Alexander III. The plot was discovered and the plotters arrested. Alexander was an eloquent, zealous defendant. He expressed an 'irrevocable resolution to die', calling for vengeance on the lawless tsarist state. He drafted a progressive programme to reflect his desires, with aspirations to liberty and equality characteristic of orthodox Marxism. It was virtually a suicide note, and in May 1887, just months after the death of his father, Alexander was hanged in St Petersburg.

The execution had an immediate and shocking impact on Vladimir: as Valentinov writes, it is 'the key to understanding how Lenin became a revolutionary'. The seventeen-year-old became 'grim and taciturn', conceiving a great hatred of those responsible for his brother's death. He pulled himself together. 'No, we will not go this way. We must not go this way' he was reported by official biographers to have said. He delved – some would say obsessively – into his dead brother's psyche, methodically quizzing Alexander's former roommate and repenting of his own disengagement. He must now understand his brother, whose political inclinations he had never grasped. He must read the books his brother read. He knew Alexander Odoevsky's remark: 'from a spark a fire will flare up' and his discovery of Marxism would inspire him to leave his own mark on the world. He decided to be the spark. He would set Russia alight, and he did.

Fifteen years later, passing through revolution and civil war, Lenin had led the Bolsheviks to victory, overthrown the three-century-old Romanov dynasty, and so ruptured the continuity of his nation's history that, beyond shaping the century that followed, the doomed communist interregnum he fathered poisoned the veins of the Russia that was to come.

Ludwig Wittgenstein

Fear of death proved to be both harrowing and clarifying.

Ludwig Wittgenstein often craved silence. The kind of silence in which he could rescue from the deeps of his mind the theories on language, meaning and logical truth which made him arguably the greatest philosopher of the twentieth century. He found this silence in different places. In a stone cabin on a Norwegian hillside, around the seminar tables at Cambridge which he could silence with a lift of his hand, and among the deafening cannon-fire and danger of the First World War, during which he prepared the drafts for his most famous work, *Tractatus Logico-Philosophicus*.

However, his desire for silence, isolation and abstraction from the common world had more fundamental motivations. In these periods of solitary contemplation and effort, Wittgenstein worked to achieve philosophical successes which he saw as necessary in justifying his own existence. From the age of ten he waged an inner war against the allure of death and a desire to 'lie down one evening and not get up again', exhibiting patterns of depressive behaviour which bore a striking resemblance to those of his two elder brothers, both of whom committed suicide when he was a teenager. It was the shock of their deaths, this original cataclysm, which set Wittgenstein on the path towards recognising his own genius; and which also created a need throughout his life to escape from the 'hell' of his own mind.

Wittgenstein was born in Vienna on 26 April 1889 into a family surrounded by the intellectual and artistic elite. His father, the steel-tycoon Karl Wittgenstein, was an extremely wealthy socialite at the apex of Austro-Hungarian high society, hosting recitals by Mahler, commissioning works by Klimt and with family connections through matrimony to figures like the Nobel Laureate Friedrich Hayek.

The Wittgenstein children were extremely gifted, furiously competitive, and obsessed with musical and academic endeavours. In his early years, Ludwig's personality would develop seemingly in opposition to this ruthless climate. Seen as the least brilliant of the Wittgenstein brood, he was impeccably conscientious, polite and practically capable, but he struggled in school and was overshadowed by the domineering personalities of his older siblings.

Karl Wittgenstein actively encouraged this corrosive competition among his children. He sought to mould his sons in his own industrialist image, home-educating the two eldest brothers in the art of business, smothering their artistic talent, and imprisoning them in journeys into careers they had no desire to enter. Ray Monk, Ludwig's most comprehensive biographer, concluded that 'on Hans and Rudolf the effects of Karl's pressure was disastrous'. Hans committed suicide in 1902, throwing himself from a ship in the Chesapeake Bay. Two years later, in a Berlin piano-bar, Rudolf, too, would publicly poison himself with a lethal concoction of milk and cyanide.

For Ludwig, a teenager at the time of his brothers' deaths, the shock must have been overwhelming. His brothers had resigned their status as honourable men (Ludwig would later describe suicide as a 'dirty thing to do'), as well as their roles as authority figures and objects of a sibling's admiration, jealousy and affection. It has become clear that the consequences of this shocking fracture would massively alter the course of Wittgenstein's life, providing him with the opportunities to become an era-defining philosopher, but with the perpetual curse of being plagued by the same mental torment which had driven his brothers to their deaths.

The shock of the suicides immediately affected Ludwig's circumstances by acting as a wake-up call to his father. He was sent to study at the Realschule in Linz, allowing him to receive a formal education alongside other students his age (including a child by the name of Adolf Hitler). There, he was able to escape the toxic atmosphere of his home, lodging with a family as he began to realise his academic potential.

Wittgenstein would then go on to study mechanical engineering in Berlin and at Manchester University, before attending Cambridge in 1911 to study philosophy under Bertrand Russell, a mentor who would later describe him as 'perhaps the most perfect example I have ever known of a genius as traditionally conceived'. In his biography, Monk writes that Wittgenstein claimed that meeting Russell and learning philosophical logic drew to a close a nine-year period of mental illness, during which he had seriously considered suicide. This is especially significant, as the date of Wittgenstein's meeting with Russell marked the end of a nine-year period since the suicide of his first brother.

At Cambridge Wittgenstein flourished academically, developing his theories on the demarcation of the boundaries of language and meaning for which he is famous today. But the lasting shock from his childhood past continued to mark his life and work. In his article, 'A Nervous Splendour', Anthony Gottlieb describes a moment when Wittgenstein 'asked a pupil if he had ever had any tragedies in his life. The pupil … inquired what he meant by "tragedy". "I mean suicides, madness, or quarrels," replied Ludwig.' It is clear that however much he felt emancipated by Russell's influence or his own intellectual progress, the shock of the suicides of his youth never left Wittgenstein's adult thinking. He may have tried to dismiss and dispel them through tireless work, but their impact was indelible.

Although we cannot enter his mind, we must ask where else the shock of such a personal childhood trauma may have led Wittgenstein's thinking. Did he believe his family possessed inherited suicidal tendencies, with which he himself was tainted? Did he retreat into academic diligence, surrendering himself totally to philosophical enquiry, in order to block out a proneness to anguish which had killed his siblings? After his death, it emerged that his brother Rudolf was gay, and had killed himself due to what he called his 'perverted disposition'. How would Wittgenstein have internalised this motive, when he himself was known to have had at least three romantic relationships with men?

These questions remain unanswered, but their importance cannot be disputed, especially when they concern a man so preoccupied with personal morality. He once wrote in a letter to Russell: '[H]ow can I be a logician before I am a human being? For the most important thing is coming to terms with myself!' But for a depressive, prone to suicidal thinking, coming to terms with himself may have proved a dangerous endeavour. Living a life of ascetic hard work and self-sacrifice may have been the safest way of avoiding questions which might otherwise have provided dangerous answers.

Wittgenstein described suicide as 'a rushing of one's own defences'. As he describes it, it seems to represent a final recourse as part of a broader need to shock himself into feeling alive: to dive into the paradox of taking control by embracing total and final vulnerability. It was this same urge which took hold during his service in the First World War, when he deliberately transferred himself to the front lines where the 'fear of death proved to be both harrowing and clarifying'. And then again, after the war was over, in a depressive episode he committed 'financial suicide' by giving away his inherited fortune. Wittgenstein's was a lifetime spent recoiling from shock by creating it for himself. He exerted control over life's uncertainties and dangers by manufacturing upheavals and losses on his own terms, all the while delving for truths about logic and life in a mind of tempest and torment.

CHAPTER SEVEN

CHILDREN'S LITERATURE

I have never written a children's story but I've had a good idea for one. It occurred as I sat on the balcony of my riverside flat in London, watching a racing spring tide suck the Thames on its 30-mile rush down to the Thames Estuary and the North Sea.

Flotsam and jetsam bobbed rapidly by. A plank, a clump of water-lilies, a polystyrene cup, all bounced past on the current and were quickly gone.

Then I spotted something out of the ordinary. A tiny speck of golden fluff. Hardly bigger than a ping-pong ball, it had a beak, and turned its head this way and that in panic. Helpless against the current, this new-hatched duckling was being swept towards Southend and the open sea. Somewhere in the shallows upstream the chick must have become detached from the rest of his mother duck's brood. Snatched by the current, he had been pulled away from security, shelter, everything he knew. Poor little thing.

But what a children's story! *The Lost Duckling*. Think of the narrative. What would this chick see on his involuntary cruise to who-knows-where? The towers and cranes of Canary Wharf, the catamaran riverbuses roaring by – perhaps he'd be whooshed between the twin blades of their hulls – the great container ships at their riverside quays, the reeds and marshes of the lower Thames, the mudbanks and islets, the (to him) giant swans, the other families of ducks and ducklings turning their tails on him as he swept helplessly on, the cruise liner towering over him, a seal, the heave of ocean waves in the estuary, night falling, the shore-lights twinkling ...

And then what? A new life ... an existence on the other side of the ebb tide now drawing him from where he'd once nestled beneath his mother's wing.

Writing for children is a very special talent which I surely lack. But, written well, I know beyond doubt that this simple plot has the makings of a tale to hold children spellbound. Why? Because it is about the loss of everything; and the smashing of the known to unlock the unknown is the archetype of a thousand stories. Children are fascinated – by turns thrilled and terrified – by the idea of their known world being wrenched away, and having to start out anew.

I suggest that most of the most famous and enduring children's stories are of this type. A large claim. But, recalling your own childhood, pluck from the air the stories, traditional or modern, that come immediately to mind, and ask yourself how many of them contain childhood hardship or wretchedness, a frightening fracture in the form of an apparent catastrophe, horrific incident or life-changing event, and a new life, new wisdom and happiness, or some other great reward.

★

The Wizard of Oz

The original film version of *The Wonderful Wizard of Oz* begins in sepia-tinted black and white. Some way in, however, the film switches to colour. And the point at which that happens is immediately after the moment when Dorothy's young life breaks apart: the story's heroine and her dog have been lifted by a tornado from Kansas and have crashed to the ground in Munchkinland. As Dorothy regains consciousness her life and the film turn from black and white to full colour. The yellow brick road stretches before her. Dorothy's wonderful adventures begin.

Synopses of *The Wonderful Wizard of Oz* often start with that crash landing on the green grass of Munchkinland. But what adults forget, children notice: that where the magic begins is not where the story begins. Dorothy is miserable in Kansas. Troubles beset her. She appears to have no parents, only foster parents. Because he bit, Toto, Dorothy's beloved dog, has been taken away by a nasty landlady to be destroyed. Toto has escaped and trotted home but must soon be sent back – by law – to his execution. Foster parents Aunty Em and Uncle Henry have let Dorothy down cruelly, failing to take her side and instead cooperating in the planned confiscation of Toto. Profoundly disillusioned, the little girl has already tried once to run away. She has lost faith in grown-ups, lost faith in their laws and their rules, is about to lose Toto, and has no-one left to turn to.

> When Dorothy stood in the doorway and looked around, she could see nothing but the great grey prairie on every side. Not a tree nor a house broke

the broad sweep of flat country that reached to the edge of the sky in all directions. The sun had baked the ploughed land into a grey mass, with little cracks running through it. Even the grass was not green.

Then comes the tornado. When Dorothy comes to, she's in another land. Her old life has been wiped. She's a new child, in a new place, setting out on a new road with new friends to new adventures, new self-confidence and a new sense of herself and her potential.

Near the end of the book Dorothy makes it back to Kansas alive – and altered. A once lonely girl, she has forged powerful friendships that have changed others' lives too. She has taken control of her destiny and that of her companions. And she has gained understanding. This transformation could not have happened without shock and violent dislocation: a catastrophic event like the tornado. The miserable start to her life and her loss of faith in homestead and homeland is an essential part of the remaking of Dorothy: they form the bedrock of the film's message. Dorothy needed first to be alone, abandoned; she needed to despair.

Children's literature understands loneliness – whether the silence of an empty room or the hubbub of a crowd of strangers. Many stories explore what it means for a child to feel solitary, deserted, persecuted, lost, or to find themselves in a strange place. Hundreds of such stories – some ancient, some modern – have imprinted themselves on our modern consciousness, as this beloved story has.

The book took American childhood by storm. By the time *The Wonderful Wizard of Oz* emerged from copyright in the middle of the twentieth century, L. Frank Baum's novel had sold more than three million copies. The illustrated edition had been a soaraway success from the day it was first published in 1900. Often censured or disapproved of by adults (and in America occasionally banned) for its escapism and indifferent literary merit, the simple tale struck a chord in the juvenile imagination that reverberated through the century and around the globe. Translated into every major world language and into film, plays and musicals, its guiding idea (set into song as 'Somewhere Over the Rainbow') helped launch Judy Garland's career. *The Wizard of Oz* has taken its place among the top children's classics of all time.

Why? First celebrated for being (quite a novelty at the time) a peculiarly 'American' children's story, its deeper claim to immortality is that it is no such thing. It is anchored not in turn-of-the-century Kansas, but in the timeless, placeless landscape of the human unconscious.

Bambi

Based on a 1923 book by an Austrian author, the Disney film *Bambi* is a story of catastrophic loss in early life. The young deer sees his mother shot by 'Man' – the human hunters – and, apparently orphaned, discovers that he is in fact the offspring of the 'Great Prince of the Forest', a heroic buck. After trauma comes the realisation of greatness, and Bambi, who finds courage and resourcefulness in the struggle to protect his kind, emerges as the new prince of the forest.

The Walt Disney film has been judged a crowning achievement for Walt himself, although his daughter complained that the opening murder was too cruel, and Bambi's mother did not need to die. Yet the film's international success and enduring fame depends critically on that early scene in which the young Bambi sees the only source of love and security in the forest, his mother, slain before his eyes.

Dick Whittington

The real Richard Whittington was (it is thought) a fourteenth-century mercer – and the grandson of a knight, so the chances of his having been the penniless wanderer with a rat-catching cat of the famous tale are slim. Indeed, the way in which re-telling has airbrushed his comfortable start from the picture, and invented his youthful woes, is significant in itself.

But the legend of Dick Whittington only needs a patina of truth. In the story that has grown up, Dick is an orphaned, impoverished young lad who falls in with a wagon team and, with only a knapsack and his cat, makes for London – where, he has heard, the streets are paved with gold.

But there he discovers the miserable truth. Dick ends up working as a scullion in a kitchen, a job he hates. In despair, he decides to leave the city. But as Dick trudges away from disappointment he hears church bells ringing, and, in their call hears the refrain: 'Turn again, Whittington, thou worthy citizen, Lord Mayor of London.' He turns – and with him his fate – returning to the capital with his cat and working his way up to riches, honour, and thrice-renewed appointment as Lord Mayor of London.

'Hansel and Gretel' by the Brothers Grimm

In this German fairy-tale Hansel and Gretel's evil step-mother has persuaded their kindly but weak father to walk them into the middle of the forest and leave them to die of starvation, or worse: a reminder of the childhood terror of getting lost – a terror we all but forget after growing up. She says there is not enough bread in the house to sustain a family of four.

In a bid to avoid starvation the children stumble on something almost as bad: in their hunger they find a gingerbread house in the forest. And, inside, a witch who tries, and fails, to eat them.

Instead they summon up their courage, kill her, find her treasure and go home, rich and confident. Even more happily, their evil stepmother is now dead and they are reunited with their father, freed from her cruel grasp.

Oliver Twist by Charles Dickens

Oliver's life begins badly and gets worse. His unmarried mother, dying as she gives birth to him, holds her infant son, and gives him a last kiss.

Oliver is raised in an unspeakable workhouse run by a hypocrite where, like the other orphans, he is starved. They draw straws to see who must ask for more and Oliver picks the shortest. He asks his famous question, and is expelled for his cheek. The story would be nothing without its beginning: in tragedy, cruelty, flight, dislocation and finally impertinence. The first and most important of many fractures, for Oliver, is drawing the short straw and being forced to ask for more. It is really where the story begins. The child's obedience breaks. Then his life, as well as Dickens's story, begins. Is it a children's story? Read to me as a child, I loved it. In musical and movie form it has always been family entertainment.

Our hero is taken in by a brutal funeral director named Sowerberry, but there things go wrong and it is not long before Oliver is beaten. He escapes to London where he falls in with the Artful Dodger and then Fagin's rascally pickpocketing crew. In criminality, however, he finds for the first time something like warmth. Oliver's life is one of risk and perpetual motion. Eventually he is rescued by a kindly gentleman and his housekeeper. His life at the close of the book is assured and happy.

The Pied Piper of Hamelin

Told in many versions and languages, the story originated in the German town of Hamelin in the Middle Ages. In the version best known today the town, plagued with rats, makes a deal with a stranger in pied garb whose magical piping talent enables him to draw the rodents away, presumably to their perdition.

But the town refuses to pay the piper. So he employs his magical musical power to steal their children by piping them away to a magic mountain (or destruction, in some versions). Depending, again, on the version, one little boy is saved because, being disabled, he cannot keep up with the herd; or three are saved, one because he is lame, one because he is blind and can't see where to go, and one because he is deaf and cannot hear the music.

'The Ugly Duckling' by Hans Christian Andersen

A mother duck sits on her brood, bored and lonely, willing her eggs to hatch. At long last the offspring all crack their eggshells and wriggle free. All, that is, save one, the biggest of the lot, which a passing duck warns her could be a turkey egg.

She perseveres because 'I have sat so long already, a few days will be nothing'. Then the egg hatches. What emerges is ugly, ungainly and unique: 'It is very large and not at all like the others,' the mother says to herself, 'I wonder if it really is a turkey.' The poor duckling, unlike his comely brothers and sisters, is scorned and driven away. He flees to live among wild waterfowl, shady humans, and then in a cave, alone. Near the end of the book he resolves to throw himself to the swans in a kind of suicide, because they will most likely kill him.

But they welcome him and he catches sight of his own reflection. At last he has matured: into a beautiful swan. Central to its appeal is its recognition of something so many children have experienced: the feeling that they are in the wrong place, the wrong company, the wrong time: trapped, caged, their true nature unrecognised.

★

Fiction is evidence of the shape we choose to give life stories. The recurring themes among most of these stories suggest that there is in all of us, and from the earliest years, a powerful subconscious understanding that the very things that, as helpless children, we crave – love, security, certainty, a trusted, accepted and familiar framework to our lives – also stifle something special and individual within us.

So in almost every case, in order for the child to break free, to become truly exceptional, the narrative equivalent of a great hammer from the sky has to come down and smash the prison walls and the low expectations within which the child is confined.

Beneath a thousand different stories this narrative template can be spotted. I am neither alone nor early in noticing this. The twentieth-century American writer and mythologist, Joseph Campbell, argues in his 1949 study, *The Hero with a Thousand Faces*, that there exists a sort of skeleton or template within most myths, and this is true through most cultures and all history: the same bones beneath the flesh of a million stories. Campbell calls it the Monomyth. He cites examples of mythical lives in stories about children, and told to children (and adults): evidence, he says, for his theory that:

> The child of destiny has to face a long period of obscurity. This is a time of extreme danger, impediment, or disgrace. He is thrown inward to his own depths or outward to the unknown; either way, what he touches is a darkness unexplored. And this is a zone of unsuspected presences, benign as well as malignant: an angel appears, a helpful animal, a fisherman, a hunter, crone, or peasant. Fostered in the animal school, or, like Siegfried, below ground among the gnomes that nourish the roots of the tree of life, or again, alone in some little room (the story has been told a thousand ways), the young world-apprentice learns the lesson of

the seed powers, which reside just beyond the sphere of the measured and the named.

[These] myths agree that an extraordinary capacity is required to face and survive such experience. The infancies abound in anecdotes of precocious strength, cleverness, and wisdom. Herakles strangled a serpent sent against his cradle by the goddess Hera. Maui of Polynesia snared and slowed the sun – to give his mother time to cook her meals. Abraham, as we have seen, arrived at the knowledge of the One God. Jesus confounded the wise men. The baby Buddha had been left one day beneath the shade of a tree; his nurses suddenly noted that the shadow had not moved all afternoon and that the child was sitting fixed in a yogic trance ...

If Campbell is right, how does the Monomyth gain entrance to children's literature in the first place? More than in any other branch of literature, children's stories are made by children: not so much by individual children (as adult novels are made by an individual novelist) as by all children; children as an audience – the Universal Child, you might say.

This is because while children's *books* are a relatively recent arrival beginning in the mid-eighteenth century, children's stories have been around since the dawn of man: handed down from generation to generation. Only much later, and three centuries after the invention of the printing press, did many of these emerge in printed form. So there's a real sense in which most enduring children's stories have been authored only partly by a particular adult, but crucially, also, by Childhood: the childish imagination in which every children's story must sink or swim.

All these tales have had to pass one essential test in order to survive: their immediate, untutored, spontaneous appeal to the listening child. This was the filter through which every children's story had to pass. The child is a merciless, rude and untutored book critic. If a story doesn't fast grip and hold the juvenile imagination, it won't be retold and it won't be remembered. Children's literature therefore presents a particularly undoctored snapshot of the longings, hatreds, resentments, sympathies, thrills, and perhaps unconscious self-knowledge, of the Universal Child. These tales are an unusually pure representation of juvenile understanding and feeling.

For most children, these stories – with their apple carts upset and things turned topsy-turvy, their horrified fascination with the idea of being lost and alone – are just fantasies. But for so many of the Great Lives I've been learning about over the last fourteen years, the apocalypse was real. Observation of children's literature teaches us that all children feel that catastrophe might open the door. Observation of the lives I've studied teaches me that sometimes they are right.

One more point must be made. Any successful children's author, and any parent who reads or invents bedtime stories for their child, will tell you that the tales that appeal most are those that the child can imagine happening to them. The kind of literature that grows out of a mother telling a story to her child has at its core the idea that this child is special, and in some way marked out. It's about the realisation and creation of the individual as a separate, special thing – often though not always by being broken off, abandoned, lost, torn away. In *Reminiscences of a Gentlewoman of the Last Century: Letters of Catherine Hutton* (1891), Mrs Hutton's childhood fantasies are altogether more cheerful:

> Nothing delighted me so much as 'The Tales of the Fairies.' I no more doubted their truth than I did my own existence – nay, how did I know that I was not a fairy myself! It was at least worth the trial, and the trial was easily made! I understood the whole perfectly, except what the mighty instrument which made all the transformations might be, and I asked my mother what a wand was. She, not being deeply versed in fairy lore, replied, 'It is a white stick.' Is that all, thought I, then I can soon get a wand! Accordingly I procured a green stick and peeled it, and, striking three times on the parlour grate, as customary with the fairies, I commanded the grate to become gold. Not a particle of the stubborn steel would change colour; I found I was not a fairy, and I was rather ashamed of the experiment.

This book is about people who, like little Catherine, decided to make their own wands. But my people are real people, not fairies. And their wands worked.

CHAPTER EIGHT

RELIGION, MYTH AND LEGEND

Messiahs and prophets: Jesus and Mohammed

> Did he not find thee an orphan and shelter thee?
> Did he not find thee erring and guide thee?
> Did he not find thee needy and suffice thee?

Abū al-Qāsim Muḥammad ibn ʿAbd Allāh ibn ʿAbd al-Muṭṭalib ibn Hāshim – the Prophet Mohammed – was probably born around AD 570, in Mecca. Little is known for a fact about his early years before (it is written) revelations started coming to him around the age of forty; but three tremendous events in infancy and childhood stand out from the accounts we have. Each one is a death.

The first was the death of his father, Abdallah, before he was born, meaning that his widow was now, as religious historian Karen Armstrong puts it, 'in such straitened circumstances that he was able to leave her only five camels and a young slave girl called Bahira'.

It is said that the child was then sent for fostering in the desert among the Bedouin, returning to his mother and paternal grandfather, Abdul-Muttalib, at the age of two.

Then, when he was six, his mother, Amina, died. Two years later, when Mohammed was eight, his grandfather died. The orphan was billeted on an uncle. According to Islamic historian William Montgomery Watt, in sixth-century Mecca there was a general disregard on the part of guardians in taking care of weaker members of the tribes. 'Mohammed's guardians saw that he did not starve to death, but it was hard for them to do more for him ....'

And so the life of the Prophet began. He would become more than a great religious leader – he would become a philosophical mould-breaker. He came to a culture that had lost its bearings, to defy the prevailing polytheism and affirm the ancient teaching that there is one God. Father-less, then motherless, finally robbed of the grandfather who loved him most and pushed into the care of people who would not cherish him, he would go on to turn his back on the world, retreat into caves, and think anew.

Of course, as with other messiahs, what we can really know about these lives is fragmentary, so interwoven with legend, interpretation and intimations of the supernat-ural that the hard facts are all but lost to us. But in one sense the facts do not matter. Unless you are a biblical or koranic literalist, you may see the lives of long-dead mes-siahs and prophets as existing in a half-light between myth and reality. From this book's point of view, the myth is as interesting as the reality because – as children's stories do in a different way – the myths and legends we construct betray humanity's own half-buried understanding of the wellsprings of individual development, human behaviour, and perhaps, exceptionality. It starts with Rejection.

Whether or not (as claimed) the breasts of the infant

Mohammed's wet nurse in the desert really did overflow with milk when the orphan's lips were pressed to her teat (legend suggests that a nearby camel's udders overflowed in a sympathetic reaction), whether or not Romulus and Remus, founders of Rome and its empire, really were suckled by a she-wolf, whether or not Moses did arrive cast adrift in the bulrushes, what interests this book is the intuitive power of those images. The hero or saviour emerges not on a gilded chariot and velvet cushions, the pampered product of sound parenting and the best education money can buy, but from the weeds, from the wilderness, from a childhood shattered by loss. What gives this archetypal storyline its universal grip on the human imagination?

The answer, I submit, is that at some deep level we know this kind of thing happens; and from our knowledge of ourselves as well as others we can sense the liberating power of loss. Freedom is born in despair. Vision, revelation, are apt to arrive in the wilderness not the boardroom.

*

In this chapter, then, we're looking at the legends that faith has spun around its messiahs, gurus and earthly deities, not with any biographical focus on real fracture in real lives that are usually so far beyond our reach, but as a route to understanding the insight that human beings have into themselves, their own nature and development; and the changes trauma can bring.

Looked at in that light, we see another story – that of Jesus – as a legend about transcendence: a transcendence born from despair; indeed, born in a stable.

Poverty, panic as a woman close to term finds herself helpless in an alien town; a stable full of beasts, unmarried motherhood, an elusive (to say the least) natural father; a visit by kings from the East who have themselves made a journey through desolation and the unknown; then boyhood as a child who had been conceived out of wedlock and who was not his earthly father's son.

And just as this life starts, in desperation, so it ends, when Jesus crucified cries out on the cross 'My God, my God, why hast thou forsaken me?' Both legends attest powerfully to something human beings believe or even, perhaps, at an unconscious level, know: that there's an important link between (on the one hand) genius, inspiration and a breaking of the chains of convention that can imprison mind and spirit, and – on the other – despair, loneliness, stigma and catastrophic loss. In the legend of faith, spiritual leaders have a habit of coming to us out of fire, abandonment and the desert.

Perhaps the God of our imagination needs to break us before we can be remade in his image. D. H. Lawrence's poem 'Shadows', written not long before his death in 1930 from the ill-health that had dogged him since youth, is an extraordinarily imaginative and powerful expression of this idea, penned by a man who was not conventionally religious.

And if tonight my soul may find her peace
in sleep, and sink in good oblivion,
and in the morning wake like a new-opened flower
then I have been dipped again in God, and new-created.

And if, as weeks go round, in the dark of the moon
my spirit darkens and goes out, and soft strange gloom
pervades my movements and my thoughts and words
then I shall know that I am walking still
with God, we are close together now the moon's in
    shadow.

And if, as autumn deepens and darkens
I feel the pain of falling leaves, and stems that break
    in storms
and trouble and dissolution and distress
and then the softness of deep shadows folding,
folding around my soul and spirit, around my lips
so sweet, like a swoon, or more like the drowse of a
    low, sad song
singing darker than the nightingale, on, on to the
    solstice
and the silence of short days, the silence of the year,
    the shadow,
then I shall know that my life is moving still
with the dark earth, and drenched
with the deep oblivion of earth's lapse and renewal.

And if, in the changing phases of man's life
I fall in sickness and in misery
my wrists seem broken and my heart seems dead
and strength is gone, and my life
is only the leavings of a life:

and still, among it all, snatches of lovely oblivion, and
    snatches of renewal

odd, wintry flowers upon the withered stem, yet
   new, strange flowers
such as my life has not brought forth before, new
   blossoms of me

then I must know that still
I am in the hands of the unknown God,
he is breaking me down to his own oblivion
to send me forth on a new morning, a new man.

The theme of redemption, rebirth and revelation through personal fracture is richly woven through Christian prose, poetry and hymn-writing. The examples are legion, and the underlying theme is clear. We must be broken before we can see God properly. Worldly success blinds us to God's truth. Pride must be humbled, human certainties banished, 'mammon' cast aside, conventional values and habits of mind blown away like fog before we can see the Celestial clearly, before we can understand. Something like a death becomes the precursor to rebirth.

    You may be inspired, unconvinced or even repelled by stories of transfiguration through the breaking down of the 'old' person; but whatever your judgement you will see beneath a thousand stories the same story. Comfort, pride and security must be shattered before we can seek and find the truth.

St Patrick

The boy was sixteen, the men were much older. They were pirates and slave-traders. One day they came for him and carried him away to an island over the sea where they sold him at auction. There, on the desolate slopes of a dead volcano, the boy began a new life as a herdsman for sheep and pigs.

It would have been lonely. Like all shepherds he was at the mercy of the elements. His thoughts no doubt wandered to his family over the sea. His father was a priest, his mother the kinswoman of a bishop. They were well born, with ancestral links to the continent. And there he was: stuck on a bare hillside, lashed by rain, with only beasts for company.

Much later in his life he wrote 'I was sixteen and knew not the true God, but in a strange land the Lord opened my unbelieving eyes, and I was converted.' God, he believed, had entered his wretched enslaved life.

Then, after six years in captivity, a miraculous escape. Somehow he got free. Fleeing on foot he reached a faraway harbour. He talked his way onto a boat and sailed for his family – a changed man.

Back home one night he lay in bed and dreamt. His dream told him to spread the word of God in the place of his captivity. He left home again – now not as a slave but as a scholar. He took religious orders and studied keenly in the cloisters of a monastery. At the end of his twelfth year, he was at last ready to fulfil the instruction of his dream.

And finally, he went back to the island where he had been enslaved and wretched. For the rest of his life he criss-crossed the green land, preaching the word of God and, slowly but surely, converting its people.

During the course of his preaching he performed many miracles and incredible feats. In the middle of a forty-day fast on top of a hill he was attacked by snakes. In retribution he drove them, and all other snakes, from the land into the sea. This was St Patrick, the sixteen-year-old boy, taken by pirates, whose life was smashed apart by captivity.

St Joseph of Copertino

Before St Joseph of Copertino was born his father suffered a fate common to many others in seventeenth-century Europe: ruin. Felix Copertino was a carpenter whose generous loan to a friend went badly wrong. Creditors came knocking and Felix had to flee, pleading for sanctuary at the altar of a church.

What Joseph's pregnant mother, Francesca Panara, thought about Felix's financial misdemeanours history has not recorded. But it is no great leap to imagine she will have been angry and despairing, penniless and pregnant as she was. Unfortunately, the son was the child of his father. He was difficult, disappointing (in his own way) and hard work.

An inward-looking child, Joseph experienced his first apparent ecstasies aged eight. They left him in a stupor, with his mouth agape (later in life he was cruelly nicknamed *boccaperta*). Worse followed: a sore on his buttocks, as 'large as a melon', and which stank to the heavens, according to biographer Michael Grosso. It was excised in a terrifying procedure undertaken by a local hermit with a reputation as a surgeon. Joseph's father himself, in one story, emerged from hiding, watched the operation, and made a vain protest as the silver forceps were heated.

Joseph's wounds were soothed with unguent. He recovered, though not well.

Grosso blames Joseph's years of sickness for making him into something of a clod: 'The bedridden years had disrupted his psychomotor development, which soon became evident in his behaviour, which at first was marked by a clumsiness and general disjointedness.'

Kinder sources blame Joseph's notorious ill-handling of pans and plates (he was thrown out of a monastery for breaking so many) on a higher calling. 'Some have ascribed this awkwardness to a defect of sight. Another and truer explanation is that his surroundings inflamed him with the fire of divine love to such a degree that his soul was continually enraptured.'[23] This generous attribution doubles as a gentle reminder of the perils involved in saintly biographies.

Joseph's melon-sized abscess didn't just leave physical scars. He had spent years in pain, unable to walk. He found solace at the altar, relief in Christ. The outer world was an unforgiving, brutish place. His inner world – introspection, reflection and meditation – made a boy, then a young man, ill-equipped for the terrestrial world. Yet as a holy man he flourished, even within his lifetime.

To St Joseph of Copertino are attributed some of the wildest tales of any saint: that he could levitate into mid-air; that stigmata appeared on his hands and bled. Unorthodox minds find themselves drawn to his story. Grosso, whose story of Joseph's life is soberly told, opens his book by reflecting that 'Joseph's story has implications for the mind-body problem, for the study of extraordinary mental and physical phenomena, for possible links to the new physics'.

But these questions and investigations need not concern us. In his life, Joseph's apparent miracles and his steady devotion to God brought him the attention of his country. And the interest of the pope. He was seen as a holy man in his lifetime; he was canonised shortly after his death.

In St Joseph's story we see yet again the tale of an individual who suffered, was nearly broken, but was made anew by their experiences. His travails pushed him away from this world, closer to heaven (either through ecstasies or by floating), closer to greatness. His fractured life made him the saint he became.

St Germaine

Scrofulous, half-orphaned, beaten, accidentally exhumed: not a great cv. This woman – who would later be canonised – had a tough life by any standards.

Germaine was perhaps still in her cradle when her mother died. Marie Laroche had married Laurent Cousin, a farmhand, and given birth to a little girl in 1579 in a village, Pibrac, not far from Toulouse.

Germaine's rotten luck got worse – and brought her that enmity peculiar to sick individuals. She had a deformed, useless right hand and was ill with scrofula, an infection of the glands of the neck which caused unsightly swellings. Everyone hated her, including her stepmother. Germaine is said to have been kept away from her brothers and sisters, sleeping in a cupboard under the stairs. What food she ate was scraps. Of what love or kindness she received we know nothing. And then she was gone – into the fields, as soon as possible, to work as a shepherd.

Out in the open air, she tended her flock well. But she had one foible. The moment church bells sounded from the village, Germaine heeded their call and entrusted her flock to a guardian angel.

'Never once on her return did she find that a sheep had strayed, or had fallen a prey to the wolves that lurked in the neighbouring forest of Bouconne, ever-ready to pounce upon unattended sheep.'

It took a while for the villagers to realise who – or what – was among them. But one day Germaine was coming home, pursued by her stepmother, who suspected her of thieving bread and hiding it in the folds of her apron. Before worried neighbours could step in, Germaine let slip the apron and out fell summer flowers. This was in the middle of a freezing winter.

It was only then, biographers relate, that 'the inhabitants of Pibrac began to realise that they had a saint in their midst'.

Germaine's short life was marked by illness, poverty and cruelty. She was found dead at the age of twenty-two on a straw pallet under the stairs. Her body was accidentally exhumed forty-three years later, and found in 'perfect preservation'. It was then placed in a special leaden coffin in the sacristy of the church at Pibrac. Sixteen years later it was apparently 'well preserved' and 'still flexible'. The miracle confirmed her status.

Martin de Porres

On his canonisation in 1962, St Martin de Porres, the patron saint of interracial harmony, was honoured in song. More than four hundred years after his death, American jazz pianist Mary Lou Williams sang of de Porres:

> This man of love, born of the flesh, yet of God
> This humble man healed the sick, raised the dead, his
>   hand is quick
> To feed beggars and sinners, the starving homeless
>   and the stray
> Oh Black Christ of the Andes, come feed and cure us
>   now we pray

Yet de Porres had begun life in distress. Born in 1579 in Lima, the illegitimate son of a white Spaniard and a black former slave, he was raised in poverty. His early life faced prejudice, struggle and suffering. But from a young age de Porres dedicated himself to the service of others and began to volunteer in the infirmary of a local monastery. Although it was unusual to accept someone of mixed race into a religious order, de Porres's dedication allowed him to join the Dominicans in 1601. He would remain there as a servant and lay brother for the rest of his life.

There, this patient and pious man served tirelessly as barber, surgeon and storekeeper. He lived simply, making the storeroom of the monastery his cell. In the small room he kept bedding to give to the sick and clothing and money to give to the poor. Without consideration of race or birth, de Porres gave alms freely to all. His charity extended to animals, with whom he was said to have had an exceptional affinity. When mosquitoes bit him, he accepted their sting willingly, declaring that 'we must also feed the little creatures of God'. In contrast to his generosity to others, de Porres's treatment of himself was unsparing. He lived a life of strict austerity; he fasted, abstained from meat, and wore a hair shirt and heavy, rough tunic next to his skin. 'Avid for suffering', as the priest Columba Ryan has described him, each night de Porres beat his naked body with a hide.

However, it was not only for his goodness or asceticism that the poor and unassuming servant's reputation began to grow; many apparently great miracles are ascribed to him. De Porres came to be known for instant and miraculous cures of the sick. He was said to levitate into the air and once even made a young novice, disappointed in his small stature, grow tall overnight. It is impossible to say whether de Porres's goodness to others – to the sick and needy, to the fractured souls of Lima – would have been enough to gather his band of devotees, but in the years that followed his death the miracles attributed to him began to multiply and his legacy was secured.

When de Porres died in 1639 he had broken barriers of birth, race and social convention to win the affection of his Dominican brothers and Christians beyond. He was finally canonised in 1962 when the church began to consider its responsibility in responding to questions of race. Yet beyond any stories of miracles and self-mortification, de Porres is perhaps best remembered for his goodness and humility; the careful keeper of the monastery storeroom, pictured, as Mary Lou Williams sang in 1962, with 'his shepherd's staff a dusty broom'. He was not raised to the company of saints despite his rough and troubled start, but because of it.

Myth and legend

In this book I have distinguished carefully between two ideas, related but different: suffering as a test and toughener-up of people; and fracture as a liberator of the extraordinary in people. The first is best encapsulated in Friederich Nietzsche's maxim that whatever doesn't kill you makes you strong. The role of fracture in myth, discussed here, has elements of both ideas. Consider David, and Goliath. To take on a fearsome giant when armed only with a stone and sling was certainly the making of David in Nietzsche's sense. The ordeal seemed likely to end the boy's life, and emerging victorious from it will have taught him to be a warrior, and later a king; and taught him a useful lesson in slingsmanship too.

But his terror in facing death and his exhilaration at escaping it will also have broken in him the chains of self-doubt, all those lessons the young shepherd boy will have learned about knowing his place and every assumption that convention suggests, that the weak are powerless in the face of the mighty; taught him that, in the words of Ecclesiastes: 'I returned and saw under the sun that the race is not to the swift, nor the battle to the strong, neither yet bread to the wise, nor yet riches to men of understanding, nor yet favour to men of skill.'

In myth and legend, what doesn't kill our heroes does indeed make them strong; but there is a death, too. Hesitation, cowardice, a precautionary sense of one's own limitations, submission to the expectations of others ... all these things die as the hero faces his horrors, surprises himself and others, and learns that he can triumph. The supreme tests of the mythological hero are the very reason we place stock in their stories. Trial, adversity and fracture are at their heart. That's why these stories have survived the ages.

Cú Chulainn

The Irish tale of Cú Chulainn and the Táin Bó Cúailnge is an early medieval mythological cycle that again sees a young man pitted against incredible odds. With the rest of his countrymen laid low by a plague, seventeen-year-old Cú Chulainn is called upon to defend Ulster's borders alone, as Queen Medb of Connacht and her armies descend on his land with all their might. Their aim? To steal the legendary Brown Bull of Cooley.

The Cattle Raid of Cooley – as the title translates – sounds rather whimsical. But, as literary critic Bruce Lincoln writes, in ancient Indo-European societies, cattle was gold. Cattle raids form the basis of countless early myths, from Iran to Ireland. Indeed, eleven other Irish stories bear the title Táin Bó (cattle raid), and cattle theft appears in the Iliad and the Odyssey. In much of rural Africa today, 'cattle' means wealth and security. And the stakes don't come much higher than they do in a raid. This is made clear in an early episode of the Táin, in which we are told how Cú Chulainn earned his name – 'Hound of Culann'. Aged seven, a young boy named Setima follows his uncle, Conchobar, the king of Ulster, to a feast on a farm belonging to a blacksmith named Culann. The boy arrives late and uninvited. Culann's fierce guard dog, perceiving an intruder, leaps on him. Setima proceeds to rip the dog limb from limb, saving his own life but leaving

Culann's cattle and property without protection. When the distraught Culann protests, Setima vows to serve in the dog's place, until he has raised another whelp to guard the farmer's property. Renamed Cú Chulainn, the boy proceeds to fight off wolves and intruders who lay siege to his new master's cattle.

By this point then, Cú Chulainn has already done plenty to prove himself. He now commands the respect of his enemies. Then, as the growing child's life unfolds, his mettle is tested again and again, and he is mocked before each contest. They scorn the 'beardless boy' only for Cú Chulainn to dispatch each adversary with ease, fighting them at a ford on Ulster's borders. The weight of the 'ordeal' soon grows heavy on the (now) young man's shoulders. He declares:

> I am alone against hordes
> I cannot stop nor let go.
> I stand here in the long cold hours
> Alone against every foe.

The ultimate reckoning and 'ordeal' comes when Cú Chulainn's 'foe' is a blood brother, friend and mentor, Fer Diad. In a three-day contest against Ireland's (until then) greatest warrior, through taunts and trials, Cú Chulainn emerges victorious but gravely wounded. It is the definitive proof of his valour: he has not only faced the ultimate in ferocity, he has also set sentimentality to one side, in service of king and country.

The Táin is a bloody and at times gruesome read but Cú Chulainn's heroics stretch beyond the battlefield. I

mentioned the importance of the human side to mythological stories. The hero's strength far exceeds ours and
his feats are exceptional; but a robot, or monster, might
achieve as much. For the myth to succeed as legend, the
hero must be all too human, must go through the pain we
suffer so that we may see ourselves in him. In Cú Chulainn's case, the emotional torment caused by the battle with
Fer Diad proves his heroism. For the love of his uncle and
king, he faces down a true friend. Inner turmoil as well as
outward pluck are at the heart of so many of these stories.
After their ordeal, our mythological heroes are different
people entirely.

In his 1957 work *Mythologies*, the French philosopher
Roland Barthes discusses the simplicity of myth. It does
nothing by half measures. It favours absolute values and
emotions, which create characters and situations that are
whole and complete. Thus any initial fracture or trauma
must always be corrected by the end of the tale. This is the
case in both 'exposure' myths, such as that of Romulus
and Remus, and in 'ordeal' myths, where the likes of Cú
Chulainn overcome an early challenge and emerge as
heroes. Barthes explains this by saying that myth is a 'form
of language, chosen by history' to serve a specific purpose.
Emptied of complications and contradictions, stories are
made that embody universal values: confidence, justice,
retribution, glory, love. Myth achieves this by 'transform-
ing history into nature', taking historical events of variable
authenticity and crystallising them in the national psyche
as epics.

This is not to say that myth is taken as historical fact.
Probably only the most fervent of Romans believed that

Romulus and Remus were suckled by a she-wolf. All, however, would have believed that Rome was born of hardship and sacrifice and worth defending with their lives.

The attraction of myth is obvious and its heroes and heroines need neither be real nor even believed to be real. But they must always be creatures with whom we can empathise. They must be recognisably human, even if also superhuman. They get shaken up, as we do; conflicted, as we do; hurt, as we do. And we see these thrusts of fortune not as mere trifles to the hero, irritations to be brushed aside by strength, but as cutting him or her sometimes to the quick. They are more than just proofs of greatness; they are part of its genesis.

Foundlings

Foundlings are everywhere in early mythology. They turn up in wild places like mountainsides, rivers and shorelines; chanced upon by peasants, kings, beasts and Pharaoh's daughter. In fact, modern readers of Greek, Roman, Himalayan, Egyptian and Mesopotamian myths can barely turn a page without stumbling over yet another forsaken baby.

Exposure of infants – abandoning babies to the world – was and is part of real life. In his way, the newborn Moses was an early forerunner of the twentieth-century baby left on a doorstep or in a phone box. But while exposure places a child in grave danger, it is not the same as infanticide: a stranger, or Fate, may save it. The possibility of salvation – victory from the jaws of death – leaves the story open.

The towering figures of myth were often exposed at birth. Soon after being born, Moses, the greatest prophet

of the Bible, finds himself inside a tiny ark made of bulrushes. He floats down the river into a reed bank and into
the arms of the Pharaoh's daughter. Sceaf, an Anglo-Lom-
bardian hero, washes up on English shores in a boat on top
of a sheaf (or in the Anglo-Saxon, 'sceaf') of grain, later to
become a king. Trakhan, a medieval king of the Himalayan mountain city of Gilgit, was sealed up inside a barrel
by his mother soon after his birth and floated downstream.
Luckily, two poor brothers see the river cargo, believe
it holds great treasure, haul it in and so save the infant
future king. The Mahābhārata, a Hindu sacred text, tells
of Karna, a child of the sun god bound up in a rush basket
which is sealed with wax and then dropped in the river.
But Karna is saved by the childless charioteer Azirath and
his wife Rhadha, who happen to see him as they walk past.

Such stories were not just told about the subjects of
myth, they were sometimes told by them. The mightiest
lords, like Sargon, an ancient king of Akkad, adopted and
embraced the foundling motif themselves. Sargon carved
the story of his early life into clay tablets which were found
by archaeologists millennia later among the ruined library
of Ashurbanipal.

The legend of his birth read:

In my city Azupirani, situated on the bank of the
Euphrates, my mother, the vestal, conceived me. In
a hidden place she gave birth to me. She laid me in a
vessel made of reeds, closed my door with pitch, and
dropped me down into the river, which did not drown
me. The river carried me to Akki, the water carrier.
In the kindness of his heart, Akki the water carrier

lifted me up. Akki the water carrier raised me as his own son.

Foundlings are the ultimate orphans of the storm, and myth-makers of all stripes loved such stories. But why has the human race been so keen to trace the greatness of the adult hero back to babes who came out of the weeds and the wilds? The answer tells us something about the persuasive power of fracture as an explanation for the exceptional in later life.

Exposure grants a terrible kind of freedom. Who has authority over a found baby, untethered in the world? Those who raise it do gain some authority, but borrowed: the child has only been placed in their path.

An exposed child is – or starts – outside all societal stricture or structure. It is not of poor parents, or rich parents, or free parents, or enslaved parents, it is of nothing and therefore can be of anything, too. It's one stroke of fortune away from annihilation or liberation. This bittersweet bleakness draws the story's audience in. The hearer pictures himself, all ties, bonds and expectations stripped away, opening his eyes to a bunch of reeds, and a clean slate. It strikes a chord.

One of my arguments has been that fracture gives those who suffer a kind of freedom. The scales fall from their eyes. They see things anew. They are freed at the very moment their world crumbles. For the foundling (however unconscious of it the baby may be), their old world has crumbled and owes them nothing. They're given a second chance in a world that can now demand nothing from them.

I don't, of course, claim that these stories are true. I don't even claim that, had they been true, the liberation I speak of would really have occurred. I am seeing the myth as an allegory, a way of explaining how we see ourselves: bound up, tied down, hemmed in, cramped and constrained, held back, obligated and in hock. The liberation through abandonment of an infant is, as it were, the last word in smashing that shell.

CHAPTER NINE

THE LITERATURE AND THE SCIENCE

Psychology

What is 'genius'? Even more problematically, what is 'a genius'? I have no answer to propose, finding the idea too elusive to categorise by reference to a single strand or element in the human makeup. But many, many writers and academics have hunted for a definition, and their hunt, even if none have succeeded in capturing the beast, may at least narrow the field of search and perhaps shed some light on what we've encountered in this book's sketches of some of those to whom the label has been attached.

But of this I'm sure. There is no distinct human sub-species called 'geniuses'. Genius is a flickering and variable flame in many, but one which burns most fiercely in those we call 'a genius'. And the reasons for that may never be fully found; certainly, we cannot argue that fracture is itself a sufficient condition for greatness. Most people who experience fracture do not go on to extraordinary achievement, and there have lived a few (not many) great women and men who appear to have had untroubled lives. Besides, boundaries are hazy, and much must remain a matter of opinion. A science of genius is well beyond our reach, and these cannot be questions for the laboratory. At least that is my view.

But, as I say, this doesn't mean people haven't tried to define the term. In fact, the pursuit of theory in this field has an ancient pedigree. Nearly two thousand years ago Plutarch, a Romanised Greek historian, published his *Parallel Lives*: 48 comparative biographies, weighing big man against big man and analysing what made them who they were. Plutarch's magnificent study is perhaps stronger on biography than it is on theory; but ever since his day people have enquired into, speculated upon and theorised about the questions his work tried to answer. So before we look at the enquiries of modern psychologists it's worth tracing their intellectual roots. Some techniques, and some putative theories – in particular the old, old debate of nature versus nurture – keep resurfacing.

Modern attempts to study the great in a systematic way were begun by the English scientist Francis Galton. Galton's 1869 *Hereditary Genius* was this polymath's disturbing and deeply flawed enquiry into the nature of what he called genius. Its title betrays the aspect of his work that would later get him into trouble, for the idea that we are born what we are has always been deeply troubling to those whose goals have been to improve, refine or 'cure' young people by education, by techniques of upbringing or by improving social conditions. Even the hint that this might be a waste of time can seem to threaten them.

Such doubters have another reason for instinctive hostility to inheritance-based theories of talent or lack of it. Aggravating their suspicions has been the evident appeal of heredity-heavy theories to a certain kind of reactionary thinking. Those whose habit of mind favours a social structure in which people know and keep their 'place'

('The rich man in his castle / The poor man at his gate / God made them, high or lowly / And ordered their estate', as the children's hymn 'All Things Bright and Beautiful' runs) are comforted to be told by scientists that social engineering and 'ladders of opportunity' are a waste of time.

More troubling still is the appeal of heredity to the incipient fascist or racist, seeming (as it may) to confirm all his or her suspicions about the superiority of races, classes or nationalities.

It has always been plain that in animals other than humans there are abilities and psychological traits that are heritable; and Galton was not the first to conclude that the human race was unlikely to be an exception. Ideas about genetic inheritance swirled in the late nineteenth century, cross-breeding with ideas about stopping the poor from reproducing, and giving birth to the science of eugenics. This study of heritability got all tangled up with racism and even fascism, reaching its nadir in the twentieth century, not least with Adolf Hitler's beliefs about the superiority of the 'Aryan' race or the inherent degeneracy of the Jewish people. Such thinking found an echo in the theory of apartheid in South Africa where I was born, spread further by elements in the Dutch Reformed Church there. Black people, claimed the DRC, were fashioned by God to be (quoting the Old Testament) 'the hewers of wood and the drawers of water'.

Eugenics, in short, acquired unsavoury associations, and it's no purpose of this book to promote a theory of inherited genius – indeed, part of my purpose is to describe the sparking of genius by circumstance rather than accident of birth. But Galton's enquiries into the nature of genius, however crude, did kick-start an academic pursuit that was to be taken up by others. Many of them appear in retrospect almost laughably crude, and vulnerable to fatal criticism.

These studies of comparative greatness are behind a good deal of modern enquiry, too, thanks to something called historiometry: the field where history, and the measurement of the personal characteristics of the men and women who make it, coincide. In 1909 the geneticist Frederick Woods defined historiometry as 'the facts of history of a personal nature subjected to statistical analysis by some more or less objective method'. It means, really, making statistics out of the personalities of figures in history. Having endured an MA course in International Relations at Yale in the 1970s (where we ended up measuring column-inches in the *New York Times*), I view the often primitive attempt to quantify simply in order to have something to feed into a computer with deep scepticism.

In the late nineteenth century the American scientist James McKeen Cattell, in unknowing anticipation of the listicle website Buzzfeed, collated and then ranked 'geniuses' before publishing his list of '1000 eminent individuals' in his 'A Statistical Study of Eminent Men' in 1894. His method, which named Napoleon III as more eminent that Confucius, the Buddha and Mozart, was based on the length of entries in biographical dictionaries and encyclopaedias. He seemed to take little account of much else, such as whether editors of nineteenth-century encyclopaedias might be biased towards more recently deceased greats.

But however flawed, Cattell's work inspired another

American psychologist in the field of studies of greatness, Lewis Terman. Working a couple of decades after Cattell, Terman began pointing the field towards childhood. A driven man, he advanced the subject with his huge longitudinal (that is, conducted over a great number of years) study, *Genetic Studies of Genius* – though not before his own personal struggle, worth reflecting on here.

Terman was the twelfth of fourteen children, his farmer parents living in a log cabin and eking out a life in the Great Plains. One night a pedlar came by the house, felt Terman's head (using the pseudoscience of phrenology) and predicted great things. The boy was educated in a one-room schoolhouse from the age of six, his parents struggling, first failing and finally succeeding in raising the funds to send him to college. After recovering from a serious tuberculosis health scare, Terman graduated from the gloriously Midwestern-sounding Central Normal College and undertook a doctorate at Indiana University: 'Genius and stupidity: A study of some of the intellectual processes of seven "bright" and seven "stupid" boys'.

As his work progressed he took it upon himself to prove to America that highly intelligent people weren't one-offs but a distinct (if fuzzily defined) section of humankind. Terman's thinking was infected by eugenicist theories about race, but he approached his research with huge energy. In 1921 he began his *Genetic Studies of Genius*, tracking 1,000 children with a high IQ across their entire lives, the lengthiest longitudinal study of all time. It continued after his death in 1956, carried on by one of its subjects and a former Terman pupil, Richard Sears.

But it was another of Terman's students, Catherine

Cox, whose work *The Early Mental Traits of Three Hundred Geniuses* is perhaps the most interesting of all of these flawed attempts to categorise the uncategorisable. More judicious with her data than Cattell, who had simply used word counts, Cox acknowledged 'the uneven value of biographies from the point of view of dependability'. Historical knowledge and judgement were also necessary, she said. Her appreciation of the difficulties of measurement in the field was welcome, but the research continued (and continues) to be undermined by the difficulty of giving any precise definition to some of its key terms – like 'genius', or even 'intelligence'.

We should remark at once that 'IQ' (Intelligence Quotient) is a much more problematic measure of mental capacity than early practitioners supposed; and, besides, 'genius' and mental ability are by no means the same thing: the former may (as some of the early case studies in this book vividly illustrate) involve leaps of the imagination, intellectual or moral courage, 'lateral thinking' and the readiness to challenge conventional wisdom. Who knows how Coco Chanel or Edward Lear would have performed at mental arithmetic. Mental ability is at the same time more measurable, and less extraordinary.

Nevertheless, and even with these limitations, Catherine Cox's work was throwing doubt on assumptions about the importance of 'input' – in the conventional sense of education, upbringing and training – in the creation of greatness. It shows a surprisingly weak relationship between levels of education and attainment, ideas of a 'perfect home' or a 'perfect education' proving fairly useless as determinants of exceptional success. Her work was useful in undermining ideas of a fixed link between genius and training, but to the extent that it seemed to suggest that genius is inborn, it runs counter to this book's argument that childhood circumstances can be midwives to extraordinary qualities of intellect or imagination. Nevertheless, wobbly though the foundations of their methodology were, Terman's and Cox's findings were usefully corrosive to the idea that greatness flows simply from the most perfect or 'best' possible upbringing.

*

Respectable science now recoils from the kind of extreme genetic claims made by Terman and others, even if they still use souped-up versions of Terman's and Cattell's methodology. But the focus of their investigations has stretched beyond mere IQ to the role of creativity in greatness, and from there to the causes of creativity. But, like greatness, creativity is a slippery, hard-to-define concept. The American academic Dean Keith Simonton attempted to sum it up thus:

> Creativity is the process by which creative ideas are generated, selected, and successfully implemented. In order to count as creative, an idea must fulfil three criteria: originality, usefulness, and surprise.

Simonton has identified a key characteristic of creativity as 'diversifying experiences', that is, experiences that make a person rethink the rules. One obvious example is moving to a new country and having to learn a new language, another might be suddenly losing a fortune, and another the loss of a parent. That these 'diversifying' experiences are more potent in childhood would stand to reason. The child is rawer, fresher, less overlaid with scar tissue, more open to the universe. 'Those bitter sorrows of childhood!' wrote George Eliot in her novel *The Mill on the Floss*, 'When sorrow is all new and strange, when hope has not yet got wings to fly beyond the days and weeks, and the space from summer to summer seems measureless.' These are the years that can make, break and re-make us.

But if our experience makes us creative people, what's the actual process? How are these creative thoughts formed? One widely accepted theory is called Blind Variation, Selective Retention (BVSR). In summary the theory is that in seeking solutions to difficult problems people employ a method of blindly (without seeing the way clearly to success) trying different solutions until one works. Like setting out down a maze and trying turning after turning. This solution, and the thinking that led to it, is then retained and the pathway between the problem and the solution remains illuminated.

The children's card game of Pelmanism is a good example of this process. One player turns over two cards at a time, looking for matching animals. When a matching pair is revealed, the player takes it. If the cards do not match, they are replaced face down and the next player takes a turn. The players selectively retain, to the best of their ability, what was on the cards. The better the child is at remembering which cards are which, and therefore the more effective they are at picking the matching card, the more they win the game.

The genius, then, is the one who can draw the links the quickest, and retain most easily the pathways that allow problem solving. This is 'combinatorial' creativity. It is best thought of as an unconscious process that takes place in the mind over hours, days, months and even years. The French mathematician Henri Poincaré captured it vividly when describing his mental state one night after drinking coffee instead of sleeping: 'Ideas rose in crowds; I felt them collide until pairs interlocked, so to speak, making a stable combination.'

One connection between Simonton's 'diversifying experiences' and the creative power of BVSR might even lie in childhood fracture. Suffering, especially in child-hood, academics have argued, is a 'diversifying experience' that opens up neural pathways which otherwise stay shut. In a joint paper on geniuses written by the University of Houston's Professor Rodica Ioana Damian and Simonton himself, the authors remark on the fact that

> ... the common denominators of these people are that they all experienced unusual and unexpected events in their childhood and adolescence, even highly trau-matic events, that set them apart.

These events, they suggest, 'push people outside the realm of "normality" and help them see the world in multiple ways, which might give them the cognitive flex-ibility necessary for coming up with creative ideas'. It is clear from the lives we examine in this book that lots of geniuses emerge from 'diversifying experiences' that you or I might now call fracture. Perhaps they're a member of an oppressed minority group (like Frederick Douglass or Tupac Shakur), suffer debilitating illness, are orphaned or are in dire financial straits. Perhaps they're gay in a homophobic culture. These crises are father to later creative achievement. As Damian and Simonton state: 'highly creative individuals stem from unconventional backgrounds'.

But a concatenation of disasters – parents dying, sickness, penury, moving abroad – does not (the authors insist) reliably produce this effect. Think of an inverted U curve, they say, where those at the top may struggle and thrive, but as traumatic events increase, the cliff edge approaches, until all possibility of success is lost and the life is well and truly wrecked.

Artists are often perceived as more 'creative' than scientists; in fact, Simonton observes that artists have more diversifying experiences than scientists. But this doesn't mean that fracture doesn't apply to scientists – or that they are not as wildly creative as any artist. I suggest that chaos or dysfunction in an artist's early years is more likely to be noticed and thought significant by commentators because we are already alive to the idea that artistic creativity and despair, catastrophe, even madness, are often allied. We are positively looking for disorder in Vincent Van Gogh's young life. We might be surprised if misery in Charles Dickens's childhood and youth had not opened his eyes to the rottenness beneath the surface in Victorian England. With scientific originality, however, we may be less likely to make an intuitive link. Other researchers have noticed that many great scientists often suffered periods of serious loneliness. Bernice Eiduson, writing in 1962, studied scientists for her book *Scientists: Their Psychological World.*

Think, as you read this, of Ada Lovelace, whom we met at the start of Chapter Two.

> I found lonely, passive, withdrawn children; aggressive, rebellious, raucous youngsters; sickly ones; and those who described themselves as ordinary and who did seem unmarked by severe traumas. Their lives appeared to be similar in most respects to those of their friends and schoolmates, except for one feature consistently mentioned throughout the interviews: periods of isolation from the customary groups with which a child might be expected to identify – an isolation sometimes lasting for years at a time. Occasionally this withdrawal was brought on by actual physical illness or disability, but more often these were merely periods during which the individual felt emotionally distant from friends of his age.

Eiduson continues: 'This commonality of isolation may not seem significant in itself. What is important, however, is that such experiences invariably led the scientists to look to their own resources for solace and amusement … what they did seemed not so crucial for later work as the fact that they had searched for resources within themselves and became comfortable being by themselves.'

Psychoanalysis and psychotherapy

Hester Solomon, a Jungian analyst and senior member of the British Psychotherapy Foundation, wrote to me after seeing an article I published in *The Times* about fracture, saying she had encountered a similar phenomenon in her years of work. When we met, Solomon gave me a definition of trauma: when 'the integrity of the self has been intruded upon'. The terrain around psychoanalytic definitions of the self is a minefield and I shall avoid it, sticking to a looser colloquial understanding.

An illness, a violent attack, and the sudden death of a loved one may all be traumatic events. But while it's easy to see that the first two violate the integrity of the self by harming the physical body, how would the third do the same? Yet these three calamities all intrude upon an individual's conception of who they are – they shake their foundations.

Let us look at one of our case studies, Rudyard Kipling, to see if we can identify the 'integrity of the self intruded upon' or 'offended', as Solomon also put it. Kipling's time in Southsea at the hands of Mrs Sarah Holloway and her son Harry saw him interrogated at the end of every day, beaten, and once even forced to parade around the town wearing a shameful placard. Sarah and Harry were attacking the young boy's person in the widest sense of the term. His sense of who he was – his self, in other words – was under siege, constantly challenged, and offended.

This is how trauma affects the psyche, by chipping away at its conception of itself. It's particularly obvious from this example how children are more vulnerable than most, but anybody who has seen, say, the bullying of a colleague in the workplace will know that traumatic events may intrude upon even an adult's self.

Solomon's view on how the individual reacts to serious trauma is based on the idea that, in order to defend themselves from this intrusion, they create an 'as if' personality.

Roughly speaking this means that they create a self for themselves as if they – and their lives – are far more stable than they really are.

In a paper on the subject, Solomon wrote that early absence of (say) parental response, or experience of abuse, led to the 'internalisation of a terrifying emptiness in that place where there had been the archetypal expectation of finding a responsive, benign other' – a mother or a father figure, for example. So where a mother has died, the child craves motherly responses and care, but finds nothing – and is too young to perceive the reasons behind this, making the suffering even worse.

Those who develop the 'as if' personality seek and find these responses elsewhere. A cousin, a grandparent, the beauty of nature, or the power of a book might all provide a kind of response, but Solomon says that none can 'stand in for the enormity of the loss of ordinarily devoted, caring and loving parents'.

The individual latches on to what they can find to make up for and cover over the absence that lies at the heart of their self. They themselves use this cover as if it were the same as the real thing. This is the self-created self, as Solomon sees it. And this type of response to trauma leaves an individual with an 'exceptional capacity for creative engagement with the world'. These people grapple with a cruel world in a unique way – they find within themselves, or they make within themselves, the resources they need not just to bear it, but to master it. For Solomon, concerned with treatment as a psychoanalyst, there is a world of difficulty associated with the 'as if' personality when that individual runs out of road (the 'as if' can only be sustained for a while, she argues), but as a theory of response to suffering, it offers significant overlap with my thesis.

But this is just one way of looking at trauma and the ego. Rather than an intrusion upon the *integrity* of the self, some see trauma more simply as a wounding of the self. This is how Martin Lloyd-Elliott, an author and a psychotherapist who works with highly successful adults, understands it. High achievers, he told me, are often 'driven by both a conscious and unconscious desire to compensate' for an ego that has been 'so wounded'.

Lloyd-Elliott finds in the wounded ego a 'disproportionate burning desire to repair the damage and cover up the cracks'. Think of the ego as a boxer: it's taken a few hefty punches to the jaw and comes back swinging. This link between trauma and success emerges here as familiar. If we take another of our case studies, Alexander Hamilton, we can see that his early suffering – absent father, dying mother, a cousin for a carer who then committed suicide – was severe. And it made him a force of a nature. His fearless soldiering, his political acumen and his sharp pen spring from that suffering and it was those skills that pressed him into the pages of history. In Hamilton, after all that early loss, we can see what Lloyd-Elliott describes: that 'disproportionate burning desire'. Alexander Hamilton had it in spades. He was not to be satisfied, even to his dying day, which he spent in the heat of a duel, refusing to fire his gun out of principle, killed by the bullet of his less scrupulous opponent.

Or take Coco Chanel, whose ego was so wounded by her callous father and the death of her mother. At the age of twelve Gabrielle (as she was then) landed on the cold stone doorstep of the Aubazine nunnery. The subsequent course of her life, its glamour and success, was a rejection of what she met in her youth. What sustained her, it seems clear to me, was exactly the will to 'repair the damage and cover up the cracks' that Lloyd-Elliott sees in those who suffer trauma. Hamilton's and Chanel's egos are, in this conception, wounded in the way we often describe somebody's pride as wounded.

I tread gingerly, however, across the terrain of psychotherapy and analysis. It is intuitively plain to me that such fields, and the men and women who toil there, offer flashes of insight; but for me these don't add up to, and cannot bear, the weight of theory that is laid upon them. The idea of fracture introduced by this book is not a developed and systematic theory, and I think cannot be. It is – if it is anything – a flash of insight, a glimpse of unexpected connections, a hunch about causation.

CHAPTER TEN

CONCLUSION

In trying to teach one learns. I cannot be the first writer to have found that setting out to explain something to other people, other minds, has helped clarify my argument in my own mind. It has also helped identify a needed clarification of which, when I set out, I was not properly aware.

My argument itself needs no repetition. It's been hammered home sufficiently – perhaps even tiresomely – throughout the book. But in the hammering home I have slipped, for the sake of simplicity and ease of expression, into the kind of type-casting which, though useful, doesn't do justice to the messiness as well as the patchiness of human attributes.

We are all basically the same kind of animal, and though the dollops of each human attribute that have been doled out to us by inheritance and training vary from individual to individual, I cannot think of a single quality – musicality, language skills, spatial reasoning, memory, fluency, patience, humour, numeracy, generosity, spite ... – that some people possess entirely and others not at all. It would be strange indeed if just one single quality, 'genius', were the exception.

Why, then, does the word, used to describe an individual

as well as a quality, occur so very frequently in this book? Because it has been my purpose to isolate and examine the possible roots of this attribute. It follows that those men and women in history who have been revered for the sheer abundance of their genius, and made famous for the use to which they put it, are a good place to start.

Starting there we've gone on to ask what else, if anything, they have in common. This is the question that Plutarch tackled some two thousand years ago in his *Parallel Lives*. *Fracture* uncovers a startling amount of shared experience in their early lives. Likewise, if we were investigating links between athletic prowess and diet we might start with champions: but that would not be to deny that to a varying degree, millions of people are quite good runners, and almost everybody can run a bit.

Millions of people have moments of genius, and almost everybody might, in the right circumstances, display a flash of the quality.

So the link I'm pointing to is really a pathway in the human brain between shock or despair, and the breaking of the shackles of habit, 'education' and others' expectations, that cramp our mind, our vision, our moral reasoning and our imagination. The earlier this happens in life, the more easily and completely those shackles may be broken.

I think as I write of the youth Abraham Lincoln, clever, self-taught (and possibly gay), boarding a riverboat for anywhere, anything, that was not his hated father, his family's book-less cabin, and the knockout loss of mother and sister.

I think of little Gabrielle Chasnel, fatherless, motherless, nameless (they got it wrong) and hungry, saying no to the nuns offering her eggs to eat because she 'had to say no to something, to say no passionately to everything around [me]'.

I think of young Maria Skłodowska, father ruined, beloved mother and sister taken from her, a nervous breakdown behind her, her Polish pride insulted, setting off on that train to Paris.

I think of Rudyard Kipling, ripped from a sunny infancy in India, pushed through the streets of Southsea with 'Liar' on a placard tied round his neck.

And I think of the child Edward Lear, facing, alone and ignorant, the unknown monsters of acute depression, epilepsy and homosexuality, the twenty-first of twenty-two children, his mother all out of energy and love and his family financially ruined: the boy whose wild imagination would burst into colour and light, into art and poetry and storytelling, and in 'The Owl and the Pussycat' would write:

'Dear Pig, are you willing to sell for one shilling
    Your ring?' Said the Piggy, 'I will'.
So they took it away, and were married next day
    By the Turkey who lives on the hill.
They dined on mince, and slices of quince,
    Which they ate with a runcible spoon;
And hand in hand, on the edge of the sand,
    They danced by the light of the moon,
        The moon,
        The moon,
They danced by the light of the moon.

NOTES

1 Kettenmann, pp. 8–10.
2 Courtney et al., p. 91.
3 Amy Fine Collins, 'Diary of a mad artist' in *Vanity Fair*, September 1995.
4 Ibid.
5 Natasha Walter, 'Feel my Pain' in *The Guardian*, 21 May 2005.
6 Herrera, p. 75.
7 Abraham Lincoln, 'My Childhood Home I See Again'.
8 Report of Mr W. M. J. Barbee, *Western Journal of Medicine and Surgery* 3, p. 185.
9 Goodwin, p. 4.
10 Dennis Hanks, second Chicago statement, quoted in Beveridge, p. 27.
11 Quoted in Bruce, p. 7.
12 Beveridge, p. 67.
13 Quoted in Allen, p. 72.
14 *Epitaphs of the War*, 'Common Form'.
15 Lycett, p. 132.
16 Macdonald Fleming, p. 345.
17 Sangeeta Dutta, 'Charlotte Brontë and the Woman Question', *Economic and Political Weekly*, 26(40), p. 2311 (1991).
18 Barker, p. 796.
19 Best, p. 18.
20 Ibid., p. 16.
21 Goldsmith, pp. 30–31.

22 Quinn, p. 52.
23 Pastrovicchi, p. 5.

BIBLIOGRAPHY

Alcántara, Tomás Polanco, *Simón Bolívar: ensayo de interpretación biográfica a través de sus documentos*, Caracas: Editorial Melvin, 1994.

Ali, Muhammad, *Muhammad Ali: The Greatest*, London: Parkgate, 1999.

Allen, Charles, *Kipling Sahib: India and the Making of Rudyard Kipling*, London: Little, Brown, 2007.

Assis Duarte, Eduardo de, 'Machado de Assis's African Descent', *Research in African Literatures*, 38(1), 2007.

Austin, Linda M., 'Emily Bronte's Homesickness', *Victorian Studies*, 55(44), 2002.

Bagby, Alberto I., 'Machado de Assis and Foreign Languages', *Luso-Brazilian Review*, 12(2), 1975.

Bair, Deirdre, *Jung: A Biography*, London: Little, Brown, 2004.

Baird, Julia, *Imagine This: Growing Up with my Brother John Lennon*, London: Hodder Paperbacks, 2008.

Barker, Juliet, *The Brontës*, New York: St Martin's Press, 1994.

Barthes, Roland (trans. Annette Lavers), *Mythologies*, London: Vintage, 2009.

Battiscombe, Georgina, *Shaftesbury: A Biography of the Seventh Earl 1801-1885*, London: Constable, 1974.

Beauvoir, Simone de, *The Second Sex*, New York: Vintage, 1989.

Best, G. F. A., *Shaftesbury*, London: B. T. Batsford Ltd, 1964.

Beveridge, Albert Jeremiah, *Abraham Lincoln, 1809-1858*, Boston

& New York: Houghton Mifflin Co.; Cambridge, MA: Riverside Press, 1928.

Blight, David W., *Frederick Douglass: Prophet of Freedom*, New York: Simon & Schuster, 2018.

Bolívar, Simón, *Carta de Jamaica*, Caracas: Ediciones de la Presidencia, 1972.

Bourgeois, Louise (ed. Marie-Laure Bernadac and Hans-Ulrich Obrist) *Deconstruction of the Father / Reconstruction of the Father (Writings and Interviews 1923–1997)*, Cambridge, MA: MIT Press, 1998.

Brady, Frank, *Citizen Welles: A Biography of Orson Welles*, New York: NY Creative Publishing, 2015.

Brontë, Emily, *Life and Works of Charlotte Brontë and Her Sisters: Wuthering Heights*, London: Scribner, Welford & Armstrong, 1873.

Bruce, Robert V., *Lincoln and the Riddle of Death*, Fort Wayne, IN: Louis A. Warren Lincoln Library and Museum, 1981.

Carr, Richard, *Charlie Chaplin: A Political Biography from Victorian Britain to Modern America*, London: Routledge, 2017.

Carson, Ciaran, *The Táin: A New Translation of the Táin Bó Cúailnge*, London: Penguin Classics, 2007.

Charles-Roux, Edmonde (trans. Nancy Amphoux), *Chanel*, London: Collins Harvill, 1989.

Charlton, James, *The Military Quotation Book*, London: St Martin's Press, 2002.

Chernow, Ron, *Alexander Hamilton*, New York: Head of Zeus, 2017.

Chitty, Susan, *That Singular Person Called Lear: A Biography*, London: Weidenfeld and Nicolson, 1988.

Chuquet, Arthur, *La jeunesse de Napoléon*, Paris: Colin, 1897–1899.

Cosgrave, Bronwyn, *Coco Chanel*, London: Quadrille, 2012.

Courtney, Carol A., O'Hearn, Michael, and Franck, Carla C., 'Frida Kahlo: Portrait of Chronic Pain', *Physical Therapy*, 97(1), 2017.

Crawford, Elisabeth, *The Beginnings of the Nobel Institution: The*

Science Prizes, 1901–1915, Cambridge: Cambridge University, 1984.

Curie, Ève (trans. Vincent Sheean), *Madame Curie – A Biography*, Garden City, NY: Doubleday, Doran & Co, 1937.

Curie, Marie, *Pierre Curie*, 2nd revised edition, New York: Dover Publications Inc., 2012.

Davies, Norman, *God's Playground: A History of Poland in Two Volumes*, Oxford and New York: Oxford University Press, 2005.

Dollfus, Ariane, *Noureev L'Insoumis*, Paris: Garnier-Flammarion, 2007.

Donald, David Herbert, *Lincoln*, London: Cape, 1995.

Douglass, Frederick, *My Bondage and My Freedom*, New York, 1855

Douglass, Frederick, *Narrative of the Life of Frederick Douglass, an American Slave*, Boston: The Anti-Slavery Office, 1845.

Eiduson, Bernice Tabackman, *Scientists: Their Psychological World*, New York: Basic Books, 1962.

Eig, Jonathan, *Ali: A Life*, London: Simon & Schuster UK, 2017.

Fairclough, Adam, *Martin Luther King, Jr*, Georgia: University of Georgia Press, 1995.

Finlayson, Geoffrey, *The Seventh Earl of Shaftesbury, 1801–1885*, Eyre Methuen Ltd: London, 1981.

Fisher, Todd, and Fremont-Barnes, Gregory, *The Napoleonic Wars: The Rise and Fall of an Empire*, London: Osprey Publishing, 2004.

Fleming, Alice Macdonald, *Trix: Kipling's Forgotten Sister*, Peterborough: Pond View, 2004.

Garapon, Paul, 'Métamorphoses de la chanson française (1945–1999)' *Esprit*, 254(7), 1999.

Garrow, David J., *Bearing the Cross: Martin Luther King, Jr., and the Southern Christian Leadership Conference*, New York: Perennial Classics, 2004.

Gaskell, Elizabeth, *The Life of Charlotte Brontë*, London: Smith, Elder and Company, 1857.

Giroud, Françoise (trans. Lydia Davis), *Marie Curie*, New York: Holmes & Meier, 1986.

Goertzel, Mildred George, Goertzel, Victor, and Goertzel, Ted George, *Three Hundred Eminent Personalities*, San Francisco and London: Jossey-Bass, 1978.

Goldsmith, Barbara, *Obsessive Genius: The Inner World of Marie Curie*, London: Phoenix, 2005.

Goodwin, Doris Kearns, *Team of Rivals: The Political Genius of Abraham Lincoln*, London: Penguin, 2009.

Grosso, Michael, *The Man who could Fly: St. Joseph of Copertino and the Mystery of Levitation*, Lanham, MD: Rowman & Littlefield, 2016.

Herndon, William Henry, and Weik, Jesse William, *Herndon's Lincoln: The True Story of a Great Life. The history and personal recollections of Abraham Lincoln*, Chicago: Belford & Co., 1889.

Herrera, Hayden, *Frida: A Biography of Frida Kahlo*, New York: Harper Perennial, 2002.

Joseph, Ellis, *Founding Brothers*, London: Faber, 2002.

Keeling, Kara, 'A Homegrown Revolutionary?: Tupac Shakur and the Legacy of the Black Panther Party', *The Black Scholar*, 29(2/3), 1999.

Kenny, Francis, *The Making of John Lennon: The Untold Story of the Rise and Fall of the Beatles*, Edinburgh: Luath Press, 2014.

Kettenmann, Andrea, *Kahlo*, Germany: Taschen, 2003.

King, Martin Luther, Jr (ed. Clayborne Carson), *Autobiography of Martin Luther King, Jr*, London: Abacus, 2000.

Kipling, Rudyard (ed. Thomas Pinney), *'Something of Myself' and Other Autobiographical Writings*, Cambridge: Cambridge University Press, 1991.

Leaming, Barbara, 'Orson Welles: The Unfulfilled Promise' in *The New York Times Magazine*, 14 July 1985.

Lear, Edward (ed. Rowena Fowler), *The Cretan Journal*, Athens, Dedham: Denise Harvey & Co., 1984.

Lear, Edward (ed. Ray Murphy), *Edward Lear's Indian Journal*, London: Jarrolds Publishers Ltd, 1953.

Bibliography

Levi, Peter, *Edward Lear: A Life*, London: Tauris Parke Paperbacks, 2013.

Lewis, David Levering, *King: A Biography*, University of Illinois Press, 2013.

Lincoln, Abraham (ed. Roy P. Basler), *Collected Works*, New Brunswick, NJ: Rutgers University Press, 1955.

Lincoln, Bruce, 'The Indo-European Cattle-Raiding Myth', *History of Religions*, 16(1), Chicago: University of Chicago Press, 1976.

Looseley, David, *Édith Piaf: A Cultural History*, Liverpool: Liverpool University Press, 2015.

Lopes, José Leme, 'Machado de Assis e a epilepsia', a publication of the Academia Cearense de Letras, November, 1975.

Lorcey, Jacques, and Monserrat, Joëlle, *Piaf et la chanson*, Paris: Séguier, 2007.

Lycett, Andrew, *Rudyard Kipling*, London: Weidenfeld & Nicolson, 1999.

Lynch, John, *Simón Bolívar: A Life*, London: Yale University Press, 2007.

Madariaga, Santiago de, *Bolívar*, Buenos Aires: Editorial Sudamericana, 1959.

Madsen, Axel, *Coco Chanel: A Biography*, London: Bloomsbury Publishing, 1990 (2nd edition 2009).

Malley, Marjorie C., *Radioactivity: A History of a Mysterious Science*, Oxford: Oxford University Press, 2011.

Man, John, *The Mongol Empire: Genghis Khan, his Heirs and the Founding of Modern China*, London: Corgi Books, 2015.

Monk, Ray, *Ludwig Wittgenstein: The Duty of Genius*, London: Vintage, 1991.

Monteiro, Pedro Meira, 'Machado de Assis, cem años depois', *Luso-Brazilian Review*, 46(1), Edição Comemorativa do Centenário da Morte de Machado de Assis, 2009.

Morand, Paul (trans. Euan Cameron), *The Allure of Chanel*, London: Pushkin Press, 2013.

Noakes, Vivien, *The Painter Edward Lear*, Newton Abbot: David & Charles, 1991.

Norman, Philip, *John Lennon: The Life*, New York: Harper Collins, 2008.

Oates, Stephen B., *Let the Trumpet Sound: A Life of Martin Luther King Jr.*, Edinburgh: Payback, 1998.

Ortiz, Alicia Dujovne, *Eva Perón*, Warner Books UK, 1997.

Pastrovicchi, the Rev. Angelo (trans. the Rev. Francis S. Laing), *St Joseph of* Copertino, OMC, 1918.

Perú de Lacroix., Luís, *Diario de Bucaramanga, vida pública y privada del Libertador*, versión sin mutilaciones, Caracas: Centauro, 1976.

Peyre, Henri, 'Napoleon: Devil, Poet, Saint', *Yale French Studies – The Myth of Napoleon*, 26, 1960.

Quinn, Susan, *Marie Curie: A Life*, London: Heinemann, 1995.

Rank, Otto (trans. Gregory C. Richter and E. James Lieberman), *The Myth of the Birth of the Hero*, London: Johns Hopkins University Press, 2004.

Rosenbaum, Jonathan, *Discovering Orson Welles*, California: University of California Press, 2017.

Salima, Pedro, *Reflexiones en torno al juramento de Monte Sacro*, Caracas: El Perro y la Rana, 2008.

Schwarz, Roberto, *A Master on the Periphery of Capitalism: Machado de Assis*, Durham: Duke University Press, 2001.

Simonton, Dean Keith (ed.), *Wiley Handbook of Genius*, Chichester, West Sussex: Wiley-Blackwell, 2014.

Stanford, Karin L., 'Keepin' It Real in Hip Hop Politics: A Political Perspective of 'Tupac Shakur', *Journal of Black Studies*, 42(1), 2011.

Storr, Robert, *Intimate Geometries: The Art and Life of Louise Bourgeois*, London: Thames & Hudson, 2016.

Strozier, Charles B., *Lincoln's Quest for Union: Public and Private Meanings*, New York: Basic Books, 1982.

Terman, Lewis, ed., *Genetic Studies of Genius*, London: G. G. Harrap & Co, 1926.

Bibliography

Trees, Andrew S., 'The Importance of Being Alexander
  Hamilton' (review of Ron Chernow's *Alexander Hamilton*),
  Reviews in American History, 33(1) 2005.

Unamuno, Miguel de, 'Don Quijote y Bolívar', *Revista de Historia
  de América*, 95, 1993.

Valentinov, Nikolai, *The Early Years of Lenin*, Michigan: University
  of Michigan Press, 1969.

Vaughan, Hal, *Sleeping With the Enemy: Coco Chanel, Nazi Agent*,
  London: Chatto & Windus, 2011.

Vaught, Seneca, 'Tupac's Law: Incarceration, T.H.U.G.L.I.F.E.,
  and the Crisis of Black Masculinity', *Spectrum: A Journal on
  Black Men*, 2(2), 2014.

Weatherford, Jack, *Genghis Khan and the Making of the Modern
  World*, New York: Crown, 2004.

White, Anthony (ed.), *Frida Kahlo, Diego Rivera and Mexican
  Modernism: The Jacques and Natasha Gelmen Collection*, Seattle:
  University of Washington Press, 2001.

Wirtén, Eva Hemmungs, *Making Marie Curie: Intellectual Property
  and Celebrity Culture in an Age of Information*, Chicago:
  University of Chicago Press, 2015.

Young, Norwood, *The Growth of Napoleon: A Study in Environment*,
  London, 1910.

Zamoyski, Adam, *Holy Madness: Romantics, Patriots and
  Revolutionaries, 1776–1871*, London: Weidenfeld & Nicolson,
  1999.

COPYRIGHT ACKNOWLEDGEMENTS

Page 108: lines from 'Alexander Hamilton' by Lin-Manuel Miranda reproduced by permission of Warner Chappell Music Ltd, © 2015 5000 Broadway Music (ASCAP); all rights administered by WC Music Corp.

Page 241: lines from 'St Martin de Porres' by Mary Lou Williams and Anthony Woods reproduced by permission of Bucks Music Group Ltd; published by Modern Works Music Publishing Ltd, administered by Bucks Music Group Ltd, Roundhouse, 212 Regent's Park Road entrance, London NW1 8AW.

INDEX